Elite Deviance

Elite Deviance

David R. Simon
University of North Florida

D. Stanley Eitzen
Colorado State University

Allyn and Bacon, Inc.
Boston   *London*   *Sydney*   *Toronto*

I dedicate this book to my family — Lynne, Molly, Danny, and Joshua — and to all those who care enough about social justice to struggle for it.

David R. Simon

I wish to dedicate this book to my wife and children: Florine, Keith, Mike, and Kelly.

D. Stanley Eitzen

Library of Congress Cataloging in Publication Data
Simon, David R., 1944-
    Elite deviance.
    1. White collar crimes — United States.   2. Deviant behavior.   3. Elite (Social Sciences) — United States.
I. Eitzen, D. Stanley.   II. Title.
HV6635.S47   364.1'6 8'0973   81-10757
ISBN 0-205-07553-3 (pbk.)   AACR2

Printed in the United States of America.
10 9 8 7 6 5 4   85 84 83

Contents

v

Preface

Public opinion polls for the past decade or so have recorded declining levels of confidence in the United States' major institutions. A majority of Americans remain cynical about the morality of politicians, especially members of Congress, and suspicious of the activities of big businesses such as the large oil companies. There is a pervasive feeling that the wealthy and powerful individuals and organizations of the U.S. receive special and unfair consideration when it comes to the passage of tax legislation and the dispensing of justice. And there is a growing concern that the voice of the average citizen goes unheard in the halls of government at all levels.

This decline in public confidence has accelerated in the past twenty years or so and continues to this day. Americans came to distrust their government during the Vietnam War, when they were constantly reassured that there was "light at the end of the tunnel." Yet we now are aware that the government lied consistently during the war about the strength of enemy troops, that the war was being waged beyond the borders of Vietnam, and much else. Vietnam was followed by the Watergate scandal — the most serious bout of presidential wrongdoing in the nation's history. During the Watergate era revelations about illegal campaign contributions by large corporations and abuses of civil liberties by the CIA, FBI, and IRS added further to the public's distrust of major institutions.

All these incidents have taken place amidst an unprecedented spiral of inflation, unemployment, and skyrocketing energy costs, which have further weakened the public's confidence in governmental and business elites to deal successfully with the economic problems of the "free-enterprise system." One might expect that all these problems would lead to a public outcry for reform and coherent policies to deal with economic and energy crises. Yet the public seems almost overwhelmed, or at least befuddled, by it all. There is evidence of a widespread alienation among the public from avenues of power. Many people believe that apathy and individual indulgence are now the dominant trends of our age.

The crisis of confidence in the United States has caught most social scientists by surprise. We lack a well-integrated body of theory and research that adequately explains the causes and predicts the consequences of the elite immorality and economic crises of our time. This void has made this book a challenge to write. Throughout the chapters that follow, we stress that the contemporary crises are not aberrations of individual personalities. Rather, their causes are structural; they stem directly from the nature of the political economy of multinational corporate capitalism. The profit motive, the ever-present stimulus of advertising on mass consumption, the massive military establishment, and the global nature of the economy of late capitalism have all contributed to a situation where deviant behavior by elites is a necessary ingredient in maintaining this system of wealth and power as we know it.

Most Americans are woefully unaware of the nature of the political economy of capitalism and its role in causing deviance on the part of elites. Even when confronted with a political-economy approach to analyzing deviance, most people tend to become fatalistic regarding the chances for changing such mammoth entities as our governmental and economic systems. This problem is magnified where most people are unaware of political ideology and of the antagonisms that are built into the very fabric of our capitalist society. Social scientists tended to exacerbate the problem by failing to point to the structured sources of societal crises and solutions that require fundamental structural changes.

This book addresses these concerns: (1) a declining public confidence caused by revelations of elite wrongdoing and economic crises; (2) the lack of social-scientific knowledge regarding elite deviance; and (3) a need to suggest solutions for the crises of contemporary politics and economics.

A basic problem we faced in writing this volume was that there is not, and probably never will be, a definition of elite deviance that is widely shared by social scientists. This is appropriate because changes in values and in technology continue to raise legal and ethical questions regarding behavior, which a generation ago were undreamed of by even the most forward looking among us. Nevertheless, we have explored in this text what we consider the most serious and representative forms of the wrongdoing by wealthy and powerful individuals in corporate and governmental organizations. We have done this in both a historical and political-economy context, and we have offered what we consider the most rational and achievable "blueprint" for social change in the closing chapter. There will doubtless be those who disagree with the analysis of the causes and solutions of elite deviance, and that is as it should be. We view the crises of elite deviance as among the most challenging of our time, and we believe that nothing less than a serious dialogue within the social-scientific community is warranted on these matters.

ACKNOWLEDGMENTS

We want to thank Alan Levitt, sociology editor of Allyn and Bacon, for his support of this project during every phase of its development. We have benefited from the constructive criticisms of various reviewers, including Jan De Amicis, Richard A. Ball, Pat Lauderdale, George Ritzer, T. P. Schwartz, Randall G. Stokes, Julia R. Schwendinger, Michael LeParte, Janet Schmidt, Lynda Ann Ewen, David Altheide, Bob Antonio, and Colin Lofton. David Simon wishes to thank certain colleagues at the University of North Florida, especially Christine Rasche, Joque Soskis, Jane Decker, Steven

DeLue, Stephen Woods, Richard Weiner, and Robert Whelan for their encouragement and support. D. Stanley Eitzen owes special thanks to some of his students at Colorado State University: Roger Davidson, Maureen Jung, Dean Purdy, and Doug Timmer. Thanks also to T. R. Young for his critique of the epilogue.

We would also like to thank Scott, Foresman & Company for permission to reproduce the material appearing in Chapter 2.

Chapter 1
The Nature of
Elite Deviance

ELITE DEVIANCE AND THE CRISIS
OF CONFIDENCE

In 1967 pollster Lou Harris asked a representative sample of adult Americans what people they considered "dangerous or harmful to the country." [1] The answers included mostly powerless individuals — people whose behavior dominated the sociological study of deviance and social problems, such as homosexuals, prostitutes, atheists, and anti-war protesters. Seven years later, at the height of the Watergate scandal, Harris posed the same question in another poll. This time the answers were strikingly different. The people considered dangerous by a majority of Americans were:

> people who hire political spies (52 percent); generals who conduct secret bombing raids (67 percent); politicians who engage in secret wiretapping (71 percent); businessmen who make illegal political contributions (81 percent); and politicians who use the Central Intelligence Agency, the Federal Bureau of Investigation, and the Secret Service for political purposes or to try to restrict freedom (88 percent). [2]

Numerous incidents between 1967 and the present have served to elevate public concern regarding the behavior of the nation's most powerful and wealthy individuals and organizations. Let's review some representative cases, beginning with those from the political arena.

1

Political Events Leading to Public Cynicism

Politicians and governmental agencies have been involved in a number of incidents that have contributed to a deep public distrust of government. Most significant was the conduct of the government during the Vietnam War (1964–1975). The Pentagon Papers, investigative reporting, and leaks from within the government had the effect of turning public opinion against the war and the government. Revealed were a number of governmental transgressions, including the manipulation of Congress by President Johnson with the Gulf of Tonkin incident; the indictment of high-ranking officers for war crimes similar to those committed by the Germans and Japanese during World War II; the deliberate destruction of civilian targets by American forces; intelligence agency suppression of information regarding enemy troop strength and sympathizers in South Vietnam;[3] falsified reports by American field commanders regarding the destruction of enemy targets; the spraying of more than five million acres of South Vietnam with defoliating chemicals; the execution of more than 40,000 so-called enemy agents by the CIA under the Phoenix Program (most without trial); and unauthorized bombing raids against North Vietnam.[4] From early 1969 until May, 1970, President Nixon assured the American people that the neutrality of Cambodia was being respected. Yet, Nixon had secretly ordered the bombing of so-called enemy sanctuaries in that country during that period. He was able to keep the bombings secret through the use of a double-entry bookkeeping system arranged between the White House and the Defense Department.

Governmental investigations revealed in 1975 that the CIA had violated its charter by engaging in domestic intelligence, opening the mail of U.S. citizens, and spying on Congressmen and newspaper reporters. Moreover, this organization plotted the assassinations of a number of foreign political officials.[5] Most significant, the Senate Intelligence Committee revealed that every American president from Eisenhower to Nixon had lied to the American people about the activities of the CIA.

Public confidence in government was also lowered when it became known that every president since Franklin Roosevelt had used the FBI for political and sometimes illegal purposes. We also found out, after J. Edgar Hoover's death, how the Bureau had been used by its longtime chief to silence his and the Bureau's critics. Hoover had also involved the Bureau in a number of illegal acts to defeat or neutralize those domestic groups that he thought were subversive.

The Watergate scandal that brought down the Nixon administration was also a most significant contributor to low public confidence in government. The litany of illegal acts by governmental officials and/or their agents in Watergate included: securing illegal campaign contributions, "dirty tricks" to discredit political opponents, burglary, bribery, perjury, wiretapping, harassment of administration opponents with tax audits, and the like.

By 1975, when the above revelations became public and just after the end of the Watergate scandal, public confidence in government was understandably low.   One poll revealed that "68 percent of the American people expressed the belief that the government regularly lies to them." [6]

Added to these incidents are the numerous cases of political corruption by individual politicians that seem to be a constant in politics. Members of Congress, state governors, and even a recent vice-president have been found guilty of tax evasion, receiving bribes, and other schemes to use their positions for economic gain.[7]   The ABSCAM scandal of 1979, where the FBI set up a number of public officials with bribes from "Arabs," once again gave the public cause for a deep sense of cynicism and distrust of government officials.   The result of these and other political scandals was that by 1979 only eighteen percent of a national sample of Americans expressed a great deal of confidence in the "people in charge of running Congress." [8]

Scandals within the Economic Sphere

The sagging confidence of the public in major American institutions extends beyond government.   Increasingly, big business has come to be viewed with distrust and cynicism.   Indeed, by 1979 big business tied with Congress as "least trusted" from a list of ten major institutions.[9] Let's review some of the incidents that have contributed to these negative feelings.   To begin, the Watergate investigation revealed that over 300 corporations illegally contributed to President Nixon's 1972 reelection campaign.[10]

Since the 1960s, when Ralph Nader launched the consumer movement, consumer unhappiness with the quality of goods and services provided by business has grown dramatically.   By 1978 it was estimated that the federal government alone received about ten million consumer complaints annually.[11]   Some corporations have willfully marketed products known to be dangerous.   There are numerous examples of this problem, the most notorious being the marketing of the Pinto by the Ford Motor Company.   This car was known by its manufacturers to have a defective gasoline tank that would ignite even in low-speed rear-end collisions, yet the company continued its sales.   Ironically and tragically, Ford continued to sell this defective and dangerous car even though the problem could have been solved for a cost of eleven dollars per vehicle.[12]

The Senate has revealed that between 1945 and 1976 approximately 350 American corporations have admitted to making bribes of some 750 million dollars to officials of foreign governments.   Many of these companies made such payments without informing their stock-holders.[13] No corporate executives were sent to prison for their involvement in concealing or making such payments.

Another problem that has turned the public against business is the relatively high incidence of fraud. Fraud in the business community takes many forms. For example, General Motors substituted Chevrolet engines in thousands of its new Oldsmobiles, without informing its customers of the switch.[14] Advertising is also full of examples of fraudulent claims for products. And the stock market has been manipulated to defraud clients: the largest case of this nature surfaced in 1975 when officials of the Equity Life Insurance Company were indicted for manipulating the price of shares by literally inventing thousands of nonexistent insurance policies. Somewhere between two and three billion dollars was lost by thousands of investors. Equity's chairman, along with several other company officials, were convicted of the crime, but received suspended sentences or prison terms that varied from only two to eight years.[15]

Perhaps the largest energizer of negative feelings toward big business has been the realization that corporations are guilty of what we might call "chemical crimes." Through their dumping of waste products into the air, water, and landfills, or through the production of products that pollute unnecessarily, businesses have assaulted the public with dangerous implications for the health of present and future generations. Of the many examples of this chemical assault, we will describe one in some detail — the infamous Love Canal.

From 1942 to 1953 the Hooker Chemical Company dumped more than 20,000 tons of toxic chemical waste into the Love Canal near Niagara Falls, New York. After Hooker sold the dump site to the Board of Education in 1953 for one dollar, an elementary school and playground were built on the site, followed by a housing development. For at least twenty years prior to 1977 the toxic chemicals had been seeping through to the land surface. It was in 1977, however, that highly toxic black sludge began seeping into the cellars of the school and nearby residences. Tests showed the existence of eighty-two chemicals in the air, water, and soil of Love Canal, among them twelve known carcinogens including ditoxin, one of the deadliest substances ever synthesized. There is evidence that Hooker Chemical knew of the problem as far back as 1958 but chose not to warn local health officials of any potential problems because cleanup costs would have increased from four to fifty million dollars.

Knowledge of the existence of toxic chemicals in the area caused a financial hardship on the residents because their homes were now worthless. But much more important, tests revealed that the inhabitants of this area had disproportionately high rates of birth defects, miscarriages, chromosomal abnormalities, liver disorders, respiratory and urinary disease, epilepsy, and suicide.[16] In one neighborhood, a few blocks from the Love Canal, a survey by the homeowner's association revealed that only one of the fifteen pregnancies begun in 1979 ended in the birth of a healthy baby — four ended in miscarriages, two babies were stillborn, and nine others were born deformed.[17]

Despite these serious threats to life, health, and the financial costs involved, Hooker Chemical has maintained that the medical evidence is inconclusive and has denied any legal liability for the site. In fact, Hooker spent more that 250,000 dollars to take out ads in twenty-three newspapers and magazines to dispute articles in *The New York Times* and *Business Week* that accused Hooker of being careless with dangerous chemicals.[18] Despite Hooker's claim of innocence, the Environmental Protection Agency is suing the company for 124.5 million dollars and the Agency has (as of 1980) some fourteen billion dollars in compensatory and punitive lawsuits pending.

The list of acts involving America's most powerful political and business organizations and their leaders could be extended almost indefinitely. Similarly, scores of additional opinion polls registering mounting public distrust, cynicism, and alienation regarding America's most powerful economic and political institutions and the individuals who head them could be discussed. What is most important for our purposes, however, is what these incidents have in common. The characteristics they share comprise what we call *elite deviance*. These are:

1. The acts are committed by persons from the *highest strata of society;* members of the upper and upper-middle classes. Some of the deeds mentioned above were committed by the heads of corporate and governmental organizations, others were committed by their employees on behalf of the employers.

2. Some of the acts are crimes in that they are "in violation of criminal statutes (which provide) for fines, terms of imprisonment, or other disabling penalties."[19] Other acts, such as American presidents lying to the public about the Vietnam War, although not illegal, are regarded by most Americans as *unethical or immoral (i.e., deviant)*. Thus, elite deviance may be either criminal or noncriminal in nature.

3. Some of the actions described above were committed by elites themselves for personal gain (e.g., congressmen who accepted bribes), or they were committed by the elites or their employees for purposes of enhancing the power, profitability, or influence of the organizations involved (e.g., when corporations made bribes overseas for the purpose of securing business deals).

4. The acts were committed with relatively little risk. When and if the elites were apprehended, the punishments inflicted were in general quite lenient compared to those given violent ("street") criminals.[20]

5. Some of the incidents posed great danger to the public's safety, health, and financial well-being.

6. In many cases, the elites in charge of the organizations mentioned were able to conceal their illegal or unethical actions for years before they became public knowledge (e.g., Hooker Chemical's dumping of poison chemicals and the presidential misuses of the FBI and the CIA). Yet the actions mentioned were quite compatible with the goals of such organizations (i.e., the maintenance or enhancement of the organization's power and/or profitability).[21]

| These features of elite deviance also involve important issues relative to: (1) composition and power of the American elite, (2) specific types of acts regarded as deviant, (3) causes of elite deviance, and (4) consequences of elite deviance for society. These issues are central to the understanding of elite deviance, and their discussion constitutes the remainder of this chapter. |

THE COMPOSITION AND NATURE OF AMERICAN ELITES

The word elite refers to "groups of persons who in any society hold positions of eminence. More specifically, it denotes persons who are eminent in a particular field — especially the governing minority and the circles from which the governing minority is recruited." [22] Such positions of eminence "are set apart from the rest of society by their" [23] rewards. These rewards generally involve the greatest amount of authority (political power) and/or material gain (wealth and/or income). Virtually all of the world's nations (modern industrial democracies, communist countries, and developing nations) are governed by elites. What distinguishes these nations from each other, in part, are the differences in the strata of society from which elites are recruited, as well as the degree of wealth and power concentrated in elite hands. There are also vast differences among the nations of the world regarding the degree of public scrutiny to which elite decisions are subject.

The social structure of contemporary America is characterized by a heavy concentration of elite wealth and power. Elites here possess not only great riches and the "ability" to make decisions that affect the conduct of nonelites (political power), but they also exert a great deal of control over such resources as:

Education, prestige, status, skills of leadership, information, knowledge of political processes, ability to communicate, and organization. [Moreover,] elites (in America) are drawn disproportionately from ... society's upper classes, which are made up

of those persons . . . who own or control a disproportionate share
of the societal institutions — industry, commerce, finance, education, the military, communications, civic affars, and law.[24]

One recent study concludes that there are 5,416 positions within
the nation's most powerful economic, governmental, military, media,
legal, civic, and educational institutions. These positions constitute a
few ten-thousandths of one percent of the population.[25] Taken collectively, however, this elite of power controls over

> half of the nation's industrial assets; half of the assets in com-
> munications, transportation, and utilities; half of all banking
> assets; and two-thirds of all insurance assets. They commanded
> nearly half of all assets of private foundations and universities,
> as well as the television networks, wire services, and major news-
> paper chains.[26]

The Economic Elite

One basis of this great concentration of power and resources stems
from the wealth possessed by the elite; that is, from its economic power.
Such wealth is owned by relatively few individuals, in families, and corporations. Regarding the wealth owned by individuals, consider that:

> only 55,400 adults have one million dollars or more in corporate
> stock;
>
> only 73,500 adults have 200,000 dollars or more in bonds and
> debt holdings;
>
> one-twentieth of one percent of adults own twenty percent of all
> corporate stock, two-thirds of the worth of all state and local
> bonds, and two-fifths of all bonds and notes; and
>
> the richest one percent own one-seventh of all real estate and one-
> seventh of all cash.[27]

Summing up the situation, two important points emerge. First, the
nation's wealth is centralized with the richest one percent of the population owning about twenty-five percent of the entire population's net
worth; and even this figure belies the real concentration of wealth, since
one-half of one percent owns twenty percent. Second, and contrary to
popular belief, the amount the wealthy own has remained stable over
the years.

> Since the end of World War II, there has been no change in
> their (the wealthy) share of the nation's wealth; it has been con-
> stant in every year studied, at roughly five-year intervals, since
> 1945. The richest 1 percent own a quarter, and the top half of
> 1 percent own a fifth, of the combined market worth of everything

owned by every American. Remarkably, economic historians
who have culled manuscript census reports on the past century
report that on the eve of the Civil War the rich had the same cut
of the total: the top 1 percent owned 24 percent in 1860 and 24.9
percent in 1969 (the latest year thoroughly studied). Through all
the tumultuous changes since then — the Civil War and the
emancipation of the slaves, the Populist and Progressive movements, the Great Depression, the New Deal, progressive taxation,
the mass organization of industrial workers, and World Wars I
and II — this class has held on to everything it had. They owned
America then and they own it now.[28]

Collectively, economic power is *centralized* in relatively few major
corporations and financial institutions:

> Out of the 2 million or so corporations, some 200 nonfinancial
> companies account for 80 percent of all resources used in manu-
> facturing; 60 percent of all assets — three-fifths of all buildings,
> equipment, and land are owned by nonfinancial companies.[29]

One recent Federal Trade Commission study demonstrated that the 200
corporations in manufacturing control assets as large as those controlled
by the largest 1,000 corporations in 1941.[30] One study of the 250
largest American corporations found that all but a handful of them
(seventeen) had at least one of their chief executives sitting on the board
of at least one additional corporation in the top 250. Some of them even
held seats on competing companies, *a practice which has been illegal
since 1914 with the passage of the Clayton Antitrust Act.* Moreover,
even people who serve on the board of directors of one company may
serve as an executive of another company. This situation has been
found to exist for over 250 directors of the top 500 corporations.[31]

More important than such interlocks is the shared ownership that
characterizes American corporate capitalism. Such ownership is concentrated among large banks and wealthy families. Out of the 14,000
commercial banks in the United States, fifty control one-half of all bank
deposits.[32] Many of these banks administer trust funds of wealthy individuals or other sources of capital with which they purchase stock.
The largest forty-nine such banks (as of the mid-1960s) held at least
five percent of the stock (often enough to gain a seat on the board) of
147 of the nation's largest 500 companies.[33] "These 49 banks held a
total of 768 directorships on the boards of 286 of the nation's 500
largest industrial corporations." [34]

And to link things thoroughly, the nation's largest banks (and other
financial institutions) own large chunks of each other. Thus, "the largest
owners of J. P. Morgan and Co. are Citibank and Chase Manhattan.
Morgan and Citibank are the largest shareholders in Bank America Corporation. And if we add Manufacturers Hanover, Chemical Bank, and

Bankers Trust to the picture, the same pattern continues." [35] These banks are owned by wealthy families (e.g., the Rockefellers, the Morgans, the Mellons), whose concern for the workings of the profit system stretches over the corporate order.

What all these facts mean is that the largest 500 or so manufacturing firms and some fifty financial institutions, controlling two-thirds of all business income and half of the nation's bank deposits, are interlocked by directorships and are controlled by less than one-half of one percent of the population. Thus a handful of people make the decisions regarding one-third of the entire gross national product.[36] It is this collectivity which we shall define as the nation's *economic elite*.

The Political Elite

Aside from the economic elite, the nation also possesses a political elite. The *political elite, to a significant extent, overlaps with, yet is independent from, the economic elite*. The corporate managers, owners (super-rich individuals and families), and directors are for the most part members of America's national *upper class*. Membership in the upper class of American society is typically measured by such indicators as (1) having one's name in the *Social Register* (an exclusive list of influential persons published in major American cities and containing the names of about 138,000 persons); (2) attendance at elite private secondary schools and universities; (3) membership in exclusive social clubs and annual attendance at upper-class vacation retreats (e.g., Bohemian Grove, Pacific Union Club, Knickerbocker Club); and, of course, (4) seats on boards of the largest, interlocked corporations.[37]

The political elite differs from the corporate (economic) elite in that it includes persons occupying "key federal government positions in the executive (presidential), judicial (the Supreme Court and lesser federal courts), and legislative (congressional) branches (and) . . . the top command positions in the Army, Navy, Air Force, and Marines." [38] Numerous studies reveal that the political elite is composed of persons from both the *upper-middle* class (e.g., lawyers, small-business people, doctors, farmers, educators, and the other professionals) and the *upper class.* The upper class tends to dominate the federal branch of the government, while upper-middle-class professionals make up the preponderance of the legislative branch. Freitag has recently performed a study of presidential cabinets from McKinley's to Nixon's, studying the degree to which cabinet heads were recruited from the ranks of big business.[39] His data indicate that from 1897 to 1973 big business supplied from 60 percent (under McKinley) to 95.7 percent (under Nixon) of presidential cabinet members.

On the other hand, the 96th Congress (which opened in January, 1979) was composed of 270 lawyers, 156 bankers and/or business people, 64 educators, and 7 doctors. The 1978 Senate had 18 million-aires, and 82 members with net worths between 500,000 and one million dollars.[40] Thus, while the Senate is made up of more affluent members, the House of Representatives is largely composed of slightly less affluent upper-middle class persons.

While it is true that economic power and the power of the state are interlinked, they are not related in a conspiratorial fashion. This is an important point, because a number of people who have written on the subjects of elite power and political corruption do believe in con-spiracies. Some members of the radical right in America believe that not only is America run by a secret clique of wealthy capitalists, but that such a clique is plotting with the Russians to lead the nation to com-munism.[41] A second distorted view of the elite has been put forth by certain "muckraking" journalists, who hold that while the state and the upper class are relatively independent, certain "moral and legal lapses in this independence" [42] occur. This view purports that the business class gets what it desires from government by engaging in all manner of cor-ruption, excessive lobbying, and other forms of illegal or unethical be-havior. The view expressed in this book is that the conspiratorial view of elite behavior is simplistic, that even though conspiracies will and do occur from time to time, such explanations do a disservice to the com-plex nature of elite power and elite deviance.

The conspiratorial view of the elite is unrealistic for a number of reasons. First, not only are the elites somewhat diverse as to class back-grounds, but they are ideologically diverse as well. That is, political opinions among elites range from conservative to social democrat. Al-though it is true that the elites agree on the basic rules of politics (i.e., free elections, the court system, and the rule of law), as well as believe in the capitalist economic system, they disagree considerably about such issues as the power of business, civil rights, welfare, foreign policy, and so on.[43]

Second, elites do not control the federal government because they do not possess a monopoly of political power. The structure of capitalist society is such that elite rule is faced with economic and other crises (e.g., inflation, unemployment, war, racism) which lead nonelite interests to demand changes consistent with their interests (e.g., unemployment bene-fits in periods of high unemployment). As William Chambliss has con-cluded, ". . . The persistence of and importance of the conflicts resolved through law necessarily create occasions where well organized groups representing (nonelite) class interests manage to effect important legis-lation." [44] Thus, in response to such cases as the Love Canal, the Ford Pinto, and a number of others mentioned above, congressional hearings are now being held on a bill (H.R. 4973) that would "impose criminal liability on corporations or corporate managers who knowingly cover up serious and harmful defects in its products and business practices, and impose an affirmative duty to disclose serious dangers to appropriate government agencies and its corporate employees." [45]

Whether this bill will become law is an open question at this point, and one can expect with confidence that the interests adversely affected by the legislation will do what they can to prevent its passage. Nevertheless, in recent years a number of measures that have been opposed by big-business lobbies have become law and/or government policy:

> *Item:* So called white-collar crime has become an investigative priority within the FBI. The Bureau's priorities within this field now include "corruption of government officials . . . frauds in federal programs . . . planned bankruptcies . . ." [46] and such items as bank fraud.
>
> *Item:* The number of public corruption cases investigated by the FBI has risen from 574 in 1978 to over 1,200 in early 1980, and resulted in the conviction of 165 public officials in 1978 alone. [47]
>
> *Item:* In 1970 the Organized Crime Control Act became law. The act involves organized criminal racketeering influence and corrupt organizations (RICO). The law's RICO statute criminalizes not only enterprises with incomes obtained from illegal sources (i.e., Mafia-related activities), but also "the use of an enterprise to commit (or conspire to commit) illegal activities," [48] thus applying to corporations. The act provides maximum penalties of twenty years in prison, and/or a 25,000 dollar fine, and requires forfeiture to the U.S. government of property that was illegally acquired or maintained.

These and other laws serve to illustrate that independent government bureaucracies, such as the FBI, often have ideologies, priorities, and interests that do not always coincide with those of the business elite. Also, interest groups are occasionally successful in getting their laws passed, even when opposed by the elite (e.g., proconsumer groups and Nader's "raiders"). [49]

Third, the conspiratorial view relating to elites dominating the state through corruption masks some of the most important unethical patterns that characterize much of elite deviance. For example, during the hearings regarding Nelson Rockefeller's appointment as vice-president in the mid-1970s, he was questioned about his gift-giving habits but was not held "accountable for the shootings at Attica (prison) or . . . for the involvement of Chase Manhattan (bank) in the repressive system of South African racism." [50]

Likewise, the right wing's conspiratorial view of a capitalist elite plotting to lead the nation into communism hides much of the unethical behavior of corporations that results as a consequence of the structure of corporate capitalism itself. As mentioned, about one-third of the economy is dominated by corporate giants. Such giantism means that in many manufacturing and financial industries (e.g., cereals, soups, autos, and tires), a handful of firms (often four or less) account for over half of the market in a particular industry or service. Such situations are often characterized by artificially high prices due, not to secret price-fixing conspiracies, but to a practice known as "price leadership." This results when one firm decides to raise prices on a given product, and such an increase is adopted by the other major firms in the same field. One Federal Trade Commission economist has estimated that such "monopolistic price distortions cost the economy $87 billion every year" [51] in inflated prices, and that was in the mid-1970s. This and other unethical practices considered in detail in this volume are not accounted for by conspiratorial views of the economy and government, and the linkages between them.

Our position is that it would be more fruitful to consider deviance within the context of the relationships between business and governmental organizations, the functions performed by government, as well as the internal organizational structure of both the corporate and political organizations that constitute the elite sectors of society. In sum, we concur with Michael Parenti's view that "elite power is principally systemic and legitimating rather than conspiratorial and secretive." [52]

ECONOMY-STATE LINKAGES AND THE FUNCTIONS OF GOVERNMENT

To understand the interrelationships between the economy and the state is to comprehend how elites attempt to formulate and implement public policy. These interrelationships are based on connections among corporations, large law firms which represent large corporations, elite colleges and universities, the mass media, private philanthropic foundations, major research organizations ("think tanks"), political parties, and the executive and legislative branch of the federal government. Key examples of these interlocks of monies, personnel, and policies are pictured in Figure 1–1.

Aside from the major corporations and the federal government, the rest of the organizations were included because:

the twelve universities and colleges listed control 50 percent of all educational endowment funds, and include some 656 corporate and other elites as their presidents and trustees;

twelve large foundations, out of 12,000, control 36.8 percent of all foundation assets. These foundations spend money to fund research on broad social problems involving domestic and foreign policy. The officers of such foundations often have experience in the elite corporations, educational institutions, and/or government.

The elite civic associations bring together elites from the corporate, educational, legal, and governmental worlds. Such organizations have been described as "central coordinating mechanisms in national policy making." [53] Such organizations issue public-position papers and investigative reports on matters of domestic and foreign policy. Membership in one or more of these organizations is sometimes a prerequisite to a high-ranking post within the executive branch of the federal government. For example, the majority of the cabinet of the Carter administration, including Jimmy Carter himself, served on the Trilateral Commission prior to assuming office. The Commission was formed by David Rockefeller (chairman of the board of the Chase Manhattan Bank; heir to the Exxon fortune; graduate of Harvard; member of the board of directors of B. F. Goodrich, Rockefeller Bros., Inc., and Equitable Life Insurance; and trustee of Harvard). Rockefeller is also the chairman of the Council on Foreign Relations. Almost all recent secretaries of state, including Cyrus Vance and Henry Kissinger, have been CFR members.[54]

The mass media are concentrated in that there are three major television and radio networks (NBC, ABC, and CBS). These networks are also multinational corporations, who own or are owned by other corporations. CBS, for example, owns the Holt, Rinehart and Winston publishing firm. NBC is owned by RCA, a major manufacturer of appliances and weapons systems components. The media also include major wire services, Associated Press and United Press International, from which most national and international news makes its way into American radio, television, and newspapers. Regarding newspapers, and news weeklies, *The New York Times, The Washington Post, Time, Newsweek* (owned by the *Washington Post*), and *U.S. News and World Report* are regarded as the most influential publications in their field.[55] Controlling shares in the three television networks are owned by five New York commercial banks (Chase Manhattan, Morgan Guaranty, Citibank, Bankers Trust, and the Bank of New York).[56]

Moreover, the major sponsors of television programs on the three networks are other large corporations. The media tend to portray deviant behavior as violent behavior which is perpetrated by powerless and poor nonelites. As one recent study concludes, the crime reported in television news and newsmagazines includes kidnappings, "mass murders, or murderers who kill their victims in usually grisley ways. . . . Ordinary people who carry out nonviolent crimes or violate the mores rarely appear in national news." [57]   On the other hand,

> the economically powerful, such as officers of large corporations and holders of great wealth, are filmed or written about rarely, and then usually for reasons having little to do with their economic power — primarily when they are involved in some conflict with the federal government or are having legal difficulties.[58]

Overall, the media function to portray crime and deviance as a problem created by nonelites and to describe corporate capitalism as a system characterized by competition, freedom, and, while flawed, the best of all existing worlds.   As a *Time Magazine* profile recently put it:

> Plainly capitalism is not working well enough.   But there is no evidence to show the fault is in the system — or that there is a better alternative. . . .   For all its obvious blemishes and needed reforms, capitalism still holds out the most creative and dynamic force that any civilization has ever discovered: the power of the free ambitious individual.[59]

Such propagandistic exercises are also characteristic of numerous television commercials and public-service announcements (often prepared by the elite National Advertising Council) which insist that the oil companies are "working to keep your trust," or that our "economics quotients" (knowledge about the American economic system) could stand improvement.   Thus one overall function of the mass media is to ensure the continuation and growth of the system of corporate capitalism.

There are twenty-eight "super" law firms, that do much of the legal work for the corporations, mass media, and educational and civic foundations.   In addition, senior lawyers in such firms often fill posts on various foundations and civic and educational institutions and from time to time assume various posts within the executive branch of the federal government.   A good example of one such "superlawyer" is Paul Warnke, President Carter's chief negotiator in the Strategic Arms Limitation Talks (SALT).   Warnke is also a member of the Trilateral Commission, a director of the Council on Foreign Relations, a former assistant secretary of defense, and partner in a Washington law firm that includes former Defense Secretary Clark Clifford.[60]

Finally, there are a host of elite-related "think tanks."   Think tanks are primarily research institutes.   In general, these operations receive monies from both public and private sources, depending on the type of research they do.   For example, about five percent of the Defense Department's Research and Development budget in the 1960s and early 1970s went to such research organizations.[61]

Such organizations perform a very wide variety of research tasks. For instance, The Rand Corporation and the Stanford Research Institute (owned by Stanford University until 1970) throughout the 1960s and 1970s performed many tasks for the Pentagon. These included everything from language training of military personnel to feasibility studies regarding the use of nuclear, chemical, and biological weapons. Such institutes were heavily involved in research on various aspects of guerrilla and counterguerrilla warfare in both Southeast Asia and other portions of the Third World during this period.

Other "think tanks," such as the American Enterprise Institute, are more closely allied with the business arm of the American power elite. The American Enterprise Institute is allied with the conservative wing of the Republican Party and Southern Democrats. Its activities primarily involve studies, the end products of which are policy proposals aimed at enhancing the profitability and power of its corporate clients.[62]

The American Enterprise Institute and other think tanks also prepare studies for influential big-business lobby groups, such as the National Association of Manufacturers and the United States Chamber of Commerce.

In short, "think tanks" provide valuable research aid in achieving the policy aims of elites both inside and outside of government.

Figure 1–1 depicts the structures which supply personnel, money, and policy to the federal government, but does not describe the processes used by or the benefits sought by elites from the state. Such means and benefits are important in that, when they are abused, they constitute forms of elite deviance. These benefits will be discussed below.

Lobbying

The principle of majority rule is sometimes violated by the special interests, which by deals, propaganda, and the financial support of political candidates, attempt to deflect the political process for their own benefit. Individuals, families, corporations, and various organizations use a variety of means to obtain numerous benefits (see below) from congressional committees, regulatory agencies, and executive bureaucracies. To accomplish their goals, lobbyists for the special interests

> along with the slick brochures, expert testimonies, and technical reports, . . . still have the slush fund, the kickback, the stock

award, the high paying job offer from industry, the lavish parties and prostitutes, the meals, transportation, housing and vacation accommodations, and the many other hustling enticements of money.[63]

The existence of lobbyists does not ensure that the national interest will be served or that the concern of all groups will be heard. Who, for example, speaks for the interests of school children, minority groups, the poor, the mentally retarded, renters, migrant workers — in short, for the relatively powerless? And if there is a voice for these people, does it match the clout of lobbyists backed by the fantastic financial resources of the elite?

In fairness it must be stressed that the success of such lobbies is not ensured:

> Big economic interests don't always win. The cargo preference bill was defeated. So was the 1979 sugar quota. The Consumer Cooperative Bank bill passed the House by one vote and became law. Sometimes scandal or the weight of evidence can push Congress in the right direction. And it must be noted that when a congressman from Michigan votes to bail out Chrysler, or a congressman from Wisconsin votes for dairy price supports, he is also voting to benefit his own constituents. This may not favor the public interest, but it is predictable politics, not personal corruption.
>
> ... To receive money from an interest doesn't mean a member of Congress is controlled, per se. There are indentured politicians and there are principled conservatives — the former virtually auction their souls to the highest bidder while the latter may truly believe that the government shouldn't be forcing pharmaceutical firms to pre-market-test their drugs.[64]

Nevertheless, corporate lobbies usually *do* exert a significant influence (see below).

The Financing of Political Campaigns

Perhaps one of the most elite dominated and undemocractic features (at least in its consequences) of the American political system is a result of the manner in which campaigns are financed. Political campaigns are expensive, with state-wide campaigns sometimes costing hundreds of thousands of dollars, and a national campaign running into the millions. These monies are raised from contributions. Nixon, for example, received 47.5 million dollars from ninety-five persons for his 1972 campaign (including two million from W. Clement Stone, an insurance executive). Such contributions are given for a number of reasons, including the hope of future favors or payoffs for past benefits. In the 1978 election campaign, for example, the American Medical Asso-

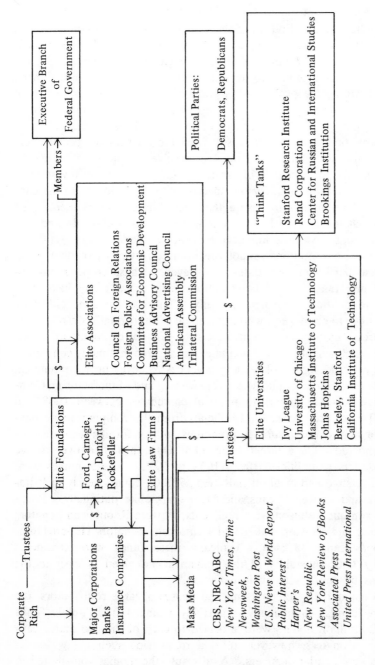

Figure 1–1. Capitalist Elite — Ruling Elite Linkages.

Source: Adapted from G. W. Domhoff, "State and Ruling Class in Corporate America," *The Insurgent Sociologist,* 3 (Spring, 1974), pp. 3–16. Used with permission.

ciation (AMA) contributed 1.79 million dollars into congressional campaign contributions. Following the election a House committee voted by a one-vote margin to kill hospital cost-containment legislation that would have saved 27 billion dollars through 1982. Interestingly, the AMA had donated money to the campaigns of all committee members, but those voting the pro-AMA position of that legislation received an average of $4,482, while those voting against the AMA had received only $1,007.[65] Thus, the passage of favorable laws or the defeat of unfavorable ones may directly result from the finances of special interests. So, too, may the special interests receive beneficial governmental rulings and the maintenance of tax loopholes. Since these investments pay off, it is only rational for the special interests to donate to the candidates of both parties to ensure that their interests are served. The result is that the wealthy have power while the less well-to-do and certainly the poor have little influence on office holders.[66]

By law, corporations cannot contribute directly any of their funds to political parties or candidates. However, because corporations apparently find that political contributions help them, many have contributed to political campaigns illegally. This can be done either by giving money to employees, who in turn make "individual" contributions, or by forcing employees to contribute to a party or candidate as a condition of employment. The Watergate case showed that many companies engaged in fraudulent bookkeeping practices to cover up their political expenditures. For example, Minnesota Mining and Manufacturing Company gave 634,000 dollars to political candidates between 1963 and 1969. To achieve such a fund, officials from the company made payments for nonexisting insurance premiums and for foreign legal services never rendered. On a larger scale, Gulf Oil contributed over twelve million dollars to politicians from 1959 to 1972. These monies were provided to state and local officials (e.g., 75,000 dollars yearly in Pennsylvania) and to Republicans and Democrats alike nationally. Presidents Nixon and Johnson were recipients, as were Republican Senators Hugh Scott and Howard Baker and Democratic Senators Hubert Humphrey and Henry Jackson. Typically these funds were channeled through a Gulf subsidiary in the Bahamas and given in cash to the politicians by couriers to avoid detection.[67]

To counter the potential and real abuses of large contributors, the 1976 presidential campaign was partially financed from public funds (about 20 million dollars were allocated to each of the two major candidates). Congress, however, refused to provide such a law for its members or potential members. As a result, the monies contributed to congressional candidates rose sharply. In 1978 the total gifts from all reporting interest groups to candidates for Congress was 35 million dollars, compared to 22.6 million in 1976 and only 12.5 million in 1974.

The evidence, then, clearly shows that the amount that interest groups spend on electing sympathetic senators and congresspersons is

growing rapidly. Moreover, this money makes a difference in elections.
In the 1978 Senate election, for example, the biggest campaign spender
won in eighty-five percent of the elections. The result is that democracy
is weakened. As Senator Edward Kennedy has said:

> Representative government on Capitol Hill is in the worst shape
> I have seen it in my sixteen years in the Senate. The heart of the
> problem is that the Senate and the House are awash in a sea of
> special-interest campaign contributions and special-interest lob-
> bying.[68]

The Candidate-selection Process

Closely related to the above discussion is the process by which
political candidates are nominated. Being wealthy or having access to
wealth are essential for victory because of the enormous cost (it costs
up to three million dollars to elect a senator and as much as 600,000
dollars for a representative). This means, then, that the candidates
tend to represent a limited constituency — the wealthy. "Recruitment
of elective elites remains closely associated, especially for the most important offices in the larger states, with the candidates' wealth or access
to large campaign contributions." [69]

The two-party system also works to limit candidates to a rather
narrow range. Each party is financed by the special interests — especially business.

> When all of these direct and indirect gifts (donations provided
> directly to candidates or through numerous political-action com-
> mittees of specific corporations and general business organiza-
> tions) are combined, the power elite can be seen to provide the
> great bulk of the financial support to both parties at the national
> level, far outspending the unions and middle-status liberals within
> the Democrats, and the mélange of physicians, dentists, engineers,
> real-estate operators, and other white-collar conservatives within
> the right wing of the Republican party.[70]

Since affluent individuals and the largest corporations dominate each
party, they influence the candidate-selection process by giving financial
aid to those sympathetic with their views and by withholding their support from those who differ. The parties, then, are constrained to choose
candidates with views congruent with the elite monied interests.

THE BENEFITS THAT ELITES
SEEK FROM THE STATE

From what we have said about lobbying, election financing, and
candidate selection, it is obvious that corporate elites devote considerable

resources to political activities, and for good reasons. The state not only regulates the capitalist economy, but also (federal, state, and local government) now accounts for 32.2 percent of the gross national product.[71] Two-thirds of these goods and services stem from spending by the federal government alone. Thus elites seek favorable legislation (or prevention of unfavorable legislation), as well as tax breaks, subsidies, and lucrative government contracts. Such contracts include everything from multibillion-dollar weapons systems to office furniture and paint. These contracts are not only influenced by the decisions of congressional members, but are often the charge of various bureaucrats with the federal government. The Government Services Administration (GSA), for example, is in charge of securing virtually all office supplies for the entire federal government. Thus favors from lobbyists are also from time to time dispensed to bureaucrats as well as elected members of Congress. These are illegal when they include kickbacks (payments by contractors that usually involve a certain percentage of the contract in which a firm is interested). Other times there may simply be the promise of a job with the company upon completion of government services. While not illegal, these types of deals are unethical.

In addition, a host of independent regulatory agencies (e.g., Federal Communications Commission, Interstate Commerce Commission, Federal Trade Commission, etc.) impact on virtually every large and small business in America. The personnel in these agencies are not infrequently the target of various lobbying and other efforts (e.g., the promise of a job in the very industry they regulate). Often, certain staff members of these agencies come from the industries they oversee, and in some cases the industries involved requested the initial regulation (for reasons explained directly below).

Finally, we cannot leave this discussion without a brief mention of the influence that elites possess over the enactment or lack of enactment of legislation which defines *what is* and *is not against* the law in the first place. Examples of such influence are legion:

> *Item:* Although the House had passed a bill to create a Federal Consumer Protective Agency by 293 to 94, it was defeated in the Senate by a filibuster. The bill was opposed by the National Association of Manufacturers, the National Association of Feed Chains, and some 300 other companies and trade associations.[72]

> *Item:* The automobile industry got the Justice Department to sign a consent decree that blocked any attempt by public or private means to sue them for damages occurring from air pollution.

> *Item:* Many of the nation's antitrust laws appear, on the surface, to be actions which regulate business. However, many of these laws were actually requested by big business. Such laws, as we shall see in Chapter 2, exclude new competitors from the market-

place, and have been used to reduce the influence of labor unions. Such laws have also functioned to increase public confidence in the quality of food and drugs by having such products certified "safe" by government inspection. For example, "The 1906 Meat Inspection Act . . . gained much popular support because of the muckraking activities of Upton Sinclair (who exposed the foul conditions in the meat-processing industry), but it also delighted the large meat-packers. It helped them export successfully by fulfilling the high safety standards demanded by European countries, but it crippled smaller companies. Americans were left with poor quality meat and wages of workers. . . ." [73] Such laws often help create uncompetitive (monopolistic) situations, and are usually welcome (even favored) by big businesses. Moreover, such laws are rarely enforced and the penalties for breaking them tend to be miniscule.

Numerous additional examples could be cited of instances where corporate officials and/or politicians have, without penalty, violated laws or prevented acts from being made public which involved the theft of great amounts of money and/or the taking of many lives. Here we have another of the great problems when it comes to dealing with the deviance of corporations, or powerful individuals: all laws are not administered equally; those laws that are administered most seriously tend to be those related to the deviance of the powerless nonelites. This process works in very subtle ways, but nevertheless that ensures a bias in favor of the more affluent.

One way in which this bias operates is illustrated by examining the priority given investigation and prosecution of corporate crimes within the federal government. Despite some advances noted above in recent years, corporate crime remains a low priority:

Item: In 1977 and 1978, the Department of Justice spent only 5.1 percent of its resources on so-called "white-collar crime" and public corruption.

Item: The Department of Justice's Criminal Fraud Section, which is responsible for federal prosecutions of illegal payments made overseas by American corporations, all government-program fraud cases, and all oil fraud cases for fiscal year 1979 possessed a total budget of only 2.4 million dollars and a staff of only fifty attorneys.

Item: As of 1979 the Law Enforcement Assistance Administration had devoted less than three percent of its discretionary research grants to programs related to elite crime, and, as of 1980, the federal government still possesses no centralized statistical capability to index the extent of elite and other "white-collar" crimes. Yet for years the FBI, via its Uniform Crime Reports, has monitored so-called "street crimes" involving both violence and crimes against property (e.g., burglary).[74]

In fact, the Criminal Justice section of the American Bar Association has issued a report concluding that:

> For the most part within the Federal agencies with direct responsibility in the economic crime offenses area, available resources are unequal to the task of combatting economic crime.
>
> The ABA . . . also found that in cases where "seemingly adequate resources exist, these resources are poorly deployed, underutilized, or frustrated by jurisdictional considerations." [75]

Thus the bias of the federal law-enforcement effort, as well as state and local efforts (see Chapter 2) remains slanted toward the crimes of non-elites.

THE CLASSIFICATION OF ELITE DEVIANCE

The bias of the law-enforcement effort in areas other than elite deviance has had dramatic consequences for the scholarly study of such acts. Federal-granting agencies and elite foundations have, historically, provided little funding for the study of elites. The first empirical study of elite deviance was not published until 1940 (Sutherland's *White Collar Crime*), and there has been what Clinard and Yeager describe as "little follow-up research, with only minimal study being carried out on illegal corporate behavior." [76]

With such minimal study devoted to the subject, such terms as "white-collar crime" have become quite ambiguous. The head of the FBI recently defined white-collar crime as "crimes that are committed by non-physical means to avoid payment or loss of money or to obtain business or personal advantage where success depends upon guile or concealment." [77] Moreover he applied the term to crimes committed by persons from "every socioeconomic stratum," [78] thus including both elites and nonelites. The view of elite deviance discussed here differs considerably from this definition. First, our concern, as we made clear above, is only with persons of the highest socioeconomic status. That is, we have defined the elites of American society as comprised of corporate and government officials. We have done this because of the enormous wealth and power that resides in the nation's political economy — the relationship between the economic and political institution. We have, therefore, not included in our discussion labor unions or organized criminal syndicates, except insofar as there are relationships between these organizations and corporate and/or governmental entities that are deviant (as when the CIA hired Mafia members to assassinate Castro). Second, we also hasten to include in the category of elite deviance unethical/immoral acts. This is not a view that is shared by all students of the subject. One criminologist described a similar classification as "definitional quicksand." [79] In a way this is true. What is criminal is often easily understood by studying only those acts that are codified in criminal statutes. This would make our task relatively easy. But such an approach overlooks many complexities. For example, in most instances "only a short step separates unethical tactics from violations of law. Many practices that were formerly considered unethical have now been made illegal and (are) punished by government." [80] Such acts include air and water pollution, bribes made overseas by multinational corporations, the disregard of safety and health standards, and false advertising. Thus what is considered unethical at one point in time often becomes illegal later.

We concede that the definition of what is unethical is, like deviance itself, often "in the eye of the beholder," [81] and is subject to intense debate. Nevertheless, as one observer of the subject states:

> It is all too human to bracket law breaking with immorality, to assume that a (person) who offends against the law is ipso facto less moral than one whose activities remain within the legally permitted. Yet a few moments' honest reflection will convince us that the mere fact of transgressing the legal code or not tells us very little about our spiritual condition.[82]

Our position is that it is unavoidable, and indeed desirable, that students of deviance concern themselves with our "spiritual condition." As Galliher and McCartney, two criminologists, have pointed out:

> If sociology makes no moral judgement independent of criminal statutes, it becomes sterile and inhumane — the work of moral eunuchs or legal technicians. . . . If moral judgements above and beyond criminal law were not made, the laws of Nazi Germany would be indistinguishable from the laws of many other nations. Yet the Nuremberg trials after World War II advanced the position that numerous officials of the Nazi government, *although admittedly acting in accordance with German laws,* were behaving in such a grossly immoral fashion as to be criminally responsible. . . . In the Nuremberg trials, *representatives of the Allied governments — France, England, the Soviet Union, and the United States — explicitly and publically supported the idea of a moral order and moral judgements independent of written law.* . . . The claim was that . . . the defendants had committed atrocities against humanity. . . . The example of Nuremberg shows that moral judgements by students of crime can be made independently of particular cultural definitions of crime.[83]

Thus the inclusion of unethical acts in the study of elite deviance represents not merely a residual category, but the cutting edge of a neglected and important field of inquiry.

Third, one view of white-collar crime differentiates acts of personal enrichment from acts that are committed on behalf of one's employer.[84] This often becomes a difficult distinction to maintain when studying the deviance of elites because some elites are owners of the organizations in which, and on behalf of whom, they commit such acts. This distinction is probably easier to maintain when discussing political corruption than it is when discussing economic deviance. However, many politicians receive illegal payments or campaign contributions for the purpose of winning elections, not necessarily for the purpose of hiding such monies in secret bank accounts, or making other personally enriching expenditures.

Also, some act of employees, committed on behalf of employers, are *indirectly* personally enriching. Often such acts are committed for the purpose of ensuring job security or for obtaining a promotion within the organization. This is not to say that employees never embezzle funds for personal use or that politicians do not take graft for the purpose of adding to their personal bank accounts. Our point is simply that the distinction between acts that are personally enriching and acts committed on behalf of maintaining and/or increasing the profitability or power of an organization in which one is owner or employer is difficult to maintain when examining various acts of elite deviance.

Therefore, our view of the types of acts that encompass the field of elite deviance include the following.[85]

Acts of Economic Domination

These are crimes and unethical deeds that are usually committed by corporations, or by corporations in league with other organizations (e.g., the CIA). Typically, such crimes include violations of antitrust laws, which prohibit the formation of monopolies, price fixing, and false advertising. These are also crimes that involve defrauding consumers, pollution of the environment, and bribing politicians, both at home and overseas. Then there are crimes committed by business, such as not correcting unsafe working conditions and the deliberate manufacture of unsafe goods and hazardous medicines and foods. And, as mentioned, there are instances where corporations illegally enter into business ventures with organized criminal syndicates.

Moreover, it is important to note that some acts of economic deviance that are crimes in the United States are legal abroad. For example, in one instance an organic mercury fungicide, which was banned (by law) for sale in the United States, was used in Iraq to coat by-products of 8,000 tons of wheat and barley. This resulted in 400 deaths and 5,000 hospitalizations among Iraqui customers.[86] This "dumping" of unsafe products is a 1.2 billion dollar business, but is perceived as unethical by journalists, government officials, and certain business people.

Finally, mention was made above concerning the *unethical* and generally unfair advantage gained by corporations in their efforts to influence government policies. Here we consider tax loopholes and other forms of corporate "welfare" including subsidies, and certain special favors granted in doing business with the government.

Crimes of Government and Governmental Control

This category includes a host of acts involving the usurpation of power. Involved here are the so-called Watergate crimes, crimes of electioneering, and other acts involving violations of civil liberties, graft, and corruption designed to perpetuate a given administration and to further enrich its members. "There are also those offenses committed by the government against persons and groups who would seemingly threaten national security. Included here are crimes of warfare and the political assassination of foreign and domestic leaders." [87]

Related to offenses against those viewed as threats to the national security are violations of civil rights of certain persons in various forms, including illegal surveillance by federal (or other) law-enforcement agencies, infiltration of law-abiding political groups by FBI/CIA agent provacateurs, and denials of due process of law.

Many unethical acts are also committed by governmental organizations and officials. Some examples include classifying certain types of information as "secret" simply to cover up embarrassing incidents, making campaign promises that candidates know they cannot or will not keep, defining a situation as a genuine crisis where no real crisis conditions exist, letting out government contracts without competitive bidding, and allowing cost overruns on such contracts.

Elite Deviance as Denials of Basic Human Rights

Related to both deviance by corporations and deviance by governments are actions that contribute to various types of social injuries. Included here are threats to the dignity and quality of life for specific groups, and humanity as a whole. Included are such practices as racism and sexism, either political or economic. In addition is the threat to the human race posed by the nuclear arms race. While such notions are not always part of a nation's laws, they do enter into any value judgments made concerning the worth and dignity of individuals.

A body of international agreement and law contains some basic notions concerning human rights. Most nations of the world, including undemocratic nations, now agree that such rights should include basic material needs being met, as well as freedom from torture, arbitrary arrest and detention, assassination, and kidnapping.

Thus the criminal and unethical acts of corporations and government, plus violations of basic human rights, which are part of certain bodies of international agreements subscribed to by the United States constitute the subject matter of elite deviance.

THE CONDITIONS LEADING
TO ELITE DEVIANCE

In the remainder of our inquiry into the various types of elite deviance, the following assumptions will be made regarding the causes, costs, and consequences of such actions:

First, organizations are often characterized by what has been termed "the shield of elitist invisibility." [88] This refers to actions, as well as heads of political organizations and governmental agencies, being frequently shrouded in secrecy. Corporate management and government officials are often shielded from the press, government investigators, and, often, from the boards of directors (in the case of corporations) by virtue of the power they possess over information. For example, the illegal payments made by the Gulf Oil Company during the 1970s were kept secret from the board of directors by Gulf's chief executive officer for over eighteen months after the scandal made headlines.

Such deceptions are possible in huge organizations. Corporations are often international organizations, characterized by "complex and varied sets of structural relationships between the boards of directors, executives, managers, and other employees on the one hand, and between parent corporation, corporate divisions, and subsidiaries on the other." [89] These complex relationships often make it impossible for outsiders and many insiders to determine who is responsible for what, and such structural complexities make it relatively easy to perform a host of acts corporate managers wish to be kept secret.

Next, the benefits involved in such deviance far outweigh the risks of apprehension and penalties. For example, it has been estimated by a Senate Judiciary Subcommittee on Antitrust and Monopoly that the dollar amount of corporate crime (i.e., antitrust violations, etc., such as price fixing and fraudulent advertising, and so on) ranges from between 174 and 231 billion dollars per year.[90] This is more than all other types of crime plus the cost of running the entire criminal justice system combined. No source can give exact estimates concerning the costs of political corruption and various kickbacks, but it has been estimated by *The New York Times* that business bribery and kickbacks, at least a portion of which goes to politicians, may run as high as 15 billion dollars per year.[91] Thus the monetary rewards of corporate and political crime are virtually without parallel.

Coupled with these rewards are minimal risks. From 1890 to 1970 only three businessmen were sent to jail for violations of the Sherman Antitrust Act (see Chapter 2 for details), and from 1946 to 1953 the average fine levied in such cases was 2,600 dollars (with 5,000 dollars being the maximum possible).[92]

From the above, one can see that there is very little incentive not to violate some laws. And as criminologist Donald Cressey has stated: "Some businessmen have so little respect for the law that they would prefer an antitrust indictment to being caught wearing argyle socks. . . . They do so because they do not believe in these laws. This is another way of saying that they consider such laws . . . illegitimate." [93] Thus the prime goal of business is to make profits, and within business's ideology, government regulation is often viewed as meddling. In summary, organizational structure, complexity, and primary goals (e.g., autonomy and profit) all help to shield top-level officials from the scrutiny of the press and the law. In addition, the lenient penalties for much elite deviance are ineffectual in deterring such deviance.

THE CONSEQUENCES OF ELITE DEVIANCE

The consequences of elite deviance to American society are thought to be monumental by most experts. Consider the following:

1. It is estimated that five times as many persons each year die from illnesses and injuries contracted on the job (100,000 to 200,000 persons) than are murdered by all street criminals[94] (see Chapters 3 and 4 for details).

2. We have observed that public confidence, as measured by numerous opinion polls, in our economic and political elites has drastically declined as revelations of elite deviance have taken place. In addition, many criminologists believe that deviance by elites provides either motivation or rationalization for non-elites to commit profit-oriented crimes.[95]

3. The power of elites to help shape criminal law and its enforcement raises serious questions regarding the racial and class biases of the criminal justice system's traditional equating of the "crime problem" in America with "street crime." [96]

4. The monetary costs of elite deviance are thought to contribute substantially to inflation. As mentioned, estimates range from 174 to 231 billion dollars in the prices added to goods and services.

5. It will be demonstrated (Chapter 2) that elite deviance has been an important cause of the persistence and growth of organized crime in America. This assistance has been provided by both economic and political elites.

Also, one sociologist has argued that there exists a symbiotic (mutually interdependent) relationship between deviance by elites and deviance by nonelites. This is because elite deviance affects greatly the distribution of power in society. As mentioned, much elite deviance is aimed at maintaining or increasing the proportion of wealth and power which rests in elite hands. Given the inequitable distribution of such resources, the most powerless and economically deprived members of society suffer from social conditions "that tend to provoke powerless individuals into criminality." [97] Likewise it is possible that elites, who view themselves as respectable members of society, view the deviance of the powerless as the genuinely dangerous type of crime faced by society. Such elite attitudes result in elites viewing themselves as morally superior to nonelites, and the crimes which they themselves commit as not "really" criminal. Thus elites may be even more likely to violate legal and ethical standards because of the deviance of nonelites, which is in part caused by the inequitable distribution of resources, the existence of which are, in turn, related to elite power.

Finally, the consequences listed above regarding elite deviance constitute a mere beginning in this regard. The relationship between the acts of the powerful and those of the powerless, especially deviant acts, are not well investigated by scholars. Moreover, the behavior of elites, insofar as it effects an alienation and loss of confidence among nonelites, undoubtedly has additional negative consequences about which we have much to learn. What is clear is that elite deviance possesses numerous important social, economic, and political consequences for all of society, only a few of the most dramatic of which will be examined in this volume.

CONCLUSION

This chapter has introduced the topic of elite deviance. Because of the Vietnam conflict, Watergate, and numerous recent incidents involving corporate and governmental wrongdoings, elite deviance has become a major concern of the public. Closer examination reveals that the deviant acts of economic and political elites are not random events. They are related to the very structure of wealth and power in America and to the processes which maintain such structures (organizations).

Moreover, aside from being illegal or unethical (at least according to the norms maintained by persons outside the organization committing the deviant act), elite deviance:

> 1. Occurs because it furthers the goals of economic and political organizations, namely, the maintenance or increase of profit and/or power.

2. Is committed with the support of the elites, who head such organizations. Such support may be open and active, or covert and implied.

3. May be committed either by elites and/or employees acting on their behalf.[98]

Finally, such deviance is important because it possesses many negative consequences for society, including high prices, dangerous products, and the increased motivation to commit deviance on the part of non-elites. Elite deviance, despite all of the public attention recently devoted to it, remains a poorly understood, and hence unresolved, social problem in our society. Since corporations and government now touch nearly every aspect of our daily lives, it behooves all of us to learn as much as possible about the dimensions and possible solutions to this type of deviant behavior.

THE ORGANIZATION OF THIS BOOK

The remainder of this book is largely devoted to an examination of the types of deviance introduced above. The next chapter discusses the "higher immorality" as a systematic aspect of the American elite. "Higher immorality" refers to a sort of systemic violation of the laws and ethics of business and politics. This includes everything from the hiring of prostitutes to close business agreements, to the hiring of members of criminal syndicates to gain a business or political advantage. In addition, the term refers to special advantages that business executives receive from government, including tax advantages, and subsidies, as well as special salary arrangements that bypass the tax laws. The term also applies to the violation of antitrust laws. Hence it covers a host of illegal and unethical practices.

Chapters 3 and 4 are devoted exclusively to economic deviance. Specifically, Chapter 3 details the problems generated by the monopolistic structure of the economy, including price fixing, price gouging, deceptive advertising, and fraud. Chapter 4 is devoted to a discussion of the more dangerous aspects of corporate deviance, including hazardous products, pollution, dangerous working conditions, and resource waste.

Chapter 5 examines the international dimensions of corporate and political deviance. Described here are discussions of America's defense policy, including defense contracting and arms sales, the bribery and product dumping of multinational corporations, and violations of human rights as they relate to American foreign policy and the questionable practices of multinational corporations.

Chapters 6 and 7 deal exclusively with various dimensions of political deviance. Chapter 6 focuses on the types of political corruption that have characterized the history of American domestic politics. Chapter 7 explores political repression in the United States, including the bias of the criminal-justice system, as well as the abuses of power perpetrated by such agencies as the FBI, the CIA, and the Internal Revenue Service.

The Epilogue grew out of the authors' mutual experiences with students. Often students become fatalistic about resolving social problems that relate to the distribution of wealth and power in the United States. Our conviction is that the United States is democratic in form, and that meaningful solutions to the problem of elite deviance can come through democratic processes. We do not believe that the necessary changes will be easy but we insist that they are worth struggling to attain. The Epilogue describes one plan for changing the economic system significantly. We feel that this proposal will eliminate or at least minimize the forms of elite deviance discussed in this book. We invite the reader to consider this plan seriously and to think of other alternatives that might be effective in diminishing elite deviance.

NOTES

1. *The New York Times* (Jan. 21, 1974), p. 16.

2. *Ibid.*

3. See Sam Adams, "Vietnam Cover-Up Playing War with Numbers," *Harper's* (May 1975), pp. 93–105, in C. Swanson, ed., *Focus: Unexplored Deviance* (Guilford, CN: Dushkin, 1978); and A. Rogow, *The Dying of the Light* (New York: Putnam, 1975), pp. 261–271.

4. Rogow, *Dying of the Light*, p. 262.

5. See Michael Parenti, *Democracy for the Few*, Third Edition (New York: St. Martins, 1980), pp. 154–155.

6. See Alan Wolfe, *The Seamy Side of Democracy*, Second Edition (New York: Longman, 1978), p. vii.

7. David Alpern, "A Question of Ethics," *Newsweek* 24 (July 14, 1976), pp. 21–22.

8. See "Opinion Roundup," *Public Opinion* 5 (Oct/Nov, 1979), p. 31.

9. *Ibid.*

10. See M. Clinard and P. Yeager, "Corporate Crime: Issues in Research," *Criminology* 2 (Aug., 1978), p. 260.

11. *Ibid.*

12. S. Balken et al., *Crime and Deviance in America: A Critical Approach* (Belmont, CA: Wadsworth, 1980), p. 170.

13. J. Roebuck and S. C. Weeber, *Political Crime in the United States: Analyzing Crime by and against Government* (New York: Praeger, 1978), p. 86.

14. "End of the Great Engine Flap: Settlement of Suit against GM for Use of Chevrolet Engines in Other Cars," *Time* 111 (January 2, 1978), p. 66.

15. See J. Conyers, Jr., "Corporate and White-Collar Crime: A View by the Chairman of the House Subcommittee on Crime," *American Criminal Law Review* 17 (March, 1980), p. 290; and W. E. Blundell, "Equity Funding: I Did It for the Jollies," pp. 153–185 in J. Johnson and J. Douglas, eds., *Crime at the Top: Deviance in Business and the Professions* (Philadelphia: Lippincott, 1978), p. 182.

16. Conyers, "Corporate and White-Collar Crime," p. 294. See also United Press International release (May 18, 1980).

17. Ralph Nader and Ronald Brownstein, "Beyond the Love Canal," *The Progressive* 44 (May 1980), p. 28.

18. *Ibid.,* p. 30.

19. G. Geis, "Upper World Crime," pp. 114–137, in A. Blumberg, ed., *Current Perspectives on Criminal Behavior: Original Essays in Criminology* (New York: Knopf, 1974), p. 116.

20. See Alex Thio, *Deviant Behavior* (Boston: Houghton Mifflin, 1978), p. 353.

21. See M. Mintz and J. Cohen, *Power, Inc.* (New York: Viking, 1976), p. xix.

22. J. Gould and W. Kolb, *A Dictionary of the Social Sciences* (New York: Free Press, 1964), p. 234.

23. Suzanne Keller, "Elites," in D. Sills, ed., *International Encyclopedia of the Social Sciences,* Volume 5 (New York: Free Press/Macmillan, 1968), p. 26.

24. T. Dye and H. Zeigler, *The Irony of Democracy,* Third Edition (N. Scituate, MA: Duxbury, 1975), p. 4. For an excellent summary of the evidence supporting the existence of an elite, see Harold Kerbo and Richard Della Fave, "The Empirical Side of the Power Elite Debate," *The Sociological Quarterly* 20 (Winter 1979), pp. 5–220.

25. *Ibid.,* pp. 14, 19, 235.

26. *Ibid.,* pp. 234–235.

27. Maurice Zeitlin, "Who Owns America? The Same Old Gang," *The Progressive* (June 1978), pp. 14–19.

28. *Ibid.*

29. *Ibid.*

30. See G. David Garson, *Power and Politics in the United States* (Lexington, MA: D. C. Heath, 1977), p. 181.

31. The figures are taken from Peter Evens and Steve Schneider, "The Political Economy of the Corporation," in Scott McNall, ed., *Critical Issues in Sociology* (Chicago: Scott, Foresman, 1980).

32. *Ibid.*

33. The Patman Committee, 1968, "Investments and Interlocks Between Major Banks and Major Corporations," pp. 70–76, in I. Zeitlin, ed., *American Society, Inc.* (Chicago: Markham, 1970), p. 74.

34. *Ibid.,* p. 75.

35. Evans and Schneider, "Political Economy of the Corporation." See also Subcommittee on Government Affairs (U.S. Senate), *Voting Rights in Major Corporations* (Washington, D.C.: U.S. Government Printing Office, 1978).

36. Garson, *Power and Politics,* pp. 181–182, 185.

37. G. William Domhoff, *Who Rules America?* (Englewood Cliffs, N.J.: Prentice-Hall, 1967), pp. 87–96.

38. T. R. Dye and J. W. Pickering, "Governmental and Corporate Elites: Convergence and Differentiation," *Journal of Politics* 36 (Nov., 1974), p. 905.

39. P. Freitag, "The Cabinet and Big Business: A Study of Interlocks," *Social Problems* 23 (December 1975), pp. 137–152. See also R. J. Barnet, *The Political Economy of Death* (New York: Antheneum, 1969), pp. 88–89.

40. R. Weissberg, *Understanding American Government* (New York: Holt, Rinehart and Winston, 1980), p. 310.

41. This point and the discussion which follows are based on R. A. Garner, *Social Change* (Chicago: Rand McNally, 1977), pp. 252ff. For a right-wing conspiratorial view see Gary Allen, *None Dare Call It Conspiracy* (Rossmoor, CA: Concord Press, 1971).

42. R. A. Garner, *Social Change.*

43. For a summary of such differences see T. R. Dye, *Who's Running America?*, Second Edition (Englewood Cliffs, N.J.: Prentice-Hall, 1979), pp. 190–195.

44. See William Chambliss, ed., *Criminal Law in Action* (Santa Barbara, CA: Hamilton, 1975), p. 230.

45. Conyers, "Corporate and White-Collar Crime," p. 293.

46. See Hon. William H. Webster, "The Examination of FBI Theory and Methodology Regarding White-Collar Crime Investigation and Prevention," *American Criminal Law Review* 17 (Winter, 1980), p. 279.

47. *Ibid.*, p. 280.

48. *Ibid.*, p. 282.

49. See Chambliss, *Criminal Law in Action,* for a discussion of such "moral entrepreneurs."

50. Garner, *Social Change,* p. 253.

51. Cited in Garson, *Power and Politics in the United States,* p. 183. A more detailed discussion of such monopolization and its effects is found in Chapter 3.

52. Michael Parenti, *Power and the Powerless* (New York: St. Martin's Press, 1978), p. 22.

53. Dye, *Who's Running America?,* p. 126.

54. *Ibid.*, p. 29.

55. See T. H. White, *The Making of the President 1972* (New York: Atheneum, 1973), Chapter 8; Domhoff, *Who Rules America?,* pp. 79–83.

56. Parenti, *Democracy for the Few,* p. 168.

57. Herbert J. Gans, *Deciding What's News* (New York: Pantheon, 1979), p. 12.

58. *Ibid.*, p. 14.

59. G. M. Tabor, "Capitalism: Is It Working?" *Time* 16 (April 21, 1980), p. 55.

60. Dye, *Who's Running America?,* pp. 115–116.

61. Michael T. Klare, *War Without End* (New York: Knopf, 1972), p. 77.

62. G. William Domhoff, *The Powers That Be: Processes of Ruling Class Domination in America* (New York: Vintage, 1978), p. 118.

63. Parenti, *Democracy for the Few,* p. 226.

64. Mark Green and Jack Newfield, "Who Owns Congress?" *The Village Voice* 16 (April 21, 1980), p. 16.

65. Michael J. McManus, "The Tyranny of Special Interests," *Rocky Mountain News* (September 9, 1979), p. 69.

66. See Warren Weaver, Jr., "What Is a Campaign Contributor Buying?" *The New York Times* (March 13, 1977), p. E2.

67. Associated Press release (January 1, 1975); and "Shake-Up at Gulf — The Ripples Spread," *U.S. News & World Report* (January 26, 1976), p. 70.

68. Cited in "TRB from Washington," *The New Republic* (November 11, 1978), p. 2. See also, "Hidden Army of Washington Lobbyists," *U.S. News & World Report* (July 25, 1977), p. 31.

69. Walter D. Burnham, "Party System and the Political Process," in William N. Chambers and Walter D. Burnham, eds., *The American Party System,* Second Edition (New York: Oxford University Press, 1975), p. 277.

70. G. William Domhoff, *The Powers That Be,* p. 148.

71. Tabor, "Capitalism," p. 54.

72. Morton C. Paulson, "What Is Business Afraid Of?" *The National Observer* (Oct. 5, 1974), p. 14.

73. Frank Pearce, *Crimes of the Powerful* (London: Pluto Press, 1976), p. 87.

74. Conyers, "Corporate and White-Collar Crime," pp. 291, 299. See also Chapter 2.

75. ABA Section on Criminal Justice, Committee on Economic Offenses (March 1977), pp. 6–7, cited in Conyers, "Corporate and White-Collar Crime," p. 290.

76. Clinard and Yeager, "Corporate Crime," p. 256.

77. Webster, "Examination of FBI Theory and Methodology," p. 276.

78. *Ibid.*

79. See Gilbert Geis, "Upper World Crime," pp. 114–137, in A. S. Blumberg, ed., *Current Perspectives on Criminal Behavior: Original Essays in Criminology* (New York: Knopf, 1974), p. 117.

80. Clinard and Yeager, "Corporate Crime," p. 264.

81. J. L. Simmons, *Deviants* (Berkeley, CA: Glendessery, 1969), p. 9.

82. John B. Mays, *Crime and the Social Structure* (London: Faber and Faber, 1967), p. 39.

83. J. F. Galliher and J. L. McCartney, *Criminology: Power, Crime, and Criminal Law* (Homewood, IL: Dorsey Press, 1977), p. 10.

84. See H. Edelhertz et al., *The Investigation of White-Collar Crime* (Washington, D.C.: U.S. Government Printing Office, 1977), p. 7.

85. See Richard Quinney, *Class, State and Crime* (New York: McKay/Longman, 1977), pp. 50–52 for an extended discussion of this typology.

86. See Mark Dowie, "The Corporate Crime of the Century," *Mother Jones* 9 (November, 1979), p. 24.

87. Quinney, *Class, State and Crime*, p. 51.

88. W. C. Scott and David K. Hart, *Organizational America* (Boston: Houghton Mifflin, 1979), p. 40.

89. Clinard and Yeager, "Corporate Crime," p. 265.

90. Ovid Demaris, *Dirty Business* (New York: Harper's Magazine Press, 1974), p. 12.

91. See "Companies' Payoffs in U.S. Come Under New Scrutiny," *The New York Times* (March 16, 1976), p. 1.

92. See Ralph Nader and Mark Green, "Crime in the Suites," *The New Republic* (April 29, 1972), p. 19. The maximum fine was raised to $50,000 in 1955, but is still a pittance compared with the multimillion-dollar profits of most large corporations.

93. Donald Cressey, "White Collar Subversives," *Center Magazine* 6 (Nov./Dec., 1978), p. 44.

94. See "Job Hazards," *Dollars and Sense* 56 (April, 1980), p. 9.

95. See, for example, Geis, "Upper World Crime," p. 114.

96. Conyers, "Corporate and White-Collar Crime," p. 293.

97. Thio, *Deviant Behavior,* pp. 85–89.

98. See N. David Ermann and Richard J. Lundman, eds., *Organization Deviance* (New York: Oxford University Press, 1978), pp. 7–9 for further discussion of these issues.

Chapter 2
Elite Deviance and the Higher Immorality

THE NATURE OF THE HIGHER IMMORALITY

Each year during the Christmas season, *The New York Times* devotes a good deal of space to a most charitable venture: it graphically describes the plight of some of New York's most destitute citizens. Through "The 100 Neediest Cases," monetary contributions are solicited by the *Times* for the less fortunate of society's members. While appreciating the *Times'* effort on behalf of the poor, *The Village Voice,* a left-wing weekly newspaper, featured in December of 1978 New York's "100 *Greediest* Cases." The greediest consisted of various elites: businessmen, celebrities, organized crime figures, union leaders, intellectuals, and politicos, all of whom were accused of making sure they experienced their own versions of a merry holiday season:

Item: ITT's recently retired chief executive, Harold Geneen (annual compensation $994,000) is a man who thinks big. When his Manhattan headquartered corporation distributed bribes, it wasn't like some small numbers banker giving a cop $400 in a brown paper bag. ITT, according to an SEC complaint made public on November 2 of this year, paid out more than $9 million in "illegal, improper, corrupt, and questionable payments." Acting as an authentic multinational corporation, ITT corrupted officials in at least nine different countries: Indonesia, Iran, the Philippines, Algeria, Nigeria, Mexico, Italy, Turkey, and, of course, Chile.

This global greed proved quite cost effective. In Indonesia alone, the bribery produced government contracts worth $157 million to two subsidiaries of ITT.

The SEC complaint placed the blame for these payoffs directly on "senior officials" in ITT's Manhattan offices, which is as close as you can come to naming Geneen as the accountable party.

Reading the SEC complaint, a skeptic might come to believe that ITT's "senior officials" were all students of the master, Meyer Lansky.

In Chile, ITT spent $400,000 between 1970 and 1972 to overthrow the democratically elected socialist government of Salvador Allende. The Chilean bribes were laundered through a dummy company called "Lonely Star Shipping," and were disguised on ITT's financial records as expenses for "public relations."

The SEC further alleged that ITT regularly used "numbered bank accounts" in Swiss banks to conceal various transactions. It also said that ITT arranged for $2 million in "black cash" to be skimmed from one deal in Italy. Nobody knows what happened to the $2 million.

Our heart goes out to ITT in its hour of humiliation. We are sure, as with almost all corporate crooks, there will be no indictments and no jail sentences. Embarrassment is always the punishment that seems to fit white-collar crime. A consent decree is the worst sanction these anonymous "senior officials" have to fear. And soon, they will be free again to play with Swiss bank accounts, laundered cash, dummy companies, skimming, and other Lansky-type schemes.[1]

Item: Judging from his books, columns, and TV show, the only federal agency that *William F. Buckley* really approves of is the CIA. He certainly doesn't like the federal agencies that monitor the ethical conduct of businessmen. Recently, we found out why Buckley doesn't like the SEC. SEC staff investigators have recommended to the full commission that Buckley be prosecuted for insider fraud and false reporting.

Buckley is a millionaire businessman. His family has extensive holdings in oil and broadcasting. Buckley has long favored more tax loopholes for the oil industry and less regulation of broadcasting.

Last month, *The Wall Street Journal* revealed that Buckley had used one of his companies — Starr Broadcasting — to help bail him out of a bad investment he had made in a chain of Texas drive-in theatres. As the *Journal* reported: "Mr. Buckley defends the transaction as an arms-length sale, even in the face of new evidence of self-dealing." Buckley was recently forced to resign as chairman of the board of Starr by the other directors, in the hope that the corporation itself won't be named in any SEC legal action.

The great benefit to humankind from this episode is not the potential civil-fraud case against Buckley. In *The Wall Street Journal* story, Buckley — who postures with the certainty of a Nobel Prize economist — admitted: "I am no good with figures. I don't understand them." . . .[2]

In 1978, Mr. Buckley signed a consent decree with the Securities and Exchange Commission. Charged with violating the federal securities laws, Mr. Buckley and two other defendants in the case agreed to make a restitution payment of 1.8 million dollars. Mr. Buckley also agreed to an order preventing him from being an officer or a director of a publicly owned company for a period of five years.

Item: The Times Square pornography business, with its attendant drugs, violence, and teenage prostitution, could not exist without the skills of upper-class professionals. Architects design the plans for the massage parlors. Accountants balance the books. And lawyers incorporate the dummy companies, get the certificates of occupancy, and handle the court cases.

One law firm represents more than half of all the porn locations in Times Square — Herbert Kassner and Seymour Detsky. They have both reportedly become millionaires through their smut clients.

And they apparently do more than pure legal work. The listed owner on the lease of one massage parlor we checked turned out to be a secretary in the office of Kassner and Detsky.

And the state senate committee on crime has played tapes at a public hearing of Detsky boasting to an undercover cop that he had two judges in his pocket and that he fixed a case by giving a law secretary $1000 in cash. On one tape, Detsky explained how he coached prostitutes on how to avoid arrests.

On another tape, Detsky detailed how he set up a dummy corporation to protect peep show equipment, leased from mobsters, from confiscation if the police raided a massage parlor.

The appellate division is now conducting an official inquiry into whether the practices of Kassner and Detsky warrant censure or disbarment on ethical grounds. When Detsky was given a chance to testify in public and explain the tapes, he invoked the Fifth Amendment 37 times. . . .[3]

Sociologist C. Wright Mills once remarked that "As news of higher immoralities breaks (people) often say, 'Well, another one got caught today,' thereby implying that the cases disclosed are symptoms of a much more widespread condition."[4] Mills used the term "higher immorality" to describe a "moral insensibility" [5] among the most wealthy and powerful members of America's corporate, political, and military elite (which he termed "the power elite"). For Mills, the higher immorality translated into a variety of unethical, corrupt, and sometimes illegal practices, which were viewed as a systematic, institutionalized feature of contemporary American society.

In business and in government, Mills felt, many transactions are accomplished via interpersonal manipulation. One type of such manipulation by the successful is using a false front: pretending to be interested in what others have to say, attempting to make others feel important, and radiating charm and self-confidence (despite one's own insecurities). Obviously, if social relations are based on insincere feelings, such activities would be characterized by a good deal of alienation on the part of the participants.

In addition, Mills believed that some business and political arrangements included the favors of prostitutes. The sexual favors of these high-priced call girls are often paid for with executive expense-account allotments[6] (see below). Aside from interpersonal manipulation and the peddling of high-priced vice, the higher immorality also includes: (1) unethical practices relating to executive salaries and expense accounts; (2) unfair executive and corporate tax advantages; (3) the *deliberate creation* of political and/or economic crises by the power elite; (4) the manipulation of public opinion; and (5) the violation of antitrust and other laws relating to political corruption. Since Mills described these various types of deviance in the 1950s, the nation has witnessed scandal after scandal involving these various forms of the higher immorality. Thus an up-to-date analysis of the nature and significance of the higher immorality is in order. This chapter is concerned with executive salaries and expense accounts, laws relating to the incomes of corporate executives and corporations, the creation of phony crises by the power elite, and violations of antitrust laws. We will also consider one form of the higher immorality only hinted at in Mills' provocative analysis — the relationships between the wealthy and powerful and members of organized crime.

The Higher Immorality and Corporate Compensation: Salaries, Taxes, and "Perks"

Since the higher immorality involves the pursuit of money, the mechanisms by which money is obtained and retained are very important. As Mills put it:

> Higher income taxes have resulted in a whole series of collusion between the big firm and higher employee. There are many ingenious ways to cheat the spirit of the tax laws, and the standards of consumption of many high-priced men are deter-

mined more by complicated expense accounts than by simple take-home pay.[7]

The accuracy of Mills' description can ge gauged by a study of all the various rewards granted top corporate executives. Table 2–1 lists the annual salaries, bonuses, and long-term income (stock options) paid to a number of top executives in 1979.

Corporate executive compensation, without expense accounts and other "perks," dwarfs the annual salaries of the highest paid politician in the United States ($200,000) and the highest paid military officers ($45,000). The data make clear that one of the most widely used and effective devices for the amassing of corporate wealth is the corporate stock option. A stock option is "a right given a corporate executive to buy his company's stock at sometime in the future, at a specified price the date the option is granted." [8] For example, suppose an executive is given an option to buy 100,000 shares of his company's stock on January 15, 1981, and on that day the price of such stock is seventy-five dollars per share. The executive may have contracted to buy the stock at fifty dollars per share back in 1979. The executive may still purchase the stock at fifty dollars per share. His profit on the stock amounts to twenty-five dollars per share on 100,000 shares, or 250,000 dollars. The executive does not pay income tax on this windfall, but he does pay capital-gains tax. Such taxes, however, are only forty percent, considerably less than the income tax one would pay on such an amount.

If the numbers in this example sound outrageous to you, consider again the data in Table 2–1.

These statistics indicate that, on the average, stock options were worth between one and four million dollars in long-term benefits in 1979. But even these figures do not tell the entire story. Consider C. C. Garvin, Jr., Exxon's chairman. The table shows that he received 248,000 dollars from the amount of stock options that he exercised in 1979. Yet, *Business Week* claims that, had he exercised *all* of his stock options, Garvin could have realized an additional 7.2 million in compensation! [9] A number of the executives on this list could have gained additional millions by the exercise of all stock options. Thus such annual compensation totals are often misleading.

Consider also the case of Harold Geneen, ITT's chairman. Geneen retired in January 1980 from the corporation. In 1980 ITT paid Geneen 450,000 dollars as a consultant. And as of 1981, with his pension plan beginning, Geneen receives 250,000 dollars in consulting fees, 130,000 dollars from various company retirement plans, and an additional 112,000 dollars from yet another employment contract.[10] This in a country where millions of average workers are still not covered by any pension plans at all!

But let us continue with our examination of stock options. Some

Table 2–1: Highest Paid Corporate Executives, 1979 (in Thousands).[†]

	Salary and Bonus	Long-term Income	Total Compensation
1. Frank E. Rosenfelt, pres. & CEO,[*] Metro-Goldwyn-Mayer	$ 194	$4,869	$5,063
2. Rawleigh Warner, Jr., chmn., Mobil	902	3,411	4,313
3. Richard W. Vieser, exec. v-p., McGraw-Edison	76	2,559	2,635
4. Barrie K. Brunet, exec. v-p., Metro-Goldwyn-Mayer	121	2,330	2,451
5. Paul P. Woolard, sr. exec. v-p., Revlon	630	1,738	2,368
6. Michel C. Bergerac, chmn., pres., & CEO, Revlon	900	1,439	2,339
7. William P. Tavoulareas, pres., Mobil	770	1,543	2,313
8. R. M. Holliday, chmn., Hughes Tool	286	1,838	2,124
9. Sidney J. Sheinberg, pres. & COO,[**] MCA	330	1,654	1,984
10. James M. Beggs, exec. v-p., General Dynamics	320	1,655	1,975
11. James D. Aljian, conslt.,[1] Metro-Goldwyn-Mayer	60	1,780	1,840
12. J. Robert Fluor, chmn., pres. & CEO, Fluor	638	1,146	1,784
13. E. Cardon Walker, pres. & CEO, Walt Disney Productions	245	92	1,521[6]
14. T. F. Bradshaw, pres., Atlantic Richfield	524	992	1,516
15. Edward B. Walker III, exec. v-p., Gulf Oil	425	1,067	1,492
16. O. C. Boileau, v-p.,[2] Boeing	167	1,171	1,338
17. Thomas D. Barrow chmn. & CEO, Kennecott Copper	834	475	1,309
18. Jesse I. Aweida, chmn. & pres., Storage Technology	500	796	1,296
19. Willard F. Rockwell, Jr., chmn.,[3] Rockwell International	578	692	1,270
20. Lee A. Iacocca, pres.,[4] Chrysler	1,266	—	1,266
21. Henry Wendt, pres. & COO, SmithKline	301	955	1,256
22. M. T. Stamper, pres., Boeing	339	820	1,159
23. Robert F. Dee, chmn. & CEO, SmithKline	406	736	1,142
24. H. S. Geneen, chmn.,[5] ITT	636	480	1,116
25. C. C. Garvin Jr., chmn., Exxon	830	248	1,078

[1] Effective May, 1979
[2] Retired Jan. 10, 1980
[3] Retired Apr. 1, 1979
[4] Includes accrued portion of $1.5 million awarded upon employment
[5] Resigned Dec. 31, 1979
[6] Includes $1.2 million received under investment participation incentive program
[*] CEO = chief executive officer
[**] COO = chief operating officer
[†] Data: Sibson & Co., BW

Source: Reprinted from the May 12, 1980, issue of *Business Week* by special permission, © 1980 by McGraw-Hill, Inc., New York, N.Y. 10020. All rights reserved.

corporations have plans that allow them to withdraw high-price stock options and publish new ones to reflect lower market prices. Some corporations even provide low-cost or no-interest loans so stock options may be purchased. Sometimes no repayment of the loan's principal (actual amount of the loan) is required until the executive "dies, retires, quits, or goes bankrupt." [11] And if the stock price falls further, executives are commonly permitted to turn their shares back to the company at the time the loan is cancelled. Hence, executives are not subject to the risks on the market that plague the bulk of the nation's stockholders.

Another innovative plan, called stock appreciation rights (SAR), further confirms Mills' claim regarding executive avoidance of taxation. Instead of paying money for stock shares, executives merely collect from the company money or stock shares equal to any increase in the stock's value. Doing this allows executives to escape paying capital-gains taxes and any money for the stock option. By 1977, eighty percent of the top 200 industrial corporations had opted for the SAR alternative. Other advances in tax avoidance have occurred in recent years. One plan, adopted by twenty-nine percent of companies with sales of over three million dollars, allows executives to choose options that make stock payments on either a spread-out or lump-sum basis, resulting in more tax savings. Such plans are usually so complex that company stockholders are unable to understand them, especially when the details are hidden in the "fine print" sections of stockholder reports. Such practices involve deceiving stockholders and prevent any stockholder "revolts."

Another stock-option plan permits executives to purchase stock at its "book-value" price. Rather than buying stock at market prices, executives buy it at a price per share equal to the company's assets minus its liabilities. This price rarely declines and usually increases greatly (regardless of the stock market's swings). Later, executives are permitted to sell the stock to the company at its new book value.

The perquisites ("perks") of corporate life are not limited to salaries, bonuses, and stock options. Indeed, the corporate-compensation landscape now represents a form of corporate socialism for top executives. Among the tax-exempt perquisites enjoyed by corporate managers are:

> financial counseling, tax and legal assistance, company automobiles and chauffeur services (for business and sometimes for personal use), company-provided planes, boats, and apartments (for business and sometimes for personal use), company paid or subsidized travel, recreation facilities, club memberships, liberal expense accounts, personal use of business credit cards . . . complete medical coverage, including . . . home health care, dental, and psychiatric care — all without outlays by the executive . . . college expenses for children, "social-service sabbaticals," and the

best and most complete form of disability, accident, and life insurance.[12]

Among the most controversial of such "perks" is the expense account. This tax-avoidance device allows individual business people to deduct from income taxes up to seventy percent of the cost of entertaining customers (for business purposes). If the account is a company account, all of it may be deducted from corporate income tax as a cost of doing business. The practice has produced some lavish deductions, fascinating justifications, and scandalous tax results. Under this practice, some corporations give gifts to customers at Christmas. Such gifts have included one billion dollars' worth of whiskey, and over two billion dollars' worth of automobiles and jewels, all tax deductible.[13]

Gifts are but one aspect of the expense account. Theater and sports tickets, nightclub outings, country-club memberships, yacht maintenance, corporate hunting lodges and other vacation retreats are paid for (in effect) by the American tax payer. In one Internal Revenue Service case a dairy owner and his wife were allowed (by the presiding judge) to deduct 16,443 dollars for a six-month African safari. The safari was claimed as an "ordinary and necessary" business expense because movies of the trip were used as advertising for the dairy.[14] Large corporations typically provide upper sales personnel with expense accounts of 700 to 900 dollars *per week*. One executive of a small eastern corporation was provided an expense account which paid his apartment rental, meals, drinks, dues at a country club, entertainment expenses, and an occasional trip overseas (for purposes of studying business methods which would make his firm more competitive). While the man's actual salary was 35,000 dollars, the expense account made his salary and benefits equivalent to a 98,000-dollar position. His 8,300-dollar income-tax bill would have been 62,600 dollars had his expense account been taxable.[15]

The symbol of the expense account is the "three-martini lunch." The claim is made by expensive restaurants that they would go out of business without the expense-account lunch. The question has been posed why business lunches are any more or less a legitimate expense than the lunches of construction workers, janitors, professors, doctors, or any other professionals. Moreover, it could be easily argued that food, housing, clothes, and entertainment are a necessary expense for any working person. Most people could not show up at their jobs without proper attire, so why should not all working people be allowed to deduct such items from taxes?

We are not saying that the "three-martini lunch," or other expense-account "perks" are deviant or immoral in the same sense that murder, bribery, and other crimes are immoral. In part, such "perks" are mere indicators of the types of advantages the business elite has been able to secure for itself, advantages which many feel are, at the least, unfair and are subject to unethical abuses for reasons just stated.

However, other advantages secured by the elite, especially those relating to tax laws and private foundations, are important because they have *in some instances* facilitated both political and economic crimes. Such advantages deserve a closer look.

The State of Welfare for the Well-Off: Tax Breaks and Subsidies

Under the American system of government has grown up what is known as a dual-welfare system. Programs for the poor are termed "relief," "welfare," "assistance," or "charity." [16] Programs for the rich, however, are called "tax expenditures," "subsidies," "price supports," "parity," and the like. The dual-welfare system is an integral part of the higher immorality, allowing the rich to become richer at the expense of the middle class and the poor. The mechanism by which the rich are allowed to retain their wealth is the tax loophole. Rich individuals and corporations were provided tax loopholes (now called "tax expenditures" by government) which amounted to 114 billion dollars in 1977.[17] In fact, corporate tax loopholes, including the expense account, allowed eleven major corporations to pay no federal corporate income taxes whatsoever. These firms and their earnings are listed in Table 2–2. About twenty years ago, one-third of the taxes collected by the federal government came from corporations, but tax breaks granted to corporations have now reduced that amount to a mere thirteen percent.

Table 2–2: Some Major Firms Paying No Corporate Income Tax in 1976.

Corporation	Earnings (in Millions)
Ford Motor Company	$148.1
Western Electric	185.6
Bethlehem Steel	225.0
Lockheed Aircraft	84.1
National Steel	43.4
Delta Airlines	73.7
Northwest Airlines	45.3
Manufacturer's Hanover	166.1
Chemical New York Corporation	90.5
Phelps-Dodge	44.6
Freeport Minerals	35.2

Source: H. R. Rodgers, Jr., "Welfare Policies for the Rich," *Dissent* 2 (Spring, 1978), p. 142. Used with permission.

Many special tax breaks have been voted by Congress to American corporations. Some of the most important are discussed below.

Investment tax credit. From 1962 to 1969 the investment tax credit saved American corporations 13.5 billion dollars in taxes. It was repealed in 1969 but reinstituted in 1971 as the "job-development credit." This tax credit allows companies to reduce its tax bill by seven percent of the amount invested in new equipment which is expected to last seven years or more.[18] This means a piece of equipment priced at 100,000 dollars saves a corporation 7,000 dollars in taxes and ends up costing (in reality) only 93,000 dollars. This break was granted corporations on the theory that buying new equipment will create additional jobs. Proof of this has yet to be demonstrated. In fact, from 1969 to 1971 the sales of corporations benefiting most from the investment tax credit rose 12.5 percent, but employment in such companies actually decreased by 500,000 (5.2 percent).[19]

The asset-depletion range. This break is expected to save American companies 30 billion dollars between 1973 and 1983. Over one-half of the benefit from this break goes to the largest 103 American manufacturing corporations. This law makes a tax-deductible allowance for wear and tear on equipment by allowing a depreciation deduction. In reality, there is no way of knowing how long a piece of equipment will last; it merely depends on how quickly a given company decides to replace a piece of equipment. Before the asset-depletion allowance, most equipment had to be depreciated (for tax purposes) over a ten-year period. Now, however, a company is allowed to depreciate equipment over an eight-year period (twenty percent faster than before). Of course, such equipment lasts eight years, ten years, or even longer. The odd thing about the asset-depletion range is that it comes at a time when twenty-five percent of the nation's plant capacity is already underused. Hence, the need for new equipment is suspect.

Taxes and multinational corporations. Many multinational corporations take advantage of foreign tax credits, which allow a company to pay taxes on profits made overseas, where taxes are usually less, and to pay no taxes on such profits in the U.S. This has made some nations (like Liechtenstein, Panama, and Liberia) "tax havens" for large corporations. The practice of setting up "dummy" corporations overseas to which items are sold only on paper (for purposes of tax avoidance) is common. Philip Stern has described one such practice:

> To understand, visualize a scene on a windswept shore of Nova Scotia. A seemingly ordinary industrial process is under way. The good ship *Gypsum Prince* is tied up to a special jetty, awaiting her cargo: gypsum rock, the stuff of which wallboard, plaster and other building materials are made. A conveyor belt

reaches across the jetty and over the ship as the rock, mined by a Canadian company named Canadian Gypsum, reaches the end of the belt . . . and tumbles into the hold of the ship. Simple. . . .

But all is not as simple as it appears. For, at the instant each piece of rock reaches the end of the conveyor belt, a sale takes place: ownership of the rock passes from the mining company, Canadian Gypsum, to Export.

But Export . . . has only the briefest use for the rock, for, the instant it hits the hold of the *Gypsum Prince,* Export sells the rock . . . — at a profit of 50 cents a ton — to U.S. Gypsum, Inc. (U.S.G.), the major American gypsum company.

And that is the sum and substance of what Export does (or did) for its million-dollar-a-year profit: it held paper ownership of a couple of million tons of gypsum rock during the fleeting instants of its fall from conveyor belt to ship hold.

Why this legal sleight of hand? It *sounds* like an exceedingly poor business . . . until you learn that Export is wholly owned by U.S. Gypsum, so that USG is, in effect, paying the million dollars to itself. . . . Export qualifies, under U.S. tax law, as a "Western Hemisphere trade corporation" (known, in the tax trade, as a WHTC) whose profits are taxed at a substantially lower rate than those of its parent, USG. Approximate tax savings during 1957 and 1958: $300,000. No wonder USG didn't mind paying the million-dollar profit to an empty corporate shell for doing nothing.

But that was not the limit of the tax-saving possibilities inherent in the situation at the Nova Scotia jetty. . . . Export was not USG's only "corporate child." The Canadian mining company was also a "child." And so was the good ship *Gypsum Prince* — or, to be more precise, the Panamanian corporation (Panama Gypsum, Inc.) that owned the *Gypsum Prince.*

Why a Panamanian corporation? Because . . . Panama imposes no taxes whatever on the profits of corporations. . . . It was all a financially incestuous arrangement: over a four-year period, USG paid its *wholly owned* shipping company (Panama) $17,-684,823 to carry gypsum from its *wholly owned* mines in Nova Scotia to its *wholly owned* processing in the United States. Now just suppose that USG chose to pay Panama something "extra" (above the lowest competitive shipping rate) for doing that — as the U.S. government alleged in a court action against USG. The government contended that the overcharge amounted to between 25 and 60 percent — but if the "extra" amounted to just 10 percent, the effect would be to reduce by nearly $2 million the profits of USG (taxable at the American 48 percent rate) and to increase by $2 million the profits of USG's corporate offspring, Panama, *which are not taxed at all.* Approximate tax saving during 1957 and 1958: about half a million dollars.[20]

Despite the tax advantages granted to corporations, individuals who own controlling interests in corporations also tend to do all they can to ensure that their fortunes are passed on to their kin. In order to escape inheritance and other taxes, a boon to such individuals has been the tax-exempt foundation.

Foundations: Charity and the Higher Immorality

The purpose of foundations is supposedly to facilitate charitable contributions. In 1972 42,000 such foundations were in the United States and showed assets of 50 billion dollars.[21] Setting up a tax-exempt foundation exempts *all* assets therein from income and capital-gains taxes, as well as most inheritance taxes. On the surface this would seem morally upright because such funds are, after all, given to worthy causes. Underneath, however, the reality has been somewhat different.

> *Item:* One millionaire, Spenser Collins, in the late 1960s established the St. Genevieve Foundation. His foundation, it seems, spent 100,000 dollars on two twin sisters. One sister was housed in a duplex, paid for by Mr. Collins' foundation, and the other was given a five bedroom house (for which she was paid 36,000 dollars as "caretaker").[22] Mr. Collins' favors, however, were not appreciated by the government, which, subsequently, tried and found Mr. Collins guilty of tax evasion. While Mr. Collins' case represents a violation of foundation law, it also demonstrates the economic crime which is *invited* by such arrangements.

> *Item:* The late Nelson Rockefeller, while governor of New York, set up a Government Affairs Foundation. Between 1961 and 1964 the governor gave 310,469 dollars to the Foundation, but it paid out exactly zero dollars in charitable causes. Instead, Frank Moore was paid 120,000 dollars in salary and 40,000 dollars in expenses, and acted largely as Rockefeller's political liaison in various state matters. Essentially, Rockefeller had gained a full-time political liaison at costs which were tax deductible.

> *Item:* From 1961 to 1964, the Standard Oil Foundation of Chicago made charitable grants of 5,459,967 dollars, but 2,059,736 dollars were donated to the American Oil Foundation of Indiana (which is owned by Standard Oil)!

Foundations excel at investing money and escaping taxation. A government study of 1,300 foundations found that 180 of them owned ten percent or more of a corporation's stock (often enough to gain controlling interest in a company).[23] Far from being strictly charitable, foundations play a major role in the corporate decisions that affect both the private sector of the economy as well as politics.

Moreover, there have been incidents of government interference in the awarding of private foundation grants. This has especially been the case with the Central Intelligence Agency (CIA). The CIA in 1966 disbursed 400,000 dollars through the J. M. Kaplan Fund to a research institute. The institute, in turn, financed research centers in Latin American countries, which also drew support from the Agency for International Development (a U.S. foreign-aid agency), Brandeis and Harvard Universities, and the Ford Foundation. The CIA also sponsored the travel of various social scientists to communist countries. The Kaplan Fund had also been financed by foundations, although it was not even listed with the Internal Revenue Service. This suggests that the foundation was fraudulently created by the CIA. Seven other foundations were discovered to have been CIA-created conduits, but the purposes of the money given or the amounts have never been made public. Why the CIA went into the charity business, which is a clear violation of its charter, has also gone unexplained.[24]

Foundation money has been used for a number of causes that have nothing whatever to do with charity, and, as such, represents one more form of the higher immorality. The Ford Foundation, for example, has lent large sums of money to private corporations, and has, in effect, gone into competition with private banks. Howard Hughes created the Hughes Medical Institute to ensure the liabilities of a number of Hughes' own companies. Other foundations have made loans to businessmen for the purpose of closing business deals. Foundation grants have also: (1) bankrolled political candidates; (2) financed experiments with school decentralization in black slums; (3) supported militant political organizations, both on the left and the right; (4) financed the foreign travels of staffs of U.S. senators; and (5) financed the activities of moderate (middle-class) civil-rights organizations, which have largely failed to understand or alleviate the problems of poor ghetto blacks (who rarely receive such money without strings).[25] In short, foundations have been used for purposes that have nothing whatever to do with charity.

Given all of the special tax privileges granted to corporations and super-rich individuals, as well as the abuse to which such privileges are subject, there is little wonder that a 1977 Harris poll found that over two-thirds of the public believed that the tax laws are written for the benefit of the wealthy rather than for the benefit of the average person.[26]

Welfare for the Rich: Subsidies

Aside from all the tax loopholes created for the rich and the corporations, many billions of dollars in benefits to rich individuals and corporations are made by the government. These are called subsidies, and they are made in the form of payments, low-interest loans, and/or "in-kind benefits" (whereby services of various kinds are provided by the government). Such generosity is extended to many different industries and tends to benefit most the largest and wealthiest interests.

In agriculture, for example, the lion's share of such payments go to the largest individual and corporate farmers "to limit the production of crops by buying up crop surpluses . . . keeping prices (to consumers) and profits high while subsidizing the expansion of giant corporate farms at the expense of family farms." [27]   Among others receiving subsidies are oil companies, a bowling alley in Dallas, an Ohio radio station, and the Queen of England (for not producing crops on the Royal Family's Mississippi plantation).[28]   As of 1973, sixty-three percent of the agricultural subsidies went to the wealthiest nineteen percent of farmers, while the bottom half of the farm population received only nine percent of such subsidies.   And some of the farm interests which receive such payments include present and former members of the Senate Agricultural Committee, which sets policy on agricultural subsidies.[29]

Among the most suspect of direct subsidies were those given International Telephone and Telegraph (ITT) and General Motors (GM) for damages inflicted on their plants in Germany during World War II. GM collected thirty-three million dollars for damages to its truck plant, trucks which were used by the Nazis throughout the war.   ITT owned plants that produced bombers for the Nazi Air Force which were (among other things) used to destroy allied shipping.   Ironically, ITT produced direction finders for the Allies that were designed to protect allied convoys from enemy attack!   ITT received twenty-seven million dollars for damages inflicted by Allied planes on its German plants.[30]   Thus inadvertently both GM and ITT aided the Nazi war effort, and were in effect reimbursed by the U.S. government for doing so.

To say the least, "subsidies go to a bewildering array of industries, seemingly without rhyme or reason." [31]   About 200 million dollars go to private aviation interests for the building of private airports (where corporate jet aircraft, among other planes, land).   Another 57 million dollars or so go to private air freight and passenger carriers as reimbursement for business losses.   About 86 million dollars are granted the cane and beet sugar producers to produce sugar.   And 6 billion dollars are handed the nation's railroads, the stockholders of which are now enjoying record dividends, despite a long history of private mismanagement.

Some interesting loans are likewise made.   Such loans have bankrolled much of the nation's hospital and private-housing construction (via FHA and VA mortgages).   Lockheed was guaranteed a 250 million-dollar loan in the early 1970s to keep from going bankrupt.   The giant firm was later involved in bribery scandals which aided in undermining U.S. foreign-policy objectives.   At the time the Lockheed loan was made the "Federal Government had outstanding . . . $56 billion in direct loans . . . $167 billion in loan guarantees . . . a total of $224 billion — twice the sum of all commercial and industrial loans that commercial banks had outstanding." [32]   This seemingly nonsensical subsidy parade takes place in part to keep inefficiently managed corporations afloat at the taxpayers' expense.

Businesses whose sole customer is the government are commonly the recipients of subsidies. Large defense contractors are often granted rent-free use of government laboratories, equipment, electricity, and so on at no cost. One study estimated the amount of government-owned facilities in the hands of various defense contractors at thirteen billion dollars.[33] This in an industry with profit margins among the highest in the private sector of the economy! The consequences of extending such benefits to defense contractors are explored in Chapter 5.

In sum, the various subsidies and tax breaks "have been totalling $117 to $125 billion a year." [34] The continuation of such advantages is dependent on large corporations and wealthy individuals being able to manipulate public opinion in their favor. Such manipulation is a very important aspect of the higher immorality.

THE HIGHER IMMORALITY AND THE CREATION OF CRISIS

One aspect of the higher immorality identified by Mills concerns crises.

> Crisis is a bankrupted term because so many men in high places have evoked it to cover up their extraordinary policies and deeds. As a matter of fact, it is precisely the absence of genuine crisis that has beset our morality. For such crises involve situations in which men at large are presented with genuine alternatives, the moral meanings of which are clearly open to public debate. Our higher immorality and general weakening of older values have not involved such crises. . . .[35]

Perhaps nothing in our recent experience so confirms Mills' words as the current energy crisis.

The oil industry is the "giant" of the capitalist system. Oil accounts for one-fifth of all profits in the manufacturing sector of the economy, making oil the richest industry in the world.[36] By the early 1970s, however, several situations at home and around the world threatened to reduce oil profits. Let's review these conditions.

At home, the oil-depletion allowance (allowing oil companies to deduct a certain percentage of their income) had been reduced (in 1969) from 27.5 to 23.5 percent. The oil companies thus expanded their overseas operations in order to take advantage of the foreign tax credit, which, between 1971 and 1974, reduced their U.S. tax bills by seventy-five percent.[37] Also at home, from 1960 to 1972, small, independent oil companies had increased their share of the domestic gasoline market from ten percent to twenty-five percent. The number of new oil wells in the U.S. had steadily declined between 1956 and 1972; indeed, total drilling had declined from 208 million to 86 million feet per year, and

20,000 flowing wells had been capped in California alone.   This reduced
U.S. oil production by five billion barrels a year.   Only one new major
oil refinery had been built in the U.S. between 1968 and 1972.[38]

Overseas, the large oil companies, which from 1948 until the late
1960s had controlled forty-two percent of the oil reserves in the Mideast,
began having problems.   By 1970, Arab nations began demanding a
larger share of control over the production of their own oil.

> In that year the new revolutionary government of Kaddafi
> in Libya withheld production in order, successfully, to force a
> price increase on Occidental, an independent whose operations
> relied on Libyan oil.   Because of the better terms offered Arab
> states by the independents, the Arab "take" had been edging up.
> But Occidental's capitulation threatened to open the gate to soar-
> ing profits for OPEC in the 1970s.
>
> In February, 1971, the Teheran Conference was called to
> deal with the rapidly shifting situation.   Here the large oil com-
> panies tried to press for a united front vis-à-vis OPEC.   They
> sought to avoid the sort of disunity marked by Occidental's caving
> in to Libyan demands.   The oil companies were undercut, how-
> ever, not only by the independents but also by the U.S. State
> Department itself.   The department, seeking better Arab-Ameri-
> can relations, let it be known that the United States was not com-
> mitted to a single-agreement approach.   Failing to reach accord,
> the oil companies agreed to concessions to the Arab govern-
> ments.[39]

The excuse to increase profits and ensure their increase for the
future came in October of 1973.   The Arab dominated OPEC nations,
during the Arab-Israeli war, announced an embargo on oil exports to
the West.   They also announced a dramatic increase in the price of
crude oil from two and one-half to about eleven dollars per barrel.   The
oil companies then announced a dramatic shortage of imported oil, and
stated that the demand for domestic oil could do nothing but increase.
Thereupon, the oil companies announced increased prices for domestic
crude oil equal to the increases in OPEC oil.   The price of oil soon
quadrupled.

This was only the beginning of the fabricated crisis.   The truth
seems to be that there was no embargo (withholding of oil) by OPEC.
Imports for the last three months of 1973 were thirty-two percent above
those for the last three months of 1972! [40]   The withholding of gasoline
from the American consumer was practiced by the oil companies resulting in:

> *Item:* From 1973 to 1974 oil-company profits increased eighty
> percent.   The oil companies claimed the profits were needed for
> new exploration of oil.   However, the oil companies invested in
> such things as real estate, entertainment, and a department-store

chain, as well as coal and uranium. Indeed, by 1975 the oil companies owned fifty percent of America's nuclear fuel, fifty-four percent of the coal reserves, and forty-five percent of the uranium reserves.[41]

Item: Oil withheld from independent dealers drove them out of business. By May of 1973, 1,200 independent gasoline stations had closed, and by the end of the year, 10,000 independent stations had ceased operations.[42]

Item: The oil companies also used the artificial crisis to exact concessions from the government. The large companies had contributed a lusty seven million dollars to the Nixon campaign of 1972, and had little problem finding sympathy for their wishes.

Item: A deal was closed with the Soviet Union and Communist China involving the purchase of 45.6 billion dollars' worth of natural gas. This involved sale by the oil companies of ten billion dollars' worth of pipeline, supertankers, and liquefaction equipment. The Soviet gas was to be sold at prices up to three times higher than domestic natural gas.

Item: Permission to build the Alaskan pipeline was granted by Congress. The pipeline was to extend, not across Canada where it would be integrated into pipelines in the Midwest, but 798 miles across Alaska. The result was, in the late 1970s, a glut of crude oil on the West Coast, some of which was exported to Japan, while shortages of unleaded gasoline developed throughout the United States, sending gasoline prices soaring. The pipeline was constructed by the oil companies themselves (in partnership with the state of Alaska, at a cost overrun which was estimated at 800 percent). Moreover, the oil companies were also granted a profit on the crude oil which flows through the pipeline, on the transporting of the oil, on its refinery, and on the final sale of the refined product.

Item: President Nixon removed all quotas and tariffs on imported (expensive) oil, and substituted scaled "license fees" (of twenty-one cents a barrel) for five years. New oil refineries, however, were allowed to use seventy-five percent of the imported oil free of such fees. Exxon thereupon announced plans to expand its domestic refining capacity by thirty percent.

Item: The annual acreage of federal lands leased for oil exploration on the U.S. Continental Shelf tripled by 1977.

Item: Mr. Nixon proposed that the oil companies be granted additional tax reliefs amounting to twelve percent of the cost of producing new wells, and a seven percent increase added to the ninety percent "dry hole" write off (thus allowing investors to deduct ninety-seven cents of every dollar lost from wells which failed to produce oil).

Item: In December of 1973, Nixon classified all oil produced over the amount produced in 1972 as "new crude" and, hence, free from any price controls. Old crude was allowed to rise one dollar a barrel to provide a further incentive to the oil companies to raise production.

The final irony in the "energy crisis" of 1973 was that in September and October, oil storage tanks in the United States were so full that many tankers were diverted to Europe, where their contents were sold at higher prices. In Holland and Israel, which were also embargoed by the Arabs, there were no lines at gas stations. But in those countries there were no government price controls that the oil companies had to fight to remove.[43]

The 1973–1974 oil crisis contained elements of the lack of public debate that Mills claimed were characteristic of crisis creation. In June, 1973, a report issued by the Federal Trade Commission stated that the oil shortage "was the result of anticompetitive practices fostered by government regulations and manipulated by major oil companies to protect their profits." [44] The report accused the oil companies of using tax breaks to make huge profits in drilling for oil, while running their refining, distributing, and marketing operations so cheaply that independent producers were undersold and outcompeted. Moreover, the FTC claimed that the large oil producers had ensured adequate gasoline supplies for their own gasoline stations, while refusing to sell gasoline to independent stations. The FTC concluded that the large oil companies obtained profits that were "substantially in excess of those they would have obtained in a competitively structured market." [45]

In response to the FTC report, Treasury Department Secretary William Simon took to the airwaves to quote a study prepared by his department's Office of Energy advisor, which characterized the FTC report as incorrect. Later, in 1974, Simon, in effect, censured, on grounds concerning national security, information that had previously been available through the Commerce Department, concerning the amounts of imported oil.

In February, 1979, came signs that a new energy crisis was being fabricated. A revolution in Iran, whose production accounted for five percent of U.S. imports, cut off oil supplies from that nation. Oil companies and pro-oil politicians immediately began threatening rationing and one-dollar-a-gallon gasoline within a year.[46] The government and the large oil companies used the crisis atmosphere to propose various plans that would benefit the oil industry in the deregulation of oil prices, the repeal of the law forbidding the export of Alaskan oil (making for more Alaskan crude and a return to full oil production in California), the exchange of Alaskan oil for Mexican petroleum, the easing of environmental regulations on coal burning, and the slowdown of the phase-out of polluting lead additives in gasoline.[47]   All this occurred when the world, and especially the United States, had a surplus of oil.   The real losers in all this, of course, are the suspicious, but, nevertheless, manipulated and ripped-off American consumers, voters, and tax payers.[48]

THE HIGHER IMMORALITY
AND ANTITRUST LAWS

Mills believed that the cause of <u>much corporate crime is that it is</u> often <u>good business to break the laws</u>.   As he said, businesses "obey these laws, when they do, not because they feel that it is morally right, but because they are afraid of being caught" and therefore such laws "exist without the support of firm moral convention.   It is merely illegal to cheat them, but it is often considered smart to get away with it." [49] There are several reasons why businesses sometimes consider it smart to break the laws that regulate their activity.   First, many of the laws are ambiguous and contain many exemptions and exclusions, leaving a great deal of room for interpretation by the courts.   Second, many laws regulating business are hardly strict in their penalties.   Indeed many violations of business laws are settled in civil, rather than criminal, courts. Imprisonment under such laws is a rarity, and the fines imposed for breaking them, many times, amount to no more than a "slap on the wrist."   Finally, the enforcement of such laws is often quite lax because government devotes comparatively few resources to catching corporate offenders.   This can be made clear by examining the Sherman Act (1890), the Federal Trade Commission Act (1914), and the Robinson-Patman Act (1936).

The Sherman Act prohibits "unreasonable restraints upon and monopolization of trade." [50]   The Act also outlaws arrangements which result in price fixing or limiting access to trade or commerce (e.g., dividing market).   However, the Act is loaded with exclusions and ambiguities.   Thus the Sherman Act only applies to monopolies in trade (commerce) and does not apply to monopolies in manufacturing.   Moreover, under a series of cases in 1911, involving American Tobacco and Standard Oil, it was ruled that the Act applied only to *unreasonable* trade combinations, and did not exclude consolidation per se.   The definition of what a reasonable combination is, of course, a matter of judicial opinion.   Under the Sherman Act's price-fixing definitions, businesses that are already regulated by the federal government (such as the Civil Aeronautics Board's regulation of the nation's airlines) are excluded from the law.   This exclusion also applies to interstate water carriers, railroads, and trucks.   Other loopholes are present in the act. While the Act specifies that it is illegal to fix the price of a product by agreement, this practice is legal in states which authorize it under "fair laws." [51]

In 1914 the Federal Trade Commission Act was passed, making it unlawful to restrict competition and to engage in unfair and deceptive trade practices. However, the power of the FTC is limited. It only has the power to issue cease and desist orders, and this it can do only on securing the permission of a federal court. The FTC can recommend prosecution of criminal cases, but it is the Justice Department which is specifically charged with this task.

In 1936 the Robinson-Patman Act made it illegal to discriminate between various buyers of products by charging different prices to different buyers. But the act (1) applies only to products, not to *services,* which are supposedly covered by other laws, and (2) specifically exempts American companies that have joined together for purposes of *export.* In addition, the antitrust laws exempt such items as bank mergers, agricultural cooperatives, and insurance companies, which are unregulated by state laws. [52]

Lack of Antitrust Enforcement

Concerning the nation's antitrust laws, the record of enforcement is quite lax. The Justice Department's Antitrust Division is charged with both the criminal and civil prosecution of these laws. The FBI has no expertise at all in antitrust violations. The Antitrust Division itself has been lax in prosecuting antitrust violations.

> In 1968 . . . the division filed 16 criminal cases involving price fixing; in 1970, with a larger staff and budget, the division brought only 4 cases; by 1975, under public pressure, prosecutions rose to 29 cases. The division has fared no better in the area of monopolies: in 1968 it brought no prosecutions; in 1975 it brought 5. This is hardly an impressive record for a unit with a budget of over $20 million. . . . The FTC (Federal Trade Commission) employs 200 attorneys in its antitrust section. . . . The record of both these agencies in the area of antitrust enforcement has been extremely poor. [53]

The facts for the 1960s and 1970s are consistent with those which comprise the entire history of antitrust regulation up to that time.

> From 1890 to 1959 there were a total of 1,499 antitrust cases begun by the Antitrust Division; only 729 of them were criminal actions. A total of 486 of the 729 cases were pursued to the imposition of sentence. . . . In recent years there has been a decline in the proportion of all antitrust cases which are criminal actions as opposed to civil actions: 59 percent of all cases were criminal actions in 1940–49; 48 percent were criminal cases in

1950–59, 31 percent were criminal cases in 1960–69, and only 9 percent were criminal cases in 1970.[54]

THE PENALTIES FOR CORPORATE CRIME: THE DOUBLE STANDARD

Corporate officials convicted of price fixing and other corporate crimes invariably receive light sentences (see Chapter 3). McCormick's data demonstrate that the heaviest jail sentence imposed in a price-fixing case from 1890 (the year the Sherman Antitrust Act was passed) until 1969 was sixty days. Actually it was not until the 1961 Electrical Conspiracy Case (discussed at length in Chapter 3) that any businessmen "were actually imprisoned purely for price-fixing and monopolization. No individuals were sent to jail until twenty years after the passage of the act." [55] In fact, in almost three-fourths of the cases (73.1 percent), convictions were gained, not by the government proving any wrongdoing, but by pleas of nolo contendere, under which defendants, instead of admitting guilt, merely refuse to acknowledge guilt, accept whatever sentence is imposed, and thereby avoid being labeled criminal by the court. Finally, only forty-five percent of the cases under the Sherman Act have been criminal in nature; the majority were tried as *civil* matters, which involved no jail terms. Of those cases in which jail terms were imposed and actually served, only two percent were tried under the Sherman Act, and almost all of these came under the Sherman Act's statutes concerning labor unions (unions assisting nonunion labor gain control over a labor market is a violation of section 6 of the Sherman Act).[56]

The laxness with which antitrust laws are enforced is in part attributable to the meager resources devoted to such enforcement. Within the Justice Department, outside Washington, local federal prosecutors — U.S. attorneys — are charged with enforcement of federal laws. In its 94 local offices, there are less than 2,000 attorneys for the entire nation, only 200 of whom prosecute fraud cases.[57] At the state level, only thirty of our fifty state prosecutors had consumer fraud units. While some white-collar prosecutions can cost over a million dollars, only forty state prosecutors had budgets that exceeded a million dollars, while three had budgets in excess of 500,000 dollars. All state prosecutors combined employ less than 7,000 attorneys. (The federal government alone employs over 10,000 lawyers.)[58] On the local level, a study of forty-one local prosecutorial offices in 1975 demonstrated that more than 100,000 complaints and inquiries were supposed to be adequately handled by 149 attorneys, 147 investigators, 89 paralegals, and 69 volunteers.[59] Obviously, American society has thus far failed to provide adequate enforcement of corporate criminal violations.

THE HIGHER IMMORALITY
AND CORPORATE CRIME

If Mills' view of corporate crime is correct, one would expect (1) widespread violations of antitrust laws, and (2) the presence of attitudes condoning such violations. There is ample evidence for both propositions.

First, several studies have documented the fact that corporate illegalities are quite widespread.

Item: One study documents that between 1945 and 1965 the Federal Trade Commission issued almost 4,000 cease-and-desist orders for legal violations by businesses for false advertising, false endorsements, removing or concealing law-required markings, false invoices, mislabeling, deceptive pricing, obtaining information by subterfuge, and a number of legally defined acts.[60]

Item: Edwin Sutherland, who coined the term "white-collar crime," studied the illegalities of seventy large corporations over a forty-year period. He found that there had been 980 decisions against these corporations. Every corporation had at least one decision against it, and the average number of decisions was fourteen.[61]

One hundred and fifty-nine of the 980 decisions were made by the criminal courts, whereas forty-five were made by courts that were either under civil or equity jurisdiction, and 361 were settled by government commission. Of the seventy corporations studied by Sutherland, thirty were either illegitimate in origin or became involved in illegal activities. Eight others, he found, were "probably" illegal in origin or in beginning policies. The finding of original illegitimacy was made with respect to twenty-one corporations in formal court decisions by "other historical evidence" in other cases. What Sutherland's study implies is that sixty percent of the corporations, or forty-two in number, with an average of four convictions each, are habitual criminals under the law.[62]

Item: A recent study of the largest 582 publicly owned corporations indicated that more than sixty percent of such firms "had at least one enforcement action initiated against them" [63] during the years 1975 and 1976. The 300 parent manufacturing firms in the study had an average of 4.8 actions initiated against them by federal agencies.[64] Yet, fewer than ten percent of the violations resulted in any criminal penalties. Moreover, in less than one percent of the federal-enforcement actions was a corporate officer sent to jail for failing to carry out corporate legal responsibilities.[65] When a jail term was imposed, "sentences almost never exceeded six months." [66]

Second, corporate executives seem well aware that many business-men engage in either criminal or unethical action. A 1961 survey in the *Harvard Business Review* of some 1,700 businessmen revealed that four out of seven believed that businessmen "would violate a code of ethics whenever they thought they could avoid detection." One-half of those sampled believed that the American businessman "tends to ignore the great ethical laws as they apply immediately to his work. He is preoccupied chiefly with gain (profit)." And eighty percent of those sampled thought that there were *accepted* business "practices" in their industries which they regarded as unethical.[67] A 1970 survey of the nation's 1,000 largest manufacturing corporations is even more shocking. Forty-seven percent of the largest 500 companies and seventy percent of the next 500 believed that price fixing is a common occurrence in their industries.[68]

There are several other reasons why corporate executives and small businessmen engage in unethical/illegal behaviors. One important factor is the capitalist economic system and its dependence on continued profits and economic growth. With antitrust and other business laws enforced with such laxness and the minimal penalties involved, viola-tions of such laws become quite rational from a profit standpoint. Quite simply, it is much more profitable to violate such laws than to obey them. Second, most corporate executives who are caught violating our laws believe often that what they have done does not violate the law in any serious sense. Typically, though found guilty, they believe that they had "not caused any harm to anyone." [69]

Third, corporate criminal behavior, like any other type of behavior, is learned. In the case of corporate executives, it is the corporate en-vironment, not the street gang or the college education, which teaches, and sometimes demands the learning of, such behavior. Thus a 1973 study by the American Management Association concluded that cor-porate executives and businessmen must often sacrifice personal morals and ethics in order to remain in business. "About 70 percent of the businessmen . . . admit they have been expected, frequently or on occa-sion, to compromise personal principles in order to conform either to organizational standards or to standards established by their corporate superiors." [70]

The convicted executives in one famous case, for example, made it clear that their motives in fixing prices were to increase the profits for the company and the furthering of their own careers.

> We did feel that this was the only way to reach part of our goals as managers. . . . We couldn't accomplish a greater percent of net profit without getting together with competitors. Part of the pressure was the desire to get ahead and the desire to have the goodwill of the man above you. He had only to get the approval of the man above *him* to replace you, and if you

wouldn't cooperate he could find lots of faults to use to get you out.[71]

Finally, corporate crime, as well as other types of "white-collar" illegalities, are made worse by the ignorance and unwitting cooperation of the public. This is not to suggest that the public is necessarily stupid or gullible. Rather, it is to confirm the fact that, until very recently, consumer education and violations of law by corporations were anything but part of the public's general knowledge or specific education in the United States. The nature of profitable crime is such that it is invisible. As Thio has stated:

> It may be difficult for the victims to know that they are victimized, even if they want to find out the true nature of their victimization. Grocery shoppers, for example, are hard put to detect unlawful substances as residues of hormones, antibiotics, pesticides, and nitrates in the meat they buy.[72]

Moreover, even when corporate criminals are caught and convicted, the news media, itself made up of corporations, has not exactly set forth with trumpets blaring when it comes to reporting such incidents. Although many criminologists believe that public shame is a key aspect of criminal penalties,[73] the media has failed to do its part:

> Even when prosecutions have resulted in conviction, most of the news media — including *Time* and *Newsweek,* the networks, and *The New York Times* — have failed repeatedly to recognize the importance of adequate reporting and have ignored the cases or have treated them trivially.[74]

The mass media, until very recently, has very much underreported corporate criminality. Such reportage may be partially responsible for convincing corporate criminals that the illegal acts they commit are not *real* crimes. This, coupled with the large majority of antitrust violations that are tried as civil matters, means little stigma and little public shame are associated with such crimes. Whether this will change in the face of growing public resentment of big business is an open question at this writing. At the moment it is safe to conclude that antitrust (and other corporate) violations are the most profitable form of crime (estimates run from 174 to 231 billion dollars, as was stated in Chapter 1) and carries little risk of detection and genuine punishment.

ORGANIZED CRIME AND THE BUSINESS ELITE

As a formal matter, organized crime is defined as "business enterprises organized for the purpose of making economic gain through illegal activities." [75] We are reminded that organized crime, to be defined as such, must display certain features:

... We have defined organized crime as an integral part of the American social system that brings together (1) a public that demands certain goods and services that are defined as illegal, (2) an organization of individuals who produce or supply those goods and services, and (3) corrupt public officials who protect such individuals for their own profit or gain.[76]

However, for most people, organized crime has taken its meaning over the past twenty years from the television series, books, movies, magazine articles, and congressional hearings (televised no less) on the Mafia or Cosa Nostra.

The image of organized crime, as presented in the mass media, is of a secret international organization of Italian and Sicilian gangsters, who, via corruption and violence, are quite successful in exerting their will in almost any task they undertake. But the media image of organized crime is probably very misleading, especially when the relationships among legitimate businesspeople, politicians, and syndicate criminals are examined. That is, an element of the higher immorality in the activities of organized crime is largely unexplored. The "higher immorality" applies to organized crime insofar as legitimate corporate and political elites utilize the services of the Mafia (or Cosa Nostra) for purposes which are unethical or illegal. This takes place when organized crime: (1) assists economic and political elites in repressing threats to the established order; (2) assists buinesses in profit-making ventures; and/or (3) assists federal officials with the carrying out of U.S. foreign-policy objectives.

Organized Crime and Repression

Organized crime has long assisted certain business and political elites in preventing and/or supressing the powerless in society. Throughout the 1920s businessmen entered into union contract negotiations with gangster-dominated unions in order to ensure themselves against upsets of any kind (e.g., union unrest). Often businessmen would join each other by creating trade associations, and the newly formed associations would negotiate with the gangster-dominated unions. Such organizations kept competition from other businesses not belonging to such associations at a minimum. The costs of such protection were usually passed on to consumers. These activities stabilized markets in small, competitive industries, such as trucking, garments, baking, and cleaning and dyeing. When prohibition ended, gangsters moved into the movie industry via these same tactics.[77]

Mafia figures have been recruited by businesses and politicians to quell labor unrest in a variety of settings:

Item: In Detroit in the 1940s the automobile companies used gangsters to suppress the efforts to unionize the auto industry.

Gangsters like D'Anna and Adonnis were given a monopoly over the haulaway business at the Ford Motor Company in return for gaining control of the auto worker unions in the city. And even after the AFL succeeded in unionizing the auto industry, Ford still hired mobsters for use as strike breakers. In 1945 and 1946 there were more strikes in the U.S. (41,750) than in the previous ten years combined, so the need for strike breakers was clear. Use of gangsters for this purpose was curtailed in the 1950s as unions supported governmental policies related to the Cold War, and militant unionism, often associated with communism, declined.[78]

Item: During the late 1930s and early 1940s the International Longshoreman's Union was infiltrated by organized criminals in New York Harbor. The docks of New York Harbor are made up of very narrow piers and grid-iron street layouts, and congestion is a continual problem. Such congested conditions make it easy to disrupt traffic on the docks. These peculiar physical conditions were part of the reason why gangsters were hired to infiltrate the local International Longshoreman's Association in the late 1930s and early 1940s. Because of the congestion, drivers did not bring their own loaders to the docks. Rather, loaders were hired at the pier. Loaders could be hired only through loading bosses, who were ILA union members. Such bosses charged high prices for using the labor they controlled, and a syndicate organization, Varick Enterprises, Inc., dominated this trade by charging all truckers a per-ton tax whether they used the loaders or not. While standardized rates were eventually worked out, the Varick organization, along with the ILA and the local Tammany Hall political machine, kept control of the loading and other rackets along the docks.

Item: In the late 1930s the West Coast ILA was a "clean" union headed by a labor radical named Harry Bridges. Bridges had taken his union out of the ranks of the American Federation of Labor to the CIO organization, an act of militant independence. Fearing such independence, as well as the strong socialist sentiment among some New York dock workers, a mobster, Albert Anastasia, murdered Peter Panto, a radical longshoreman leader, who worked on the Brooklyn docks. Militant left-wing union activity continued throughout the 1940s until 1951, when over "a million trade unionists in 12 unions, one fifth of its membership, were expelled from the CIO"[79] in response to the Report of the Investigation of Communism in New York City Distributive Trades.

Other brutal attacks on union dissidents by mobsters occurred throughout the 1940s. This fear concerning socialism within the American labor movement is responsible for the persistence of organized crime's involvement in labor racketeering and violence, at the behest of certain corporate elites. Of course

> Both employers and unions have hired gangsters to help them in industrial disputes. It has been employers who have benefited the most. One of the underlying factors was a desire to keep real wages down, and the constant use of terror to destroy rank and file organizations was condoned because of the general American fear of radicalism in the docks — so crucial to the working of the system.[80]

But labor unions are not the only entities that have been repressed by syndicate criminals. For example, some sociologists feel that organized crime has significantly contributed to the controlling of the American ghettos. Michael Tabor has argued that a conspiracy exists in the American ghetto between organized crime and the police, who are corrupted by organized criminals. Tabor's analysis centers on the role of organized crime in the distribution of heroin in ghetto areas. His contention is that the selling of heroin and the creation of a small army of heroin addicts within the ghetto keeps persons who might otherwise challenge the existing social order "strung out" on dope, and in a state of perpetual escapism from inhumane conditions in the ghetto.[81]

Moreover, Stephen Spitzer has argued that organized crime helps control problem populations in a number of ways. First, organized crime creates a parallel opportunity structure, a means of employment in illegal activities for persons who might otherwise be unemployed, and possibly politically discontent. The goods and services provided by organized crime to the under classes in society do deflect their energies from the sources of their oppression.[82] In this view, organized crime, insofar as it gains a monopoly over illegal goods and services, actually aids and maintains the public order, because monopoly brings with it security that one will make profits and, as a result, lessens the need for violence.

There is some evidence that the theses of both Spitzer and Tabor are correct. We know that heroin addiction is highly concentrated in the ghetto areas of America, and that certain illegitimate gambling activities, such as numbers running, not only give poor people a source of hope that they will become wealthy, but also provide a source of employment. *The New York Times* has estimated, for example, that thousands of people are employed in Harlem alone in the numbers racket.[83]

Organized Crime and Profits

Aside from aiding with the control of so-called problem populations, organized crime has increased the profits for certain legitimate businesses. The most obvious source of profit provided by organized crime is as an important "customer" of corporations. It was estimated, for example, that by 1940 bookies were "the fifth largest customer of the American Telephone and Telegraph Company." [84] Moreover the members of organized crime are themselves consumers of many goods and services. Given the multibillion-dollar estimates of organized criminal enterprise (i.e., fifty to eighty billion dollars), the amount of money spent by syndicate members as both profits capitalists *and* consumers serves as a rather significant market. As Quinney has stated:

> . . . Organized crime and legitimate business may mutually assist one another, as in regulating prices or commodities or enforcing labor contracts. Interdependence between the underworld of crime and the upperworld of business ensures that both systems will be maintained. Mutual assistance accompanied by the profit motive provides assured immunity.
>
> Organized crime has grown into a huge business in the United States and is an integral part of the political economy. Enormous amounts of illegitimate money are passed annually into socially acceptable endeavors. An elaborate corporate and financial structure is now tied to organized crime.[85]

Likewise, it has been reported that a number of large corporations (e.g., Pan American Airways and the Howard Hughes Corporation), have entered into partnership with organized crime in a number of gambling casinos and resort ventures in both Las Vegas and the Caribbean.[86] Apparently certain members of the corporate elite are not above obtaining capital for purposes of expanding markets. It is not known how much capital has come from criminal syndicates for ventures of this types, but, as mentioned in Chapter 1, obtaining such capital is now against the law under the RICO statute.

Organized Crime and the Political Elite

Revelations by the Senate Intelligence Committee in 1975 revealed the hiring of organized crime members by the CIA in the 1960s for the expressed purpose of assassinating Premier Castro of Cuba.[87] Thus, organized crime (at certain times at least) has functioned as an instrument of American foreign policy. Such escapades allegedly began during World War II when the underworld figures in control of the New York docks were contacted by Navy intelligence officials in order to ensure that German submarines or foreign agents did not infiltrate the area. It was thought that the waterfront pimps and prostitutes could act as a sort of counterintelligence corps. The man whose aid was sought for this purpose was Lucky Luciano, and he was reportedly quite successful in preventing sabotage or any other outbreaks of trouble on the New York docks during the war. Following his arrest and conviction for compulsory prostitution in 1936, Luciano was granted a parole and given exile for life in 1954 in exchange for the aid he provided during the war.

Mafiosi assistance was enlisted in other war-related efforts. Some locals were used by the Allies during the invasion of Sicily in 1943. Vito Genovese, a New York gangster, who had earlier escaped to Italy to flee a murder charge, became an "unofficial advisor to the American military government." [88]   After the war, local Mafiosi were installed as mayors in many locations in Sicily because they were antisocialist. And in France in 1950 the CIA recruited a Corsican gangster, Ferri-Pisani, to recruit an elite terror squad for use on the Marseilles docks. Socialist dock workers had refused to move shipments of U.S. arms bound for use in Vietnam (in support of the French military effort there). Corsican gangsters had also been used to assault the picket lines of communist unions in France and to harass union officials. The concession granted these international criminals in exchange for such aid was the privilege of using Marseilles as the center for Corsican heroin traffic. In Pearce's words, "The CIA had helped build the French Connection." [89]

In Cuba, it is known that the dictator Batista allowed Mafia financier Meyer Lanski to set up gambling casinos in Havana in 1933. Following Castro's closing of the casinos in the early 1960s, organized-crime figures were recruited by the CIA to aid in carrying out assassination plans on Castro's life. Finally, in Vietnam in the 1960s and early 1970s, organized-crime figures and the CIA cooperated in setting up Asia's Golden Triangle, Southeast Asia's center for heroin distribution. The triangle stretches for some 150,000 square miles across northeast Burma, northern Thailand, and northern Laos. The CIA's involvement includes the transporting of opium "in their own airline, Air America." [90]   These illustrations have led some criminologists to conclude that organized crime has served and continues to serve the domestic and foreign political goals of the American political and economic elites.

CONCLUSION: SOME CONSEQUENCES OF THE HIGHER IMMORALITY

This chapter has discussed a series of acts which involve the exercise of elite power. C. Wright Mills coined the term "higher immorality" to denote what he felt was a systematic corruption among the American economic and political elite. The features of the higher immorality discussed above are unique in that most of the acts are not against the law. Indeed, certain types of executive compensation (e.g., expense accounts and stock options), corporate income taxes, and government subsidies to businesses and wealthy individuals represent special favors which elites have secured for themselves via the passage of special legislation, and are, therefore, perfectly legal.

But, as mentioned in Chapter 1, what is legal does not necessarily represent what is moral or just. Consider the tax situation for a moment. Stern estimated in 1972 that of the 77.3 billion dollars in tax favors granted by the federal government, only 92 million in "loopholes" went to the nation's six million poorest families, while twenty-four times that amount went to 3,000 families with incomes over one million dollars.[91] In another study by economist Joseph Peckham, it was concluded that people who earned less than 2,000 dollars per year paid forty-four percent of their incomes in state, federal, and local taxes. People earning 2,000 to 15,000 dollars paid about twenty-seven percent of their incomes in these various taxes, and those who earned over 15,000 dollars paid about thirty-eight percent of their incomes for taxes. Thus the highest tax rates were paid by the lowest income group, and the second highest rates were paid by the highest group. This violates the spirit of our tax laws which are supposedly based on the ability to pay (i.e., progressive taxation).[92]

What these examples indicate is that "those who have the power and wealth have been able to influence the law for their personal benefit." [93]

The consequences of these tax loopholes are serious. First, such privilege creates cynicism among the majority of taxpayers, who are very much aware that the nation's tax laws favor the rich and powerful. Second, special loopholes for the wealthy create larger government deficits and increase inflation by billions of dollars per year. Third, government subsidies, which go largely to big businesses, violate the basic principles of "free enterprise." Why, for example, should Lockheed and Chrysler be allowed loan guarantees to ensure that they will remain in business while only about one in ten of the new businesses beginning in this country survives more than five years (on average)? [94]

We also indicated that political and economic elites attempted to convince the public of the reality of the energy crisis. Yet when one looks at the facts, as well as who profited from this so-called crisis, such reality becomes suspect. The energy crisis has clearly resulted in huge increases in oil-company profits, elimination of competition from independent oil dealers, and fuel bill increases in the billions for consumers serviced by multinational oil companies. Even the government's own studies indicated that the energy crisis of 1973–1974 was the result of the oil companies' anticompetitive practices, and not due to a genuine shortage of crude oil. Such manipulation by elites, involving the creation of favorable media images of their activities and the suppression of important facts, is not illegal, unless lied about under oath. Yet how many of the people reading these words consider such activities moral, ethical, or just?

Finally, we have described the long history of goods and services provided political and economic elites by members of organized criminal syndicates. It can be seen that members of Mafia families have suppressed labor unions, lower-class ghetto dwellers, and anticapitalist political movements; provided capital for certain business ventures; and, on numerous occasions, aided political elites in the execution of American foreign and military policy. In return for such services and capital, certain (not all) elites have allowed the activities of organized-criminal syndicates to grow and prosper. This, in turn, has contributed to the flourishing of trade in many American cities, as well as the corruption of politicians on all levels by organized-crime members (see Chapter 6). The use of capital from illegal businesses is now against the law, and the CIA suffered no little embarrassment when it was revealed that Mafia members had been recruited to assassinate Fidel Castro. Thus, the use of organized criminal syndicates to further the goals of economic and political elites contributes to criminal activity at all levels of American society, and, occasionally, results in scandal for elites. This further contributes to the decline of public confidence in elite rule.

Thus, while many of the activities which constitute the higher immorality are not illegal, they are widely regarded as unethical and often possess serious consequences for nonelites. Obviously, our discussion tends to confirm Mills' thesis that the higher immorality is an institutionalized feature of elite power in America.

NOTES

1. *The Village Voice* (Dec. 11, 1978), p. 11. Reprinted by permission of The Village Voice. Copyright © News Group Publications, Inc., 1978.
2. *Ibid.*, p. 16. Reprinted by permission of The Village Voice. Copyright © News Group Publications, Inc., 1978.
3. *The Village Voice* (Dec. 18, 1978), p. 28. Reprinted by permission of The Village Voice. Copyright © News Group Publications, Inc., 1978.
4. C. Wright Mills, 1952, "A Diagnosis of Our Moral Uneasiness," pp. 330–339, in I. H. Horowitz, ed., *Power, Politics and People* (New York: Ballantine, 1963), p. 331.
5. Barry Kreisberg, *Crime and Privilege* (Englewood Cliffs, N.J.: Prentice-Hall, 1975), p. 4. See also S. Balkan et al., *Crime and Deviance in America* (Belmont, CA: Wadsworth, 1980), pp. 182–184 for a brief historical view of the higher immorality and corporate crime.
6. C. Wright Mills, "Plain Talk on Fancy Sex," pp. 324–329, in Horowitz, *Power, Politics, and People.* For some recent statements by expense-account girls themselves, see Elizabeth L. Ray, *The Washington Fringe Benefit* (New York: Dell, 1976). Ms. Ray's "services" on the payroll of Congressman Wayne Hayes touched off a scandal in Washington which resulted in Hayes' leaving Congress. Ms. Ray's account closely parallels Mills' description of the goals and means of the expense-account girl. An anonymous article, "The Corporation Prostitute," pp. 354–359, in Judson Landis, *Sociology: Concepts and Characteristics,* Fourth Edition (Belmont, CA: Wadsworth, 1980), claims that some corporations hire prostitutes on a permanent basis for "closing" a variety of deals, including: bidding on factory sites, mergers with other companies, lobbying political issues,

undercutting competitors, gathering stockholders' proxy votes, and securing oil leases (p. 355).

7. Mills, "Diagnosis of Our Moral Uneasiness," p. 334.

8. P. Blumberg, "Another Day, Another $3,000: Executive Rip-Off in Corporate America," *Dissent* 2 (Spring, 1978), p. 159.

9. "Annual Survey of Executive Compensation," *Business Week* (May 12, 1980), p. 57.

10. *Ibid.*

11. See also "It Ain't Hay, But Is It Clover?", *Forbes* 125 (June 9, 1980), pp. 116–148.

12. *Ibid.*, p. 164.

13. F. Lundberg, *The Rich and the Super-Rich* (New York: Bantam, 1968).

14. *Ibid.*, p. 433.

15. *Ibid.*, pp. 434–435.

16. D. Tussing, "The Dual Welfare System," *Society* 2 (Jan./Feb. 1974), pp. 50–58.

17. Associated Press Release (April 9, 1977). See also H. Rodgers, "Welfare Policies for the Rich," *Dissent* 2 (Spring, 1978), p. 141; and Gary Hart, "The Economy Is Decaying, the Free Lunch Is Over," *The New York Times* (April 21, 1975).

18. Philip Stern, *The Rape of the Taxpayer* (New York: Random House, 1973), p. 214.

19. *Ibid.*, p. 232.

20. *Ibid.*, pp. 259–260. Copyright © 1973 by Philip Stern. Reprinted by permission of Random House, Inc.

21. Ovid Demaris, *Dirty Business* (New York: Harper's Magazine Press, 1974), p. 257.

22. Lundberg, *The Rich and the Super-Rich*, p. 284.

23. *Ibid.*, p. 292.

24. Examples cited in Demaris, *Dirty Business*, pp. 303–304.

25. Cited in *ibid.*, pp. 317–318.

26. See M. Clinard and R. F. Meier, *The Sociology of Deviant Behavior*, Fifth Edition (New York: Holt, Rinehart, and Winston, 1979), p. 568.

27. Michael Parenti, *Democracy for the Few*, Second Edition (New York: St. Martin's, 1977), p. 76.

28. *Ibid.*

29. See Robert Sherrill, *Why They Call It Politics*, Second Edition (New York: Harcourt, Brace, Jovanovich, 1974), pp. 126–127; and H. R. Rodgers, Jr., *Crisis in Democracy* (Reading, MA: Addison-Wesley, 1978), p. 126.

30. Cited in Parenti, *Democracy for the Few*, p. 77.

31. Ira Katznelson and Mark Kesselman, *The Politics of Power* (New York: Harcourt, Brace, Jovanovich, 1975), p. 142.

32. Sidney Lens, "Socialism for the Rich," *The Progressive* 91 (September, 1975), p. 14.

33. Cited in Donald McDonald, "Militarism in America," *The Center Magazine* 3:1 (January, 1970), pp. 31–54, in Robert Perrucci and Mark Pilisuk, *The Triple Revolution Emerging* (Boston: Little, Brown, 1971), p. 42.

34. Rodgers, *Crisis in Democracy*, p. 127.

35. Mills, "Diagnosis of Our Moral Uneasiness," p. 338.

36. David Mermelstein, "The 'Energy Crisis,'" in D. Mermelstein, ed., *The Economic Crisis Reader* (New York: Random House, 1975), p. 268.

37. Cited in Demaris, *Dirty Business*, p. 228. The oil-depletion allowance was repealed in 1975.

38. Dave Pugh and Mitch Zimmerman, "The 'Energy Crisis' and the Real

Crisis Behind It" (San Francisco: United Front Press, 1974), pp. 274–380, in Mermelstein, *Economic Crisis Reader,* pp. 275–276.

39. See G. David Garson, *Power and Politics in the United States* (Lexington, MA: D. C. Heath, 1977), pp. 251–252. See also Robert Scheer, *America after Nixon: The Age of the Multinationals* (New York: McGraw-Hill), p. 143.

40. Michael Tanzer, "The International Oil Crisis: A Tightrope Between Depression and War," *Social Policy* (Nov.–Dec., 1974), pp. 291–305, in Mermelstein, *Economic Crisis Reader,* pp. 293–294.

41. K. Dolbeare and M. Edelman, *American Politics,* Third Edition (Lexington, MA: D. C. Heath, 1977), p. 51.

42. Pugh and Zimmerman, "The 'Energy Crisis,' " p. 257.

43. Demaris, *Dirty Business,* p. 229. The above examples of oil-company profit sources due to the crisis are based on Demaris' discussion, pp. 229–249.

44. S. F. Singer, "The Oil Crisis That Isn't," *New Republic,* 8 (Feb. 24, 1979), p. 13.

45. Cited in Demaris, *Dirty Business,* pp. 228–229.

46. *Ibid.,* p. 229.

47. See Alexander Cockburn and James Ridgeway, "The Worst Domino," *The Village Voice* (Feb. 19, 1979), pp. 1, 7–8.

48. See S. F. Singer, "The Oil Crisis That Isn't," pp. 14–15.

49. Mills, "Diagnosis of Our Moral Uneasiness," pp. 335–336.

50. J. G. Vancise, *The Federal Antitrust Laws,* Third Revised Edition (Washington, D.C.: American Enterprise Institute, 1979), p. 7.

51. August Bequai, *White Collar Crime: A 20th Century Crisis* (Lexington, MA: D. C. Heath, 1978), p. 96.

52. *Ibid.,* pp. 100–101.

53. *Ibid.,* p. 102.

54. John E. Conklin, *"Illegal But Not Criminal": Business Crime in America* (Englewood Cliffs, N.J.: Prentice-Hall, 1977), pp. 104–105.

55. A. E. McCormick, "Rule Enforcement and Moral Indignation: Some Observations on Antitrust Convictions Upon the Societal Reaction Process," *Social Problems* 25 (Oct., 1977), p. 34.

56. *Ibid.*

57. Bequai, *White Collar Crime,* p. 150.

58. *Ibid.,* p. 148.

59. *Ibid.*

60. Lundberg, *The Rich and the Super-Rich,* p. 137.

61. Quoted in Lundberg, *The Rich and the Super-Rich,* p. 137.

62. E. Sutherland, "Crimes of Corporations," pp. 71–84, in G. Geis and R. F. Meier, *White-Collar Crime,* Revised Edition (New York: Free Press), p. 73.

63. Lundberg, *The Rich and the Super-Rich,* p. 148.

64. M. B. Clinard, *Illegal Corporate Behavior* (Washington, D.C.: Law Enforcement Assistance Administration, 1979), p. 108.

65. *Ibid.*

66. National Council on Crime and Delinquency, *Criminal Justice News Letter* 7 (March 26, 1979), p. 2.

67. Cited in A. Rogow, *The Dying of the Light* (New York: Putnam, 1975), p. 89.

68. M. Green et al., *The Closed Enterprise System* (New York: Grossman, 1972), pp. 149–150, 472.

69. M. Clinard and R. Quinney, *Criminal Behavior Systems: A Typology,* Second Edition (New York: Holt, Rinehart, and Winston, 1973), p. 211.

70. Cited in Rogow, *The Dying of the Light.*

71. R. Smith, "The Incredible Electrical Conspiracy," pp. 357–372, in

M. Wolfgang et al., eds., *The Sociology of Crime and Delinquency* (New York: Wiley, 1970), p. 363.

72. A. Thio, *Deviant Behavior* (Boston: Houghton, Mifflin, 1978), p. 352.

73. G. Geis, "Upper World Crime," in A. S. Blumberg, *Current Perspectives on Criminal Behavior* (New York: Knopf, 1974), pp. 132–133.

74. *Ibid.*, p. 116.

75. F. A. J. Ianni and F. Ianni, eds., *The Crime Society: Organized Crime and Corruption in America* (New York: New American Library, 1976), p. xvi.

76. Clinard and Quinney, *Criminal Behavior Systems*, p. 225.

77. See Mary McIntosh, "The Growth of Racketeering," *Economy and Society* 2 (1973), pp. 63–64.

78. Frank Pearce, *Crimes of the Powerful* (London: Pluto Press, 1976), p. 140. The items in this section are from Pearce's discussion.

79. *Ibid.*, p. 143.

80. McIntosh, "The Growth of Racketeering," p. 64.

81. See M. Tabor, "The Plague: Capitalism and Dope Genocide," pp. 241–249, in R. Perrucci and M. Pilisuk, eds., *The Triple Revolution Emerging* (Boston: Little, Brown), 1971.

82. Stephen Spitzer, "Toward a Marxian Theory of Deviance," *Social Problems* (February, 1975), p. 649.

83. See *The New York Times* (Jan. 30, 1975), p. 1; (March 21, 1975), p. 41; (August 7, 1975), p. 38; and (Nov. 4, 1975), p. 38 for details.

84. R. King, "Gambling and Crime," in L. J. Kaplan and D. Kessler, eds., *An Economic Analysis of Crime* (Springfield, IL: Charles C. Thomas, 1936), p. 40.

85. R. Quinney, *Criminology: Analysis and Critique of Crime in America* (Boston: Little, Brown, 1975), p. 145.

86. See E. Reid, *The Grim Reapers* (New York: Bantam Books, 1969), pp. 138–139 and H. Kohn, "The Nixon-Hughes-Lansky Connection," *Rolling Stone* (May 20, 1976): 41-50+, pp. 77–78.

87. See Dolbeare and Edelman, *American Politics*, pp. 85–89, for Senate Intelligence Committee Report excerpts on this and other CIA assassination plots.

88. Pearce, *Crimes of the Powerful*, p. 149.

89. *Ibid.*, p. 150.

90. *Ibid.*, p. 151.

91. See Philip Stern, "Uncle Sam's Welfare Program for the Rich," *The New York Times Magazine* (April 16, 1972), p. 26.

92. See this and other studies cited in Richard Parker, *The Myth of the Middle Class* (New York: Liveright, 1972).

93. J. Victor Baldridge, *Sociology: A Critical Approach to Power, Conflict, and Change,* Second Edition (New York: Wiley, 1980), p. 489.

94. See Michael Maccoby and K. A. Terzi, "Character and Work in America," pp. 116–161, in Philip Brenner et al., eds., *Exploring Contradictions: Political Economy in the Corporate State* (New York: McKay/Longman, 1974), p. 128.

Chapter 3
Corporate Deviance: Monopoly, Manipulation, and Fraud

Sociologist Stanton Wheeler, in his presidential address to the 1975 annual meeting of the Society for the Study of Social Problems, chided his colleagues for their neglect of one particular area of criminality — "the patterns of illegal activity that lie at the core of large-scale corporate, industrial society." [1] The magnitude of this omission was revealed by the first (in 1978) comprehensive investigation of corporate crime. Sociologist Marshall Clinard and his associates gathered data on the illegal actions of the 582 largest publicly owned corporations in the United States. Among their findings were that, during a twenty-four month period: (1) sixty percent of these corporations had a legal action instituted against them by a federal agency for criminal activity; (2) of those corporations having had at least one violation, the average number of violations was 4.2 — with one corporation being formally accused by the government on sixty-two occasions; and (3) almost one-half of all the violations occurred in the oil refining, automobile, and drug industries (a rate 300 percent greater than their size in the sample indicated). [2]

The neglected subject of corporate deviance is the focus of this and the next chapter. Specifically, this chapter is devoted to five areas of corporate deviance: (1) the problems generated by monopoly; (2) price fixing; (3) price gouging; (4) deceptive advertising; and (5) fraud.

THE COSTS OF MONOPOLIES

As noted in Chapter 1, the United States has moved from competitive capitalism to a stage of monopoly capitalism. Karl Marx, well over 100 years ago, correctly predicted this current stage.[3] Free enterprise, he argued, will result in some firms becoming bigger and bigger as they eliminate their opposition or absorb smaller competing firms. The ultimate result of this process is the existence of a monopoly in each of the various sectors of the economy. Monopolies, of course, are antithetical to the free-enterprise system because they, not supply and demand, determine the price and the quality of the products. This, as we will see, increases the benefits for the few at the expense of the many.

For the most part, American society upholds Marx's prediction. Although there are a few corporations that are virtual monopolies (Xerox, American Telephone and Telegraph, and IBM), most sectors of the American economy are dominated by "shared monopolies." Instead of a single corporation controlling an industry, the situation is one in which a small number of large firms dominate an industry.

> When four or fewer firms supply 50% or more of a particular market, a shared monopoly results, one which performs much as a monopoly or cartel would. Most economists agree that above this level of concentration — a four-firm ratio of 50% — the economic costs of shared monopoly are most manifest. Familiar examples of such oligopolistic industries are automobiles (GM, Ford, and Chrysler), aluminum (Alcoa, Kaiser, and Reynolds), rubber tires (Goodyear, Firestone, U.S. Rubber, and Goodrich), soaps and detergents (Procter and Gamble, Colgate, and Lever Brothers), cigarettes (Reynolds, American, Philip Morris, L and M), and electric bulbs (GE, Westinghouse, Sylvania).[4]

Shared monopolies exist also in subparts of a larger industry. In the food industry, for example, four or fewer corporations control many of the various sectors. This is true of the breakfast cereals (where four firms control ninety percent of sales), bread and prepared flour (seventy-five percent of sales by the shared monopoly), baking (sixty-five percent), fluid milk (sixty percent), dairy products (seventy percent), processed meats (fifty-six percent), sugar (sixty-five percent), canned goods (eighty percent), and soups (ninety percent by just one company, Campbell's).[5]

The existence of shared monopolies indicates the extent of concentration of American business. The evidence is clear that the assets of America's businesses are highly concentrated in the hands of a few giants. The 200 largest, for instance, have increased their share of U.S. industry from forty-five percent in 1945 to sixty percent in 1979. "Back in 1960 the 450 major firms controlled about 50 percent of the nation's manufacturing assets and took in 59 percent of the profits. Today it is around 70 percent control, and 72 percent of all profits." [6]   Examined another way:

> Of the almost two million corporations in America, one-tenth of 1 percent controls 55 percent of the total assets; 1.1 percent controls 82 percent.   At the other end of the spectrum, 94 percent of the corporations own only 9 percent of the total assets. [7]

This fantastic concentration of assets among a few giants is a relatively recent phenomenon.   General Motors, the largest corporation in sales, is but some sixty years old, yet it has grown in rank to be a bigger economic enterprise than such nations as Argentina, Belgium, and Czechoslovakia. [8]   Two processes account for the superconcentration of assets among a few corporations: growth through competition, where the "fittest" survive, and growth through mergers.

Between 1968 and 1971 approximately 20,000 mergers took place. An obvious result is that the big companies get bigger.   The assets of the top 500 companies increased in that three-year period by thirty-five percent.   This trend has continued as the 500 largest manufacturing companies increased their assets from eighty-three percent of all manufacturing and mining assets in 1975 to eighty-nine percent by 1977.   This is the result of the involvement of the largest corporations in mergers. In 1975, for instance, fourteen mergers involved a purchase price of 100 million dollars or more.   In 1977 the number had increased to forty-one and in 1978 there were eighty mergers of that size or larger. [9] But why is there the urge to merge among the biggest?   The goal of bigness appears to be *control*.   As Eugene Rostow has put it: "The history of corporations is the best evidence of the motivation for their growth.   In instance after instance (it) appears to have been quest for monopoly power, not the technological advances of scale." [10]

The ever greater concentration of power and resources in a few corporations has important negative consequences for American society, exacerbating many social problems. [11]   Foremost is the overpricing that occurs when four or fewer firms control a particular market.   A study by the Federal Trade Commission has estimated that if industries with the four largest firms were reduced in control from fifty to forty percent of sales, prices would fall by at least twenty-five percent.   When industries are so concentrated that four or fewer firms account for seventy percent of sales, they are found to have profits fifty percent higher than the lesser concentrated industries. [12]

The existence of monopolies is costly to consumers in other ways, since the costs of advertising and product changes are borne by them. The irony is that consumers, even though squeezed by monopolies, are forced to finance the continuation of monopolies.

Overpricing leads to lost output because of fewer sales and excess capacity.   Based on 1970 national income, several economists have calculated that lost production due to shared monopolies cost between forty-eight and sixty billion dollars annually. Lost output is deleterious for three reasons. First, it reduces the potential economic activity. Second, lower output substantially reduces tax revenues that, if not reduced because of lower output, could either reduce the tax burden for all or be spent to alleviate social problems. Third, another negative consequence of overcharging by monopolies is inequitable transfer cost. Excessive prices bring excessive profits. These profits then redistribute income from purchasers to the stockholders of the corporations. Although some thirty-one million persons own stock, two percent of all individual stockholders own about two-thirds of all stocks held by individuals.[13] The result is that a relative handful of stockholders (the already wealthy) reap the dividends. Thus, overcharging redistributes wealth, but in the direction of greater inequalities. As Newfield and Greenfield have put it:

> It is this tiny minority of shareholding Americans that gather in the super-profits generated by the power of big business to stifle competition and manipulate prices without fear of challenge. When we recognize that officers of these superbusinesses often collect more money from their stockholdings and stock-option privileges than from their salaries, we can see where much of our money goes: not to the community at large, not to wage earners, not into more efficient products, but into the bank accounts, trust funds, and holdings of the richest 1.6 percent of Americans.[14]

Put another way — and one that is stronger and even more compelling — two Stanford economists have argued that were there an absence of monopolies: (1) 2.4 percent of American families would control not forty percent of the total wealth, but only 16.6 to 27.5 percent, and (2) 93.3 percent of American families would be better off, and only the wealthier 6.7 percent worse off. Without monopoly, they have estimated that our current maldistribution of wealth would be as much as *fifty percent less*.[15]

Heavily concentrated industries are also sources of inflation. When consumer demand falls, for example, the prices of products in concentrated industries tend to rise.

> Economist John Blair studied 16 pairs of products, one from a concentrated industry [i.e., where a shared monopoly existed], the other from a more competitive one (e.g., steel building materials vs. lumber; pig iron vs. steel scraps). During the two recessions of the 1950's, the price of every unconcentrated product fell, while the price of 13 of the 16 concentrated products actually rose.[16]

In other words, where a few corporations are large enough to control an industry, they are immune from the rules of a competitive economy.

The immediate consequences for consumers is that they will pay artificially high prices.

Inflation is also caused by shared monopolies because they can automatically pass on increased labor costs or increased taxes to the consumer. In competitive industries, on the other hand, a corporation may be forced to reduce its profit if it wants to continue to get a share of the market. Moreover, the tendency toward "parallel pricing" in concentrated industries means that prices only rise. When an industry leader like General Motors or U.S. Steel announces a price increase of seven percent within a few days, similar increases are announced by their "competitors." As Ralph Nader and his associates have noted, "Each firm gladly increases its profit margin by getting the same share of a larger pie. There is no incentive to keep prices down, for then all the other firms will have to come down to that price — which means the same share of a smaller pie." [17]

It is impossible to know exactly how much monopolies contribute to inflation. Certainly the profits generated by lack of competition rather than efficiency or product superiority are hidden contributors.

The existence of monopolies also has important political consequences. The concentration of economic power undermines the democratic process in two fundamental ways. The first is overt, as the powerful marshall their vast resources to achieve favorable laws, court decisions, and rulings by regulatory agencies. They have the lobbyists, lawyers, and politicians (as noted in Chapter 1) to work for their interests. More subtly, but real nonetheless, is that the powerful get their way because of the bias of the politico-economic system. Such time-honored notions as "our economic interests abroad must be protected," or "tax incentives to business will benefit everyone," and "bigness is goodness," go unchallenged because we have been socialized to accept the current system as "proper." Thus, decisions continue to be based on precedent and the idea of "what is good for General Motors is good for the country" prevails. As long as such notions guide decision making, the interests of the wealthy will be served at the expense of the nonwealthy.[18]

For defenders of a free and competitive enterprise system, the existence of monopolies and shared monopolies should be attacked as un-American because the economy has become neither free nor competitive. There should be strong support of governmental efforts to break up the largest and most powerful corporations. As Green put it:

> Huey Long once prophesied that fascism would come to the United States first in the form of anti-fascism. So too with socialism — corporate socialism. Under the banner of free enterprise, up to two-thirds of American manufacturing has been metamorphosed into a "closed enterprise system." Although businessmen spoke the language of competitive capitalism, each sought refuge for themselves: price-fixing, parallel pricing,

mergers, excessive advertising, quotas, subsidies, and tax favoritism. While defenders of the American dream guarded against
socialism from the left, it arrived unannounced from the right.[19]

In summary, the negative consequences of shared monopolies are
important to our understanding of elite deviance in two ways: (1)
monopolies are themselves deviant because they disproportionately redistribute wealth and advantage toward the already advantaged; and
(2) the existence of monopolies aids in creating an environment where
deviant acts are encouraged. An examination of the automobile industry
will illustrate these interrelated phenomena.

Case Study: The Automobile Industry

The automobile industry is the nation's largest. One out of six
businesses is related directly or indirectly to the automobile. The data
from 1979 for the top 500 corporations listed General Motors second in
sales (66.3 billion dollars), Ford fifth (43.5 billion dollars), and Chrysler
twenty-second (12.0 billion). The major oil companies, whose fortunes
are directly related to automobile usage, ranked first, fourth, sixth, sev-
enth, and eighth in sales (a total of 216 billion).[20]

> The pivotal position of the industry in the U.S. economy is un-
> derscored by such considerations as the following: One out of
> every seven workers in this country is said to be dependent directly
> or indirectly on the automobile industry; the industry consumes
> about one fifth of the nation's steel production, one out of every
> fourteen tons of copper, more than two out of every five tons of
> lead, more than one out of every four tons of zinc, one pound in
> seven of nickel, one-half of the reclaimed rubber, almost three
> fourths of the upholstery leather, and substantial proportions of
> total national output of glass, machine tools, general industrial
> equipment, and forgings.[21]

The important point is that the automobile industry is one of the
nation's most highly concentrated. In the early 1900s, 181 companies
manufactured and sold automobiles. By 1927 there were forty-four,
by 1935 there were ten, and now there are only four domestic manufacturers.

The automobile industry has become a shared monopoly. But
even this shared monopoly is in danger of even greater concentration.[22]
In 1979, GM, for example, had fifty percent of all U.S. sales (and a
fifty-nine percent share of all domestically built cars), Ford had twenty-
seven percent, Chrysler had twelve percent, and American Motors had
less than one and one-half percent of all passenger-car sales. These
differences are highly significant, as each percentage point means a difference of approximately 700 million dollars in revenues. GM's share
of the market will likely increase because of the government's insistence
that the automobile industry reduce gasoline consumption in all cars sold

in the U.S.   In 1974 the average car sold by domestic manufacturers
went fourteen miles to the gallon.   Federal regulations now insist the
fuel economy be boosted in stages until each manufacturer sells cars
averaging 27.5 miles per gallon in 1985.   This will require massive costs
for downsizing and new technologies.   The bigger the company, the
less these costs will hurt.   GM, with 30.4 billion dollars in assets (400
percent greater than Chrysler's), for example, can afford the huge costs
and, since the 1974 edict, it has spent a yearly average of 3.2 billion to
overhaul its models.   These huge expenditures have given GM a lead
in the fuel-economy race and an ever greater share of the market.
Figure 3–1 contrasts the domestic-market share, by company, for 1974

It was stuck with big cars during
the oil embargo

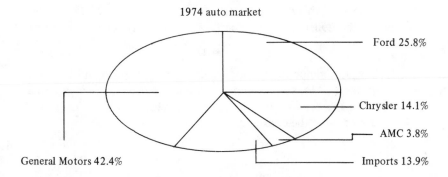

1974 auto market

Ford 25.8%

Chrysler 14.1%

AMC 3.8%

General Motors 42.4%   Imports 13.9%

But its new smaller cars paid off handsomely
last year despite growing imports

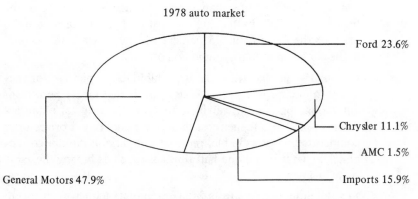

1978 auto market

Ford 23.6%

Chrysler 11.1%

AMC 1.5%

General Motors 47.9%   Imports 15.9%

Figure 3–1. How Downsizing Helped Boost GM's Market Share.

Source: Reprinted from the March 26, 1979, issue of *Business Week* by special permission, © 1979 by McGraw-Hill, Inc., New York, NY 10020.   All rights reserved.   Data from Motor Vehicles Manufacturers Association.

and 1978. Thus we see that a positive governmental policy, aimed at solving the problem of petroleum shortages and waste, has the negative effect of increasing the dominance of one corporation.

The other advantages of being big are illustrated by the two largest automobile companies — GM and Ford. These companies had in 1979, respectively, assets worth 32.023 billion and 23.510 billion and profits of 2.892 and 1.169 billion.[23] Such huge sums allow these companies to make big capital outlays, to provide credit to their suppliers, and to pay great sums for advertising. Moreover, they can afford a high degree of product differentiation (i.e., a number of different models and options), which further reduces competition. As a result of these barriers it has been estimated that a new company would need at least one billion dollars for manufacturing and another 200 million to set up a dealership network. The result of these high-entry barriers is that since 1923 there has not been a successful new domestic entrant into the automobile market.[24]

But how does this market control affect the consumer? The answer is simple — the consumer pays dearly. Let's briefly look at some examples:

1. Because competition is limited to four companies and in reality to one (GM), the companies do not compete in price and quality of the product but do compete in advertising. This cost is passed on to the consumer.

2. Yearly style changes (planned obsolescence) is the industry's strategy for continued growth in sales and profits. This policy has at least three important negative effects: (1) it increases the waste of resources; (2) it increases the likelihood of unsafe products because of insufficient time for planning and testing; and (3) the huge costs of style changes are paid for by the consumer. "The cost of dynamic obsolescence is passed on to the buyer twice: first, by tacking the cost of style changes onto the price of the car (about 25 percent of the price), and, second, in the car's unnecessarily rapid loss of value." [25]

3. Frequent style changes make it prohibitively expensive for outsiders to make spare parts. The result is that ninety percent of automobile parts are available only from the original manufacturers — and at a higher cost than one would pay if prices were competitive. For example, replacement parts, if purchased separately, cost two and one-half times as much as buying the same parts in a new car.[26]

4. Finally, monopoly control of the automobile industry has meant that prices tend to rise regardless of the demand. During the 1973–1974 recession, the number of cars sold fell by twenty

percent, yet the prices of domestic new cars were raised nine percent.[27] Obviously the law of supply and demand is rescinded in monopoly industries. That monopoly conditions, rather than the market, control prices is also shown in the similar price increases among the auto makers. In a typical instance, when one manufacturer announces its price increase, within weeks the others will make similar increases. If one is out of line with the others, there is a period of adjustment toward the GM price.[28] The result is higher profits for each of the companies — an average annual return on net worth between 1946 and 1967 of 16.67 percent in the automobile industry compared to 9.02 percent in other manufacturing corporations.[29] "In sum, the automobile industry imposes classic oligopolistic costs on its consumers." [30]

But the costs to consumers do not end here. There is considerable evidence that the automobile manufacturers actually create a deviant market structure. Sociologist Harvey Farberman has suggested that the auto makers impose on their new-car dealers a pricing policy that requires high volume and low per-unit profit.[31] The dealer is at the mercy of the manufacturers. If the dealer protests the situation, then he or she might lose the dealership or receive unfavorable treatment (slow delivery or not enough of the most popular models). Thus when the manufacturers demand high volume and a low-profit margin, the dealers are forced to look for profits elsewhere in their operations and these solutions are often deviant.

One way to increase profit is to minimize one's taxes. The "short sale" allows both buyer and seller to escape taxes. This is a tactic whereby the customer pays part of the car's cost by check and the remainder in cash. The sales manager, in turn, records the sale as the amount paid by check. The customer pays sales tax on that amount only, and the dealer does not pay income tax on the cash received. This excess cash is "buried" or "laundered."

When an automobile agency has an abundance of trade-ins, the best are recycled back to the agency's used-car retail line, while the surplus is sold to used-car wholesalers. The dispersal of cars into the wholesale market often involves the receipt of "kickbacks" by the used-car manager, as independent wholesalers must pay graft for their supply.

Another tactic to increase profits in used-car sales is to provide cosmetic changes rather than improve the mechanical condition. This practice is based on the knowledge that customers are especially impressed by observables such as the paint job and the interior.

Car dealers also make unusually high profits from their repair shops. These profits are elevated by two practices — flat-rate labor costs and the parts monopoly.[32] Under the industry-wide tactic of the flat rate, labor for repairs is charged according to the standard amount of time a given job is supposed to take — not the time it actually takes. The result is that the customer typically pays for shop and mechanic time that were never used.

The other "scam" is the charging for parts at the inflated retail cost. As noted earlier, the monopoly pricing of parts is exorbitant. Of course, another tactic to increase profits is the unnecessary replacement of parts.[33] The totals are impressive, with nearly forty percent of all auto repairs wasted. The National Highway Traffic Safety Administration released the data in Table 3–1 on auto repair deviance in 1978.

The automobile industry, in sum, is permeated by a "rip-off" mentality. Two aspects of this we have not discussed — the actual manipulative sales techniques used in the new and used-car dealerships to maximize profits[34] and the unsafe cars that kill and maim (which we will discuss in the next chapter). The important point for now is that monopoly control has costly consequences for consumers.

PRICE FIXING

The *sine qua non* of capitalism is competition. We have seen, though, that the tendency toward concentration makes a mockery of the claim that the American version of capitalism is competitive. The existence of shared monopolies allows the few corporations that control an industry to eliminate price wars by parallel pricing and product homo-

---

Table 3–1: How Billions Are Wasted on Auto Repairs.

Of 50 billion dollars spent yearly for auto repairs, nearly 20 billion may be wasted for a variety of reasons, including owners' lack of care, according to a study by the National Highway Traffic Safety Administration released in July. Where the money goes —

Undermaintenance, failure to make needed replacements	$4.5 bil.
Faulty repairs	$3.8 bil.
Unneeded repairs in package deals	$3.4 bil.
Repairs made fraudulently	$2.3 bil.
Unnecessary use of nonstandard parts	$2.2 bil.
Overmaintenance, unnecessary replacement of parts	$2.1 bil.
Bad diagnoses	$1.2 bil.
Total	**$19.7 bil.**

Note: Details do not add to total because of rounding.

Source: Reprinted from *U.S. News & World Report* (September 18, 1978), p. 72. Copyright 1978, U.S. News & World Report, Inc.

geneity. The former depicts the practice where tacit collusion by "competitors" achieves a common price, while the latter means that prices are going to be roughly equal because the "competitors" produce products with similar specifications. Both practices are common and have the consequence of equal prices regardless of whether the leading companies in an industry conspire to do so or not.

Prices are also manipulated to maximize profits through collusive activities of the companies supposedly in competition with each other. This practice is called price fixing. It refers to the explicit agreement among "competitors" to keep prices artificially high to maximize profits. Price fixing is illegal and complaints are monitored and brought to court by the Antitrust Division of the Justice Department. The illegality of price fixing, however, has not deterred competing companies from conspiring to make abnormal profits through this practice. One review of cases where price fixing was proved from 1963 to 1972 revealed that the practice occurred among companies producing and marketing the following: steel wheels, pipe, bed springs, metal shelving, steel castings, self-locking nuts, liquified petroleum gas delivery, refuse collection, linoleum installation, swimsuits, structural steel, carbon steel, baking flour, fertilizer, railroads, welding electrodes, acoustical ceiling materials, hydraulic hose, beer, gasoline, asphalt, book matches, concrete pipe, drill bushings, linen, school construction, plumbing fixtures, dairy products, fuel oil, auto repair, brass fittings, plumbing contracting, bread, athletic equipment, maple floors, vending machines, ready-mix concrete, industrial chemicals, rendering, shoes, garage doors, automobile glass, and wholesale meat.[35] Examining these and other cases, the researchers tried to determine if there was a pattern associated with price fixing. They concluded that "conspiracy among competitors may arise in any number of situations but it is most likely to occur and endure when numbers are small [few companies involved], concentration is high [when four or fewer firms control fifty percent or more of the market], and the product is homogeneous." [36]

We should not forget, however, that collusive arrangements to keep prices or fees artificially high are not limited to industrial sales. Price fixing in one form or another often occurs in real-estate fees, doctors' fees, lawyers' fees, and tax accountants' fees, to name a few.

Although the government continues to prosecute price-fixing cases, the problem continues. Apparently the potential for increased profits is too tempting. Moreover, when found guilty the punishment has been more symbolic than real. Thus the incentives have been too tempting for many. Once again profit is the primary source of motivation — and the customer be damned.

The extra profits garnered through price-fixing arrangements have the obvious impact on customers — they pay extraordinary prices for goods and services — but it also has some negative indirect effects. Two of these subtle consequences are especially noteworthy. The first is that larger than necessary expenditures fuel inflation. The second is that extra profits exacerbate the gap between the haves and the have-nots.

For an illustration of price fixing, let's examine the most blatant incident in modern American history.

Case Study: The Electrical Conspiracy

From the mid-1940s through the 1950s, virtually all electrical manufacturing firms were actively involved in collusive activities to keep prices high.[37] Twenty-nine companies, but principally General Electric and Westinghouse, eventually were found guilty of conspiring to fix prices, rig bids, and divide markets on electrical equipment valued at 1.75 billion dollars annually. The amount of profit generated from the price fixing in the electrical industry was considerable.

> The result of these machinations was grossly inflated prices. Generator prices rose 50 percent from 1951 to 1959, while wholesale prices on all commodities rose only 5 percent. The Senate Small Business Committee later asserted that Westinghouse had bilked the Navy by a 500 percent overcharge on certain gear assemblies, and GE had charged 446 percent too much on another contract.[38]

An example of how the prices were fixed occurred in so-called competitive bidding for new business. Public agencies (e.g., utilities, school districts, and the government) required companies to make sealed bids for the cost of their products. The conspiring companies used this seemingly competitive practice to ensure high prices. They did this by rotating business on a fixed-percentage basis (i.e., each company was allowed the proportion of the sales equal to the proportion of the market they had controlled prior to the conspiracy). For sealed bids on circuit breakers, for example, the four participating companies divided the sales so that GE received forty-five percent, Westinghouse thirty-five percent, Allis-Chalmers ten percent, and Federal Pacific ten percent.

Every ten days to two weeks, working-level meetings were called, in order to decide whose turn was next. Turns were determined by the "ledger list," a table of who had got what in recent weeks, and after that the only thing left to decide was the price that the company picked to "win" would submit as the lowest bid.[39]

Four grand juries investigated the price-fixing allegations in the electrical industry and handed down twenty indictments involving forty-five individuals and twenty-nine corporations. At the sentencing hearing in 1961, Judge Ganey levied fines of $1,787,000 on the corporations and $137,000 on different individuals. The highest corporate fines were against General Electric ($437,500) and Westinghouse ($372,500).

Seven individuals were given jail sentences of thirty days (later reduced to twenty-five for good behavior). Twenty others received suspended sentences. In addition, the individuals were assessed fines ranging from $1,000 to $12,500. The corporations also faced settlements to injured parties. By 1964, for example, some ninety percent of the 1,800 claims against GE had been settled for a total of 160 million dollars.

In conclusion, several facts are especially noteworthy about the electrical conspiracy case. First, and most obvious, this antitrust conspiracy illustrates the willful and blatant violation of the law by some of the leading corporations of the United States.

Second, the highest officials in the guilty corporations escaped without fines and jail sentences. Those found guilty were vice-presidents, division managers, and sales managers, but *not* presidents and chief executive officers.

The sentences levied were mild considering the huge amounts of money involved. The government even ruled that when the companies paid their fines and settlements, then the payments could be considered *a business expense and therefore tax deductible.*[40]

This type of crime is underplayed by the media compared to street crimes. For example, on the day that the defendants pleaded guilty or *nolo contendere* ("no contest"), only four of the largest twenty-two newspapers made the story front-page news, and four well-known papers — the *Boston Globe, New York Daily News, Christian Science Monitor,* and the *Kansas City Times* — completely omitted the story. Five days later, when the sentencing occurred, forty-five percent of the twenty newspapers with one-fifth of all the newspaper circulation in the U.S. did not consider the story front-page news.[41]

The parties convicted did not consider their acts immoral. Two quotes make this point: (1) the president of Allen-Bradley, Fred L. Loock, said, "It is the only way a business can be run. It is free enterprise";[42] and (2) a GE official said, "Sure, collusion was illegal, but it wasn't unethical." [43]

The punishment for those judged guilty was incredibly light given the magnitude of the case (a maximum of 12,500 dollars and thirty days in jail). But more important is the discrepancy when the sentences for these types of crimes are compared to those given to individuals found guilty of street crimes. Some extreme examples are provided by Nader and Green:

> A year after seven electrical manufacturers were sent to jail for 30 days apiece, a man in Asbury Park, New Jersey, stole a $2.98 pair of sunglasses and a $1 box of soap and was sent to jail for four months. A George Jackson was sent to prison for ten years to life for stealing $70 from a gas station, his third minor offense; and in Dallas one Joseph Sills received a 1000-year sentence for stealing $73.10. Many states send young students who are mari-

juana first offenders to jail for five to ten years' sentence. But the *total* amount of time spent in jail by all businessmen who have ever violated antitrust laws is a little under two years.[44]

In all probability, antitrust cases like the electrical conspiracy represent only a small portion of the actual amount of price fixing in American industry.[45] The potential profits are too tempting for many business executives and the chances of getting caught are slim. The likelihood of escaping conviction, if caught, is great because of two factors. First, the deals are made in secret and masked by apparently legal activity (e.g., sealed bids). Second, the government's antitrust budget is very small. In 1971, for instance, this budget was only 11.5 million dollars — one-twentieth of Procter and Gamble's advertising budget.[46]

PRICE GOUGING

Because private corporations are entirely profit oriented, they take whatever advantage they can to sell products or services at the highest possible prices. Shared monopolies, as we have seen, use their control of the market to increase prices an average of twenty-five percent. Price fixing, of course, is another tactic to maximize profits. In this section, we want to describe yet another manifestation of profit-maximizing behavior — price gouging. This term refers to the practice of taking extraordinary advantage of consumers because of the bias of the law, monopoly of the market, manipulation of the market, or because of contrived or real shortages. Whatever the means used, price gouging is a form of deviancy. Let's examine the procedures used in three areas: (1) selling to the disadvantaged; (2) taking advantage of events; and (3) extraordinary profits through convenient laws and manipulation.

Taking Advantage of the Disadvantaged

Low-income consumers are the victims of price gouging from a variety of merchants, banks and finance companies, landlords, and the like. Some plausible reasons why the poor pay more might include higher rates of street crimes in their neighborhoods, which raise the cost of doing business, and the economic marginality of the poor, making their credit especially risky. But even when these rationales are accounted for, the poor are the victims of unusually high prices, which of course tend to perpetuate their poverty. Many food chains find that it costs two or three percent more to operate in poor neighborhoods, yet low-income consumers pay between five and ten percent more for their groceries than would those living in middle-income areas.[47] Perhaps the best example of price gouging by ghetto stores is that they tend to raise prices on the first and the fifteenth of each month because these are the days when welfare checks are received.[48]   Similarly, there is evidence that grocers in the Mississippi Delta raised prices when food stamps were introduced.[49]

Banks and other financial organizations also take advantage of the poor. Because they are not affluent and therefore have inadequate collateral or credit reference, the poor must pay higher interest rates or may be forced to deal with loan sharks because they are denied resources through the legitimate financial outlets.

The greater risk of loaning to the poor is used to justify extremely high prices in poor neighborhoods. In the jewelry business, for example, the normal markup is 100 percent, but for jewelry sold in poor neighborhoods, the markup often is 300 percent or higher. A ring selling wholesale for fifty dollars will sell for as much as 300 dollars in the poverty market. In order to protect themselves from possible default, credit jewelers in such a situation will try to get the maximum down payment — say sixty dollars. If so, the dealer has already made a ten-dollar profit and the future payments are all profit.[50]

The merchants in poor areas engage in such price gouging because (1) the stores are essentially monopolies (no competition present); (2) the stores can argue legitimately that their costs are higher than in middle-class areas (although their prices, as we have seen, tend to exceed their increased risks by a wide margin); (3) the poor are unorganized and have no access to the powerful in society; (4) the poor are often unaware of the available avenues to complain of abusive practices; and (5) the poor tend to be apathetic because of the hopelessness of trying to change the practices of powerful banks, supermarket chains, finance companies, and other seemingly monolithic organizations. Cross has summarized the economic plight of the poor as

> Caught in a vicious cycle of poverty, the poor and the stores which serve them are trapped by the worst aspects of the free enterprise system. And it is likely that the poor are also at the receiving end of a greater amount of deliberate fraud and price discrimination than the suburban middle class.[51]

Taking Advantage of Unusual Events

The sharp entrepreneur is always looking for the special events that might lead to spectacular profits. For example, when California passed Proposition 13 in 1978, local property taxes were dramatically reduced by seven billion dollars. This event was used by some people to increase profits substantially. Landlords, for example, did not reduce rents accordingly but tended to pocket the difference. The California-based corporations made an instant additional profit of two billion dollars, yet did not lower prices on their products.

A few years ago a worldwide shortage of sugar caused the price to increase rapidly for U.S. consumers. This caused a concomitant rise in a number of products using sugar. The cost of candy bars increased while their size dwindled (the price tripled while the size shrunk to one-third its former size). The cost of soda pop also increased markedly during this period. Canned pop from vending machines went from fifteen to twenty-five cents a can. Interestingly, and revealing of the tendency of corporations to gouge whenever possible, the cost of diet pop (which, of course, contained no sugar) went up in price to twenty-five cents as well. Moreover, when the sugar shortage subsided, the cost of pop stayed at the shortage-created level. Also, all major pop companies had the same pricing strategy — a form of parallel pricing or price fixing.

But the best example of using a crisis to one's economic advantage, and the one that has had the greatest impact on the American consumer, is the price gouging by the oil companies following the oil boycott of the OPEC countries in 1973–1974 and the shortages caused by the up-heavals in Iran in 1979 (which were discussed in detail in Chapter 2).

Extraordinary Profits through Deception

Although there are many examples of price gouging because of deception, we will focus on this phenomenon in one industry — the pharmaceutical industry.

The sale of prescription and nonprescription drugs is a large industry, representing ten percent of all medical costs in the U.S. (approximately 1.2 billion dollars annually). About half of all prescription drugs come in two forms — under a brand name or under the generic name. Although a drug is identical chemically, if marketed under a brand name it is very much more expensive — and therefore profitable. Some examples:

> *Item:* The tranquilizer Librium, made by Hoffman-LaRoche, sells wholesale for $9.06 per 100 10-mg. tablets, while its generic substitute lists for $1.10.[52]
>
> *Item:* Hydroduiral, a drug for blood pressure made by Merck, costs $6.09 per 100 50-mg. tablets under its trade name but sells for .45 under its generic equivalent.[53]
>
> *Item:* Abbott wholesales 100 tablets of crythromyacin for $15.50 while its generic counterpart wholesales for $6.20.[54]
>
> *Item:* In 1971 the drug PETN, sold under its brand name, grossed fifteen million dollars, but it would have brought only four million if purchased generically.[55]

Obviously, customers would save enormous sums if every prescription were filled with an available generic, yet only about ten percent are filled with the less expensive alternative.[56]   The question is why, and the answer is that the drug manufacturers have done all in their power to get doctors and the public to buy the branded and more expensive drugs. Let's elaborate.

The situation in drug sales is very different from the typical purchaser-seller relationship.   The sale of prescription drugs is not the choice of the consumer but one made by the physician, whose choice is not based on price but on knowledge.   Doctors prescribe drugs they know about, and most of their information is supplied by the large pharmaceutical firms which spend from 3,000 to 5,000 dollars per doctor, per year, promoting their own brand-name drugs.[57]

The drug manufacturers also benefit by the proliferation of drugs (e.g., sixty-one firms offered their own version of one chemical compound, PETN), which leaves physicians inundated with a virtual sea of drugs and drug names.   Busy physicians will opt, in most cases, for the drugs that are most familiar, and the drug firms do all they can to familiarize them with their branded (and expensive) products.

But the drug companies have done more than just advertise their products to physicians.   According to Ben Gordon, a drug consultant to the U.S. Senate for twenty years, ". . . The larger drug manufacturers have been misleading and lying to the American public, to the medical profession, and to the Congress, about the quality of their drugs, as against that of the generic drugs." [58]   They have used several scare tactics, such as films in which generic drugs were compared to defective cars and warnings to pharmacists that the increased use of generic drugs would cause the druggists' insurance rates to increase.[59]

Another tactic of the drug firms has been to lobby for laws prohibiting generics to be substituted for the branded drugs prescribed by physicians.   At one time all fifty states had such a law but in recent years many have been changed.   In late 1978, some forty states and the District of Columbia allowed pharmacists to substitute generic drugs for the brand-name prescription drugs.

This shift in the laws and the greater consumer familiarity with generic drugs has brought about a shift in policy by the large drug firms. They are fighting generics with what they call "branded generics."   These are prescription drugs that carry a different name and are priced midway between the brand-name drugs and the products that come from the generic drug houses.   Although the chemicals used are identical, the large drug firms argue that the higher price of the branded generics is justified.   In the words of Joseph Stetler, president of the Pharmaceutical Manufacturers Association: "Those larger companies have heavy investments in quality control research, which is relatively incidental, but they have a backup capability that is of value to a consumer.   So there's a justification for a price differential." [60]

That reasoning sounds good but in many cases the large companies do not manufacture their highly advertised products. "20/20," the ABC Newsmagazine, visited the Mylan Pharmaceutical Company and found one machine producing erythromycin tablets. Some of the tablets were then dyed pink, others were colored yellow, while still others were made orange. The only difference among the three sets of tablets was the color, yet the three would be priced very differently. The pink version is the generic and sells for $6.20; the yellow pills are marketed by Smith-Kline and sell for $9.20; and the orange ones are called Bristamycin and are marketed for $14.00. Similarly, at the Phillips-Roxanne Laboratories, 60-mg cidamenphene-todene tablets are placed in a Smith-Kline bottle to be sold wholesale for $13.20 a hundred, but when they are put in a Phillips-Roxanne package, they sell for $10.80. Again, the products are precisely identical — even manufactured at the same place.[61] The only difference is in color, packaging, price, and "man in the plant." As Jack Anderson has put it:

> . . . Many large drug companies actually don't manufacture some of their highly advertised products. Usually, officials from a big drug company will hire a smaller firm to manufacture a product for them. Then the big firm will stamp its brand name on the product, jack up the price and sell the drug as its own. The big name firm is required only to send someone to the factory to watch over the manufacturing process. The ruse is known as "man in the plant." Thus, the industry giants are able to charge consumers millions of dollars more than generic firms for products that are essentially the same.[62]

To counteract the problem, the Department of Health, Education, and Welfare published in 1978 a *Guide to Drug Prices* to provide information for consumers, pharmacists, and doctors. Former HEW Secretary Joseph A. Califano, Jr., has said that "If one of five physicians uses this *Guide* to cut the costs of prescriptions by 10 percent, that would save consumers $120 million a year in prescription drug costs." [63]

DECEPTIVE ADVERTISING

One tenet of capitalism is expansion. Each corporation wishes to produce an increasing amount so that profits likewise will inflate. The problem, of course, is that the public must be convinced to consume this ever-larger surplus.[64] One way to create demand is through advertising. Advertising expenditures in 1973 amounted to twenty-six billion dollars and by 1979 they had increased to 48.5 billion. A strong argument could be made that advertising expenditures are wasteful in three ways: (1) they create a demand to consume that increases the waste of natural resources; (2) they increase the cost of products, as consumers pay all the advertising costs; and (3) the money spent serves no useful purpose (other than profits).

But advertising is a problem to the public in another way — it is sometimes designed to deceive the public. In a fundamental way all advertising is deceptive because it is designed to manipulate. Symbols are used to create in the observer a concern with his or her status, beauty, age, or to associate sex appeal with a certain look, or whatever. Advertising deceives because that is how desires to consume new products are created. But the deception we want to consider goes beyond this type of illusion. We are concerned with a more willful form of deception, where the goal is to sell, even through lies.[65]

Talking about advertising in the U.S., a retired advertising executive has said that the cardinal principle is:

> Don't worry whether it's true or not. Will it sell? ... The American people ... are now being had from every bewildering direction. All the way from trying to persuade us to put dubious drug products and questionable foods into our stomachs to urging young men to lay down their lives in Indochina, the key will-it-sell principle and the employed techniques are the same. *Caveat emptor* has never had more profound significance than today, whether someone is trying to sell us war, God, anti-Communism or a new improved deodorant. Deceit is the accepted order of the hour.[66]

The tendency toward deception in advertising takes two forms — blatantly false advertising and "puffery." Let's examine these in turn. Several examples will show the ways advertising can be outright false:

> *Item:* The Federal Trade Commission ruled that Anacin had falsely advertised its product by claiming that it: (1) relieved nervousness, tension, stress, fatigue, and depression; (2) was stronger than aspirin; (3) brought relief within twenty-two seconds; (4) was highly recommended over aspirin by doctors; and (5) was more effective for relieving pain than any other analgesic available without prescription.[67]

> *Item:* The attorney general of Colorado filed suit against Montgomery Ward alleging that Ward's had regularly advertised items such as television sets and major appliances at a sale price below the "regular price" when in reality the "regular price" was substantially inflated.[68]

> *Item:* A common tactic companies use is called "bait and switch" advertising, although it is a clear violation of FTC rules. This is the practice of advertising a product at an extremely low price; but when customers arrive to buy it, there is none available and the salespersons pressure people to buy more expensive articles.

Item: Products are advertised at exaggerated sizes.[69]   Lumber is uniformly shorter than advertised — e.g., a twelve-inch board really is eleven and one-quarter inches wide.   The quarter-pounder advertised by McDonald's is really three and seven-eighths ounces. Nine-inch pies are in truth seven and three-quarters inches in diameter, because the pie industry includes the rim of the pan in determining the stated size.[70]

Item: When Libby-Owens-Ford Glass Company wanted to demonstrate the superiority of its automobile safety glass, it smeared a competing brand with streaks of vaseline to create distortion, then photographed it at oblique camera angles to enhance the effect.   The distortion-free marvels of the company's own glass were "shown" by taking photographs of a car with the windows rolled down.[71]

Item: An analysis of news items appearing in *The New York Times* during 1974 revealed court cases of FTC rulings concerning deceptive advertising for the following: Air France, Fram Oil Filters, Ford, GM, Chrysler, American Cynamid, Clorox, Calgon, Listerine, Lysol, A&P, Sterling Drug, Kayser Pantyhose, Hardees, Carte Blanche, California Milk Producers, Skippy Peanut Butter, Sugar Association, Viceroy Cigarettes, and Jack LaLanne Health Spas.[72]

A more subtle form of deceptive advertising is called "puffery." This term refers to the practice of making exaggerated claims for a product.   Although advertisers routinely make such false claims, and the result is deception, the law considers such practices as legal.   Some examples:

"Blatz is Milwaukee's finest beer"

"Nestlé's make the very best chocolate"

"Ford gives you better ideas"

"GM — always a step ahead"

"Zenith Chromacolor is the biggest breakthrough in color TV"

"The world's number one station" (KDKA, Pittsburgh)

"Breakfast of Champions" (Wheaties)

"You can trust your car to the man who wears the star" (Texaco)

"You can be sure if it's Westinghouse"

"The greatest show on earth" (Barnum and Bailey)

"The world's greatest newspaper" (Chicago Tribune)

"The world's most experienced airline" (Pan Am)

"Prudential has the strength of Gibraltar"

"Every kid in America loves Jello brand gelatin" [73]

Such claims are false or unsubstantiated. Even though they are considered legal, their intent is to mislead. The goal, as is always the case with advertising, is to use whatever will sell the product. If that means trifling with the truth — then so be it.

FRAUD

Fraud is committed when one is induced to part with money or valuables through deceit, lies, or misrepresentation.[74] Although the law recognizes fraud as a crime, it has traditionally assumed that a fraud directed against a private individual was not a crime because of the principle of *caveat emptor*. Preston has summarized this principle as:

> The buyer must accept full responsibility for a sales transaction; the seller accepts none. He must rely upon and trust nothing but his own personal inspection of his purchase, ignoring any representations of the seller which he does not confirm for himself. Any buyer who does other than this must suffer all consequences of purchases which turn out badly.[75]

This principle of the marketplace is an open invitation for fraud and some criminologists have contended that fraud is probably "the most prevalent crime in America." [76]

The types of frauds perpetrated on victims involve a host of schemes applied to a wide variety of economic activities. The following are some representative cases:

Item: A 1979 government survey found that motorists were overcharged an average of 150 dollars per car per year for repairs. The result is that fifty-three cents of every dollar spent on car repairs is wasted because of overcharges, work not performed, wrong repairs, and incompetent work performed.[77]

Item: Medicaid sets the allowable profit in nursing homes at only one dollar per patient per day. Given this small margin, some nursing home operators cut down on the cost of running the home (fewer employees, lower thermostat settings, poor-quality food, overcrowding), but charge Medicaid for the full amount. Medicaid abuse by doctors, hospitals, nursing homes, and druggists was estimated in 1979 to total eight billion dollars annually.[78]

Item: Fraud in medicine includes outright quackery, fee splitting (kickbacks from specialists to general practitioners who recommend them), unnecessary surgery, and claiming payment for services never rendered.[79]

Item: Land fraud has occurred most commonly in areas of special allure such as in the desert, mountains, or by the sea. Land, represented in brochures, media presentations, and by salespersons as having favorable characteristics, has been sold to unsuspecting buyers even though it was without the amenities claimed. As an example of such sales deception, a newspaper ad for Lake Mead Rancheros claimed: "The Rancheros are livable now. . . . You can own a king-sized western estate with roads and electricity, water and phones available. . . . Build now and move in." In actuality, though, power and phone lines were six miles away and the nearest water was from a coin-operated pump twelve miles away.[80] Often several elements of the legitimate business community are extensively involved in land fraud: law firms, banks, title companies, real-estate firms, contractors, the media, and investors. Moreover, public officials are sometimes "bought" to solve problems such as zoning, road construction, and to curb regulatory zeal.

Item: The American Knitting Center sold imported knitting machines to persons with the promise that they in turn would market the garments manufactured at high prices. Twelve hundred women purchased these machines for 550 dollars each, while they had cost the sellers between 60 and 90 dollars each.[81]

Item: A dance studio signed a sixty-nine-year-old widow to eight "lifetime" memberships, entitling her to 3,100 hours of instruction at a cost of 34,193 dollars.[82]

Item: In a fifteen-year span, some 100,000 Americans paid over seventy million dollars for lightbulbs sold under the Torch brand. The sales were made over the phone with the salesperson claiming to be handicapped and often tearfully pleading for a sale. The bulbs were overpriced by 300 percent and were substandard in quality. Moreover, an investigation by New Jersey revealed that some of the doctor-certified "disabilities" of the salespersons were: acne, excess weight, nervousness, hernia, hay fever, and dislocated shoulder.[83]

Item: Many fraudulent schemes are based on the classic one perfected by Bostonian Charles Ponzi in the 1920s. This is a pyramid system whereby early investors are paid off handsomely with proceeds of sales by later ones. The result is often a rush of new investors greedy for easy profits. A recent example of the Ponzi scam was the Home-Stake swindle perpetrated by Robert Trippet. This scheme consisted of selling participation rights in the drilling of sometimes hypothetical oil wells. The beauty of this plan was that, since oil exploration was involved, it provided a tax shelter for the investors. Thus the plan appealed especially to the wealthy. As a result, many important persons were swindled of a good deal of money (e.g., the chairman of Citibank, the head of United States

Trust, the former chair of Morgan Guarantee Trust, the former chair of General Electric, and entertainers such as Jack Benny, Candice Bergen, Faye Dunaway, Bob Dylan, and Liza Minnelli). John Kenneth Galbraith, the noted economist, in reviewing a book about the Home-Stake swindle, said that it should have been titled *How the Rich Swindled Each Other and Themselves.*[84]

Item: The Equity Funding Corporation of America began in 1960 as a legitimate insurance business with 10,000 dollars.[85] In the mid-sixties it became the fastest growing life-insurance company in America. From 1967 to 1972 sales increased from 54 million to 1.32 billion, and insurance in force from 109 million to 6.5 billion. The stock in the company went public in 1964 at six dollars a share and during the company's phenomenal growth period sold for as high as eighty dollars. In April, 1973, this growth was found to be the result of fraud. The corporation filed for bankruptcy and the stock was declared of "no value." At a representative price of forty dollars a share, the shareholders lost 300 million. Since 1967 it had *never* made any money. Its earnings all of those years had been false. What appeared to be growth was the result of issuing 64,000 phony policies with a face value of two billion dollars. These bogus policies were then sold to other insurance companies for cash. In addition, Equity Funding routinely faked assets and earnings in its annual reports, sold counterfeit bonds, and forged death certificates. The result was that policy holders, stockholders, and other insurance firms lost between two and three billion dollars. Other money was also indirectly lost because of the resulting scandal. For example, in the week that the *Wall Street Journal* published the story of the scandal, the value of all shares on the New York Stock Exchange dropped by fifteen billion dollars.

CONCLUSION

Two problems that especially concern Americans are street crimes and inflation. Our discussion in this chapter should provide new insight into these problems. Street crimes, for example, are miniscule in their economic costs when compared to the costs of illegal activities by corporations. To cite just one example, the two to three billion dollars lost in the Equity Funding fraud involved more money "than the total losses of *all* street crimes in the United States for one year." [86]

The primary sources of inflation, many argue, are huge governmental expenditures. Of course these do impact the inflationary spiral, but the blame lies elsewhere as well. Ignored by most critics are the sources of inflation found in our corporate economy. Speaking of the economic situation in 1969, Senator Philip Hart estimated that, of the

780 billion dollars spent by consumers, about 200 billion purchased *nothing of value.*[87] We have seen that the existence of shared monopolies increases prices by twenty-five percent. We have seen that consumers pay, in addition, all the costs of advertising, which amounted to thirty billion dollars in 1978. We have seen that consumers pay inflated prices brought about by price fixing and other collusive arrangements by "competitors." Finally, we have seen that consumers spend billions on products sold under false pretenses, products that do not perform as claimed, products identical to cheaper ones but unavailable or unknown, and the like. The point is that these extra costs to consumers do not bring anything of value back to them. What could be more inflationary than that? Put another way, the corporate economy diverts scarce resources to uses that have little human benefit.

To conclude, Edwin Sutherland, the sociologist who first examined white-collar crime extensively, made several observations relevant to the understanding of such corporate deviant behavior as price fixing, misleading advertising, and fraud.[88]

1. The criminality of corporations tends to be persistent. Recidivism (repeat offenses) is the norm. Of the seventy largest industrial and merchandising U.S. corporations, ninety-seven percent have had two or more adverse court decisions.

2. The illegal behavior is much more extensive than the prosecutions and complaints indicate.

3. Businesspeople who violate the laws designed to regulate business do not typically lose status among their associates. In other words, the business code does not coincide with the legal code. Thus, even when they violate the law, they do not perceive themselves as criminals.

NOTES

1. Stanton Wheeler, "Trends and Problems in the Sociological Study of Crime," *Social Problems* 23 (June 1976), p. 525. This criticism has been made by others as well. See especially Alexander Liazos, "The Poverty of the Sociology of Deviance: Nuts, Sluts, and Preverts," *Social Problems* 20 (Summer 1972), pp. 103–120.

2. Marshall B. Clinard, *Illegal Corporate Behavior* (Washington, D.C.: U.S. Department of Justice, Law Enforcement Assistance Administration, 1979). See also Marshall B. Clinard and Peter C. Yeager, "Corporate Crime: Issues in Research," *Criminology* 16 (August 1978), pp. 255–272.

3. Karl Marx, *Capital: A Critique of Political Economy* (New York: International Publishers, 1967). Originally published in 1866.

4. Mark J. Green, Beverly C. Moore, Jr., and Bruce Wasserstein, *The Closed Enterprise System* (New York: Bantam Books, 1972), p. 7. Copyright © 1972 by The Center for Study of Responsive Law. Reprinted by permission of Viking Penguin Inc.

5. Daniel Zwerdling, "The Food Monopolies," *The Progressive* 39 (January, 1975), p. 15. See also Louis M. Kohlmeier, "Snap, Crackle and Divestiture," *The New York Times* (April 25, 1976), Section 3, pp. 1, 9.

6. From a statement by the chairperson of the Federal Trade Commission, quoted in TRB, "Bartered Brides," *New Republic* (March 17, 1979), p. 3.

7. Herbert J. Gans, "The New Egalitarianism," *Saturday Review* (May 6, 1972), p. 43.

8. Ralph Andreano, "Multi-National Corporation: The New Globalism," *Superconcentration/Supercorporation* (Andover, Mass.: Warner Modular Publications, 1973), p. 331d.

9. Edward M. Kennedy, quoted in "Pro and Con: A Ban on Big Company Mergers," *U.S. News and World Report* (March 26, 1979), p. 67.

10. Quoted in Green et al., *The Closed Enterprise System,* pp. 13–14.

11. This section on the consequences of shared monopolies is taken primarily from Green et al., *The Closed Enterprise System,* pp. 14–26; and Jack Newfield and Jeff Greenfield, *A Populist Manifesto* (New York: Warner Paperback Library, 1972), pp. 48–56.

12. Green et al., *The Closed Enterprise System,* p. 14.

13. Gans, "The New Egalitarianism," p. 43.

14. Newfield and Greenfield, *A Populist Manifesto,* p. 51.

15. William Conner and Robert Smiley, quoted in Ralph Nader, Mark Green, and Joel Seligman, *Taming the Giant Corporation* (New York: W. W. Norton, 1976), p. 216.

16. Green et al., *The Closed Enterprise System,* p. 15. See also "The Monopoly Inflation Game," *Dollars and Sense,* no. 23 (January, 1977), pp. 12–13. Copyright © 1972 by The Center for Study of Responsive Law. Reprinted by permission of Viking Penguin Inc.

17. Nader et al., *Taming the Giant Corporation,* p. 213.

18. Cf., Michael Parenti, *Power and the Powerless* (New York: St. Martin's, 1978).

19. Mark J. Green, "The High Cost of Monopoly," *The Progressive* (March, 1972), p. 4.

20. "The Forbes Sales 500," *Forbes* 125 (May 12, 1980), pp. 214–215.

21. Robert F. Lanzillotti, "The Automobile Industry," *The Structure of American Industry,* Fourth Edition, Walter Adams, ed. (New York: Macmillan, 1971), p. 256.

22. "GM's Juggernaut," *Business Week,* no. 2578 (March 26, 1979), pp. 62–77.

23. "The Forbes Assets and Earnings 500," *Forbes* 125 (May 12, 1980), pp. 223, 240.

24. Green et al., *The Closed Enterprise System,* p. 244.

25. David Hapgood, *The Screwing of the Average Man: How the Rich Get Richer and You Get Poorer* (New York: Bantam, 1975), p. 152.

26. *Ibid.,* pp. 165–166.

27. "The Monopoly Inflation Game," p. 12.

28. Lanzillotti, "The Automobile Industry," p. 282.

29. Green et al., *The Closed Enterprise System,* p. 246.

30. *Ibid.,* p. 246. Copyright © 1972 by The Center for Study of Responsive Law. Reprinted by permission of Viking Penguin Inc.

31. The following is taken primarily from Harvey A. Farberman, "A Criminogenic Market Structure: The Automobile Industry," *The Sociological Quarterly* 16 (Autumn 1975), pp. 438–457. See also W. N. Leonard and N. G. Weber, "Automakers and Dealers: A Study of Criminogenic Market Forces," *Law and Society* 4 (February, 1970), pp. 407–424.

32. Cf. Hapgood, *The Screwing of the Average Man,* pp. 164–167.

33. Cf. Gerald F. Seib, "Dallas Ordinance against Car Repair Frauds," *Crime at the Top: Deviance in Business and the Professions,* John M. Johnson and Jack D. Douglas, eds. (Philadelphia: J. B. Lippincott, 1978), pp. 319–322.

34. For a description of these techniques, see Roger Rapoport, "How I Made $193.85 Selling Cars," in *The Marketplace: Consumerism in America,* edited by the editors of *Ramparts* with Frank Browning (San Francisco: Canfield, 1972), pp. 39–47.

35. George A. Hay and Daniel Kelley, "An Empirical Survey of Price Fixing Conspiracies," *The Journal of Law and Economics* 17 (April, 1974), pp. 13–38.

36. *Ibid.,* pp. 26–27.

37. The following account is taken primarily from three sources: Gilbert Geis, "White Collar Crime: The Heavy Electrical Equipment Cases of 1961," *Corporate and Governmental Deviance,* M. David Ermann and Richard J. Lundman, eds. (New York: Oxford University Press, 1978), pp. 59–79; Richard Austin Smith, "The Incredible Electrical Conspiracy," Parts I and II, *Fortune* 63 (April, 1961), pp. 132–137, 170–180; (May, 1961), pp. 161–164, 210–224; and Green et al., *The Closed Enterprise System,* pp. 154–157.

38. Green et al., *The Closed Enterprise System,* p. 155. Copyright © 1972 by The Center for Study of Responsive Law. Reprinted by permission of Viking Penguin Inc.

39. Smith, "The Incredible Electrical Conspiracy," Part I, p. 137.

40. Cf. *Wall Street Journal* (July 27, 1964), p. 22. For the account of more recent cases of corporations and their executives receiving little if any punishment for their crimes, see Robert Stuart Nathan, "Coddled Criminals," *Harper's* 260 (January, 1980), pp. 30–35; and "Crime in the Suites: On the Rise," *Newsweek* (December 3, 1979), pp. 114–121.

41. Green et al., *The Closed Enterprise System,* p. 152; and *New Republic* (February 20, 1961), p. 7.

42. Quoted in Smith, "The Incredible Electrical Conspiracy," p. 133.

43. *Ibid.,* p. 135.

44. Ralph Nader and Mark Green, "Crime in the Suites," *New Republic* (April 29, 1972), pp. 20–21.

45. For a recent price-fixing violation in the forest-products industry, see Jean A. Briggs, "For Whom Does the Bell Toll?" *Forbes* (June 25, 1979), pp. 33–36.

46. Nader and Green, "Crime in the Suites," pp. 17–21.

47. Cf. Jennifer Cross, *The Supermarket Trap,* Revised Edition (Bloomington: Indiana University Press, 1976), p. 119; and Eric Schnapper, "Consumer Legislation and the Poor," *Consumerism,* Second Edition, David A. Aaker and George S. Day, eds. (New York: The Free Press, 1974), p. 87.

48. Cross, *The Supermarket Trap,* p. 123.

49. *Ibid.,* p. 124.

50. Paul Jacobs, "Keeping the Poor Poor," *Crisis in American Institutions,* Fourth Edition, Jerome H. Skolnick and Elliott Currie, eds. (Boston: Little, Brown, 1979), p. 96.

51. Cross, *The Supermarket Trap,* p. 122.

52. "The Drugmakers Rx for Living with Generics," *Business Week,* No. 2559 (November 6, 1978), p. 205.

53. *Ibid.*

54. "20/20," the ABC Newsmagazine broadcast (November 30, 1978).

55. Ronald S. Bond and David F. Lean, *Sales, Promotion, and Product Differentiation in Two Prescription Drug Markets,* staff report of the Federal

Trade Commission (Washington, D.C.: U.S. Government Printing Office, February, 1977), pp. 76, 79.

56. "Generics Pose No Threat to Big Drug Firms," *Chemical and Engineering News* (November 11, 1974), p. 71.

57. "20/20," p. 19.

58. *Ibid.*

59. *Ibid.,* pp. 19–20.

60. *Ibid.,* p. 21.

61. *Ibid.,* pp. 21–23.

62. Jack Anderson, "Secret Documents that Unveil the Drug Industry's Deception," *Rocky Mountain News* (September 28, 1978), p. 65.

63. Quoted in William Steif, "Drug Price Relief," *The Progressive* 42 (November, 1978), p. 13.

64. Harold Freeman, "On Consuming the Surplus," *The Progressive* 41 (February, 1977), pp. 20–21.

65. For an elaboration of the role of television in the manipulation of people, see Rose K. Goldsen, *The Show and Tell Machine: How Television Works and Works You Over* (New York: The Dial Press, 1975).

66. John Philip Cohane, "The American Predicament: Truth No Longer Counts," *Los Angeles Times* (October 1, 1972), quoted in Martin R. Haskell and Lewis Yablonsky, *Criminology: Crime and Criminality,* Second Edition (Chicago: Rand McNally, 1978), p. 172.

67. Associated Press release (September 17, 1978).

68. Associated Press release (December 15, 1978).

69. Ivan L. Preston, *The Great American Blow-Up: Puffery in Advertising and Selling* (Madison: University of Wisconsin Press, 1975), p. 220.

70. *Ibid.,* pp. 229–231.

71. *Ibid.,* p. 235.

72. Hugh D. Barlow, *Introduction to Criminology* (Boston: Little, Brown, 1978), pp. 252–253.

73. Preston, *The Great American Blow-Up,* pp. 18–20.

74. Barlow, *Introduction to Criminology,* p. 228.

75. Preston, *The Great American Blow-Up,* pp. 32–33.

76. Edwin H. Sutherland and Donald R. Cressey, *Criminology,* Ninth Edition (Philadelphia: Lippincott, 1974), p. 42.

77. Associated Press release (May 7, 1979); Ralph Blumenthal, "Automobile Repair Is Due for a Major Overhaul Soon," *The New York Times* (July 15, 1979), p. E9.

78. Andrea Fontana, "Ripping Off the Elderly: Inside the Nursing Home," in John M. Johnson and Jack D. Douglas, eds., *Crime at the Top: Deviance in Business and the Professions* (Philadelphia: J. B. Lippincott, 1978), pp. 125–132; and "Medicaid Abuse: Even Worse Than Feared," *U.S. News and World Report* (June 4, 1979), pp. 43–45.

79. See Charles H. McCaghy, *Deviant Behavior* (New York: Macmillan, 1976), pp. 228–229.

80. Quoted in Robert P. Snow, "The Golden Fleece: Arizona Land Fraud," in Johnson and Douglas, eds., *Crime at the Top,* p. 138.

81. Reported in Haskell and Yablonsky, *Criminology,* pp. 111–112.

82. *Ibid.,* p. 112.

83. Robert J. Flaherty and Tedd A. Cohen, "Rascality Springs Eternal," *Forbes* (April 20, 1979), pp. 87–88.

84. John Kenneth Galbraith, "Crime and No Punishment," *Esquire* 88 (December, 1977), pp. 102–106. See also David McClintick, "The Biggest Ponzi Scheme: A Reporter's Journal," in *Swindled,* Donald Moffett, ed. (New York: Dow-Jones Books, 1976), pp. 90–126.

85. The following is based on Raymond L. Dirks and Leonard Gross, *The Great Wall Street Scandal* (New York: McGraw-Hill, 1974); and William E. Blundell, "Equity Funding: I Did It for the Jollies," in Moffett, *Swindled,* pp. 42–89.

86. Johnson and Douglas, *Crime at the Top,* p. 151.

87. Quoted in Ralph Nader, "A Citizen's Guide to the American Economy," *The Consumer and Corporate Accountability,* p. 18.

88. The following is taken from Edwin H. Sutherland, *White Collar Crime* (New York: Holt, Rinehart, and Winston, 1961), pp. 217–233.

Chapter 4
Corporate Deviance: Human Jeopardy

The topic of this chapter is the corporate disregard for the welfare of people — involving the abuse of consumers, workers, and society itself. Our thesis is that the profit-maximizing behaviors by corporations under monopoly capitalism are hazardous to our individual and collective health, and therefore constitute another manifestation of elite deviance. The first part of the chapter examines three manifestations of corporate deviance that jeopardize individual health — dangerous products, food pollution, and hazardous working conditions. The second part focuses on the problems society faces from various corporate activities — the waste of natural resources and ecological contamination.

INDIVIDUAL JEOPARDY

Unsafe Products

Commonly, the concern over violence in society is directed toward murder, rape, child abuse, and riots. We do not include in the context of violence the harm inflicted on people by unsafe products. The National Commission on Product Safety has revealed that twenty million Americans are injured in the home as a result of incidents connected with consumer products. "Of the total, 110,000 are permanently disabled and 30,000 are killed. A significant number could have been spared if more attention had been paid to hazard reduction." [1] Two additional points were made by that Commission:

> Manufacturers have it in their power to design, build, and market products in ways that will reduce if not eliminate most unreasonable and unnecessary hazards. Manufacturers are best able to take the longest strides to safety in the least time. . . .[2] [However] competitive forces may require management to subordinate safety factors to cost considerations, styling, and other marketing imperatives.[3]

Considerable evidence points to unsafe products from clothing to toys to tires, but nowhere has the poor corporate safety record been more visible than in the automobile industry and we will therefore concentrate on it. The indictment against this industry involves two basic charges: (1) faulty design and (2) working against governmental and consumer efforts to add safety devices as basic equipment.

The production of dangerously defective vehicles. In 1929 the president of DuPont tried to induce the president of General Motors to use safety glass in Chevrolets, as Ford was already doing. The president of GM felt that this addition was too costly and would therefore hinder sales. In his reply to DuPont, he said:

> I would very much rather spend the same amount of money in improving our car in other ways because I think, from the standpoint of selfish business, it would be a very much better investment. You can say, perhaps, that I am selfish, but business is selfish. We are not a charitable institution — we are trying to make a profit for our stockholders.[4]

This example shows how the profit motive superseded the possibility of preventing deaths and serious injuries. It is not an isolated instance in this industry. We will review two representative cases, one involving GM and the other, Ford.

Ralph Nader in his attack on GM's Corvair in *Unsafe at Any Speed* showed how that car had many dangerous defects, including a heater that gave off carbon monoxide and an instability that increased its likelihood of overturning.[5] GM's response to this indictment was to attack the credibility of Nader and to hide evidence that supported Nader's allegations.[6]

The fastest selling domestic subcompact has been Ford's Pinto. From the very beginning, however, the Pinto was flawed by a fuel system that ruptured easily in a rear-end collision.[7] Preproduction crash tests established this problem, but since the assembly-line machinery was already tooled, Ford decided to manufacture the car as it was — *"even though Ford owned the patent on a much safer gas tank."* [8] This decision was made partly because the Pinto was on a tight production sched-ule. Ford was trying to enter the lucrative subcompact market domi-nated by Volkswagen as quickly as possible. The time span from the conception of the Pinto to production was targeted at twenty-five months, when the normal time for a new car was forty-three months. Also in-volved in the decision to go with the original gas tank were styling con-siderations and the effort to maximize trunk space.

The profits-over-human considerations is clearly evident in the reluctance of Ford to change the design of the Pinto as fatalities and injuries occurred because of the faulty gas tank. Although the com-pany calculated that eleven dollars per car would make the car safe, it decided that this *was too costly.* They reasoned that 180 burn deaths and 180 serious burn injuries and 2,100 burned vehicles would cost 49.5 million dollars (each death was figured at 200,000 dollars) but that a recall of all Pintos and the eleven-dollar repair would amount to 137 million.[9] (See Table 4–1.) In addition to the decision to leave the Pinto alone, Ford lobbied in Washington to convince government regu-latory agencies and Congress that:

> ... Auto accidents are caused not by *cars,* but by (1) people and (2) highway conditions. This philosophy is rather like blaming a robbery on the victim. Well, what did you expect? You were carrying money, weren't you? It is an extraordinary experience to hear automotive "safety engineers" talk for hours without ever

Table 4–1: $11 vs. a Burn Death (Benefits and Costs Relating to Fuel Leakage Associated with the Static Rollover Test Portion of FMVSS 208).

Benefits
Savings: 180 burn deaths, 180 serious burn injuries, 2,100 burned vehicles.
Unit Cost: $200,000 per death, $67,000 per injury, $700 per vehicle.
Total Benefit: 180 × ($200,000) + 180 × ($67,000) + 2,100 × ($700) = $49.5 million.

Costs
Sales: 11 million cars, 1.5 million light trucks.
Unit Cost: $11 per car, $11 per truck.
Total Cost: 11,000,000 × ($11) + 1,500,000 × ($11) = $137 million.

Source: Ford Motor Company internal memorandum, "Fatalities Associated with Crash-Induced Fuel Leakage and Fires," cited in Mark Dowie, "Pinto Madness," *Mother Jones* 2 (September/October, 1977), p. 24. © *Mother Jones.* Used by permission.

mentioning cars. They will advocate spending billions educating youngsters, punishing drunks, and redesigning street signs. Listening to them, you can momentarily begin to think that it is easier to control 100 million drivers than a handful of manufacturers. They show movies about guardrail design and advocate the clear-cutting of trees 100 feet back from every highway in the nation. If a car is unsafe, they argue, it is because its owner doesn't properly drive it. Or, perhaps, maintain it.[10]

Meanwhile, fiery crashes involving Pintos were occurring with some regularity. Liability suits against Ford increased, with judgments routinely found against Ford. In 1978 a jury in California awarded 127.8 million dollars — including 125 million in punitive damages — to a teenager badly burned when his 1972 Pinto burst into flame after being hit in the rear by a car traveling thirty-five miles per hour. At that time up to fifty Pinto-related civil suits were pending in various courts.[11]

In that same year, ten years after the government had begun investigating the Pinto problem, the Department of Transportation finally announced that its tests showed conclusively that the Pinto was unsafe and ordered a recall of all 1971 to 1976 Pintos. One critic of Ford's outright defiance of human considerations made this telling observation: "One wonders how long Ford Motor Company would continue to market lethal cars were Henry Ford II and Lee Iacocca [the top Ford officials] serving twenty-year terms in Leavenworth for consumer homicide." [12]

✦ **Resistance to consumer and governmental pressures to provide safety devices.** The automobile industry has traditionally resisted new safety devices because the added cost might hurt sales.[13] Following tests conducted by the government and the insurance industry in the late 1950s, the government ruled that lap belts must be installed in all new cars built after January 1, 1965. The auto industry resisted (as it has since resisted other requirements such as lap-and-shoulder belts, ignition interlocks, and buzzers), despite clear evidence that these devices are effective in saving lives: "Between 1968 and 1977, the stock of cars on the road grew from 83 million to 112 million, an increase of 35 percent. Over the same period, traffic fatalities declined 6 percent." [14]

Since lap belts are effective only when used, and relatively few are used, the government reasoned that safety could be improved significantly if a passive restraint such as the air bag were standard equipment. A study by Allstate Insurance concluded that air bags would reduce occupant crash deaths by sixty-five percent. Had all cars been so equipped in 1975, 9,500 persons would have died in car crashes in that year instead of the 27,200 who did. Additionally, 104,000 serious injuries could be prevented each year.[15] The increased safety argument led the National Highway Traffic Safety Administration to recommend air bags be required on all cars manufactured after April, 1973. The argument that air bags save lives was not as compelling to the automobile industry, however.

The expense of tooling up for such a life-saving system was considered too high. They countered with strategies such as advertising in the major newspapers and high-level lobbying in Washington. As a result, the date requiring air bags was moved back two years to August, 1975. Because of further pressure from the automobile industry, the Department of Transportation continued to move the date back when all new U.S. cars must be equipped with passive restraints. One of President Reagan's early decisions was to delay further the requirement.

Dangerous Nutrition

The food industry is obviously big business, with 145 billion dollars in sales (1977). One corporation — Beatrice Foods — made 261 million dollars in profits in 1979 (up from 150 million in 1976). The thesis of this section is that the food industry, in its search for more profits, often disregards the health of consumers, and therefore constitutes deviance. We will explore four areas in which human considerations are often secondary to profit: (1) the sale of adulterated products; (2) the extensive use of chemical additives; (3) the increased use of sugar and fats; and (4) the sale of products known to be harmful.

√ **Adulterated products.** We will use the meat industry as our illustration of blatant disregard for the health of consumers. Upton Sinclair's exposé of the Chicago stockyards and meat-packing houses around 1900 showed how spoiled meat was sold, how dangerous ingredients were in sausage (such as rats and dung), and how rats overran piles of meat stored under leaking roofs.[16] President Theodore Roosevelt commissioned an investigation of Chicago meat packers and, as a result, the Meat Inspection Act of 1906 required that meat sold in interstate commerce had to be inspected according to federal standards. However, meat processed and sold within a state was not subject to the law (omitting as late as 1967 nearly fifteen percent of the meat slaughtered and twenty-five percent of all the meat processed in the U.S. As a result:

> Surveys of packing houses in Delaware, Virginia, and North Carolina found the following tidbits in the meat: animal hair, sawdust, flies, abscessed pork livers, and snuff spit out by the meat workers. To add even further flavoring, packing houses whose meat did not cross state lines could use 4-D meat (dead, dying, diseased, and disabled) and chemical additives that would not pass federal inspection. Such plants were not all minor operations; some were run by the giants — Armour, Swift, and Wilson.[17]

At the end of 1967 the Wholesome Meat Act was passed, specifying that state inspection standards must at least match federal standards.

This was accomplished in 1971 but there have been continuing violations. One problem is "Number 2" meat — meat returned by a retailer to a packer as unsatisfactory, which is then resold as Number 2 meat to another customer if it meets standards of wholesomeness. As an example of how this can be abused, consider the following occurrence in a Los Angeles Hormel plant:

> When the original customers returned the meat to Hormel, they used the following terms to describe it: "moldy liverloaf, sour party hams, leaking bologna, discolored bacon, off-condition hams, and slick and slimy spareribs." Hormel renewed these products with cosmetic measures (reconditioning, trimming, and washing). Spareribs returned for sliminess, discoloration, and stickiness were rejuvenated through curing and smoking, renamed Windsor Loins, and sold in ghetto stores for more than fresh pork chops.[18]

This Hormel situation occurred because the U.S. Department of Agriculture inspector, who was paid 6,000 dollars annually by Hormel for "overtime," looked the other way.[19]

Meat packers are also deceptive about what is included in their products. The labels on the package are not always complete. Consider, for instance, the ingredients of the hot dog.

> The hot dog . . . by law can contain 69 percent water, salt, spices, corn syrup and cereal, and 15 percent chicken; that still leaves a little room for goat meat, pigs' ears, eyes, stomachs, snouts, udders, bladders and esophagus — all legally okay. There is no more all-American way to take a break at the old ball game than to have water and pigs' snouts on bun, but you might prefer to go heavier on the mustard from now on.[20]

The extensive use of additives in food. The profits from the food industry come mainly from the processing of farm goods through fortifying, enriching, and reformulation into products that look appealing, have the right taste and aroma, and will not spoil. In 1977 there were more than 1,300 food additives approved as flavors, colors, thickeners, preservatives, and other agents for controlling the properties of food. Let's briefly look at some of these additives.[21]

Sodium nitrites and nitrates are chemicals added to keep meat products appearing blood red. Nitrites are also used to preserve smoked fish.

A variety of preservatives are used to prevent the spoilage of bread, cereals, margarine, fish, confections, jellies, and soft drinks. The most commonly used are BHT, BHA, sodium benzoate, and benzoic acid.

About ninety-five percent of the color in the food we eat is the result of synthetic colors added. Red dye No. 2 was prohibited by the government when it was found to cause cancer in mice, although it is still allowed in maraschino cherries because it is assumed that no one will eat more than one or two at a time.

Flour, that all-purpose staple, is bleached and conditioned by a number of potent poisons — hydrogen acetone, benzyl peroxide, chlorine dioxide, nitrogen oxide, and nitrosyl chloride. Also added to flour are such strengtheners as potassium bromate and ammonium presulfate.

An indirect additive that affects the health of consumers is one that is fed to animals. Diethylstilbestrol (DES), an artificial female sex hormone, fattens about seventy-five percent of the beef cattle in the U.S. This hormone is added because it causes dramatic weight gain on less feed. It has been outlawed for poultry, although hens are fed arsenic because it makes them lay more eggs.

There is a great deal of controversy among scientists about the results of these additives in our diet. "Altogether, laboratory tests have produced evidence that some 1,400 substances — drugs, food additives, pesticides, industrial chemicals, cosmetics — might cause cancer. But there are only a few chemicals which *all* the experts see as linked to human cancer." [22] Typically, government scientists disagree with the scientists hired by industry.[23] Several considerations, though, should cause us to be cautious about what we eat. First, many of the additives are poisons. The quantities in food are minute, but just what is the tolerance level? Is any poison, in any amount, appropriate in a food? Is there the possibility of a residue buildup in vital organs?

A second caution flag is signaled in what happens to laboratory animals fed relatively large quantities of these additives. They are poisoned; they do get cancer; and they do suffer from other maladies induced by the additives.

Finally, there is the serious question of what happens with the interaction of these additives on humans. Scientists may be able to test the effects of a few chemicals but what about the hundreds of thousands of possible combinations? In a slice of bread, for example, there can be as many as ninety-three possible different additives. The danger is that it takes years — maybe twenty or thirty — of a particular diet for an individual to develop cancer. Since most of the additives are of recent origin, we do not know the eventual outcome. We do know that the average American has increased his/her yearly intake of food additives from three pounds in 1965 [24] to about five pounds in 1977.[25] Also known is that the cancer rate continues to rise.

Why, then, do the food companies insist on adding these potentially harmful chemicals to our food? One possibility is that consumers demand more variety and convenience. But more important, the food industry has found that the processing of synthetic foods is *very* profitable. As one food marketer has remarked: "The profit margin on food additives is fantastically good, much better than the profit margins on basic, traditional foods." [26] Hightower has shown how this works:

It gets down to this: Processing and packaging of food are becoming more important pricing factors than the food itself.

Why would food corporations rather sell highly processed and packaged food than the much simpler matter of selling basics? Because processing and packaging spell profits.

First, the more you do to a product, the more chances there are to build in profit margins — Heinz can sell tomatoes for a profit, or it can bottle the tomatoes for a bigger profit, or it can process the tomatoes into ketchup for still more profit, or it can add spices to the ketchup and sell it as barbeque sauce for a fat profit, or it can add flavors and meat tenderizer to the barbeque sauce for the fattest profit of all.

Second, processing and packaging allows artificial differentiation of one company's product from that of another — in other words, selling on the basis of brand names. Potatoes can be sold in bulk, or they can be put in a sack and labeled Sun Giant, which will bring a higher price and more profit.

Third, processing and packaging allow the use of additives to keep the same item on the shelf much longer and they allow for shipment over long distances, thus expanding the geographic reach of a corporation.

Fourth, processing and packaging separate consumers from the price of raw food, allowing oligopolistic middlemen to hold up the consumer price of their products even when the farm price falls. When the spinach crop is so abundant that spinach prices tumble at the farm level, the supermarket price of Stouffer's frozen spinach souffle does not go down.[27]

American corporations, in their quest for profits, have knowingly marketed defective medical devices, lethal drugs, known carcinogens, toxic pesticides, and other harmful products overseas when they have been banned here. For example, when the government banned cyclamates in 1969 because laboratory tests had shown that the drug caused grotesque malformations in chick embryos, Libby, McNeil, and Libby sold 300,000 cases of cyclamate-sweetened fruit to customers in West Germany, Spain, and elsewhere.[28] A more detailed discussion of such practices is found in Chapter 5.

✳ **The increased use of unhealthy substances in foods and the efforts to convince the young to use such products.** This section discusses the types of food provided by the food industry and the advertising efforts to push certain questionable items. In particular we will address how the food industry has increased the consumption of sugar and fats.

The previous section noted the problem with chemical additives. That discussion neglected to mention the foremost food additive — sugar. The introduction of processed foods has increased the annual amount of refined sugar consumed by the average individual from 76.4

pounds in 1909–13 to 94.1 pounds in 1978 (even though the average annual household purchase of sugar itself declined in that period).[29]

One of the biggest sources of sugar intake is the ingestion of soft drinks. For example, the number of gallons, per capita, consumed per year increased from 16.8 in 1962 to 31.4 in 1975.[30]

The increased use of sugars presents three health dangers. Dental disease such as cavities and gum problems are clearly exacerbated by sugar. Another problem is that refined sugar, although an energy source, offers little nutritional value. Not only does it deprive the body of essential nutrients found in complex carbohydrates, but it actually increases the body's need for certain vitamins.[31] Finally, there appears to be a relationship between the increasingly larger proportion of refined sugar calories in the diet and the higher incidence of diabetes.[32] These problems, plus the problem of weight control, led the Senate Select Committee on Nutrition and Human Needs to recommend that Americans reduce their consumption of processed sugars by forty-five percent to the level consumed by Americans in the early 1900s.[33]

Another trend in the American diet is the increased consumption of fats. From the beginning of this century to 1973, the average daily amount of fats consumed per person rose from 125 grams to 156 grams (the equivalent of about twenty-four pounds more per year).[34] One source of this fat for modern Americans is the potato chip. Potato chips are forty percent fat compared to 0.1 percent fat in baked potatoes.[35] The food processors push us to eat potato chips rather than fresh potatoes because the profit is 1,100 percent more.[36] The Senate Select Committee on Nutrition recommended that Americans reduce their consumption of fats by forty percent because fat consumption leads to problems of obesity, cancer (breast and colon), and heart disease.[37]

The increased consumption of additives, sugar, and fats in food by children is a special health concern. But children are an important market, and food producers have spent multi-millions in advertising aimed at children. In 1979, the estimate for money spent on television advertising for children was 600 million dollars,[38] up from 400 million in 1973.[39] Obviously, the corporations believe that their advertising influences children in their interests, needs, and demands. This belief is backed by research findings which show that children are susceptible to the messages. One study of youngsters in grades one to five found that seventy-five percent had asked their mothers to purchase the cereals they had seen on television.[40] In another study eighty percent of the mothers of children aged two to six expressed the conviction that television ads did cause their children to ask for certain products.[41]

The nutritional problem emanating from the television advertising blitz aimed at children is that the most advertised food products are sugar-coated cereals, candies, and other sweet snack foods. One study, for example, found that ninety-six percent of all food advertising on

Saturday and Sunday children's TV programs in 1975 was for sweets.[42] This report by the Federal Trade Commission shows that these advertisements are effective in that:

> (a) children's requests for specific, brand-name cereals and snack foods are frequently, if not usually, honored by their parents; (b) very high proportions of children are able to name specific (heavily advertised) brands as their favorites; (c) when asked to list acceptable snacks, high proportions of children mention cookies, candy, cake, and ice cream, including specific (heavily advertised) products; (d) U.S. consumption of snack desserts has increased markedly since 1962, and significant proportions of the purchases are made by children.[43]

The television directed at children is effective because the advertisers have done their research.   Social-science techniques have been used by motivation researchers in laboratory situations to determine how children of various ages react to different visual and auditory stimuli.   Children are watched through two-way mirrors, their behavior is photographed, and their autonomic responses (e.g., eye-pupil dilation) are recorded to see what sustains their interest, their subconscious involvement, and the degree of pleasure they experience.[44]   Thus, advertisers have found that if one can associate fun with a product, or power, or a fascinating animated character, then children will want that product.

The staff of the Federal Trade Commission has argued that all television commercials aimed at children are inherently unfair and deceptive. The young, they contend, are unable to be rational consumers.   Therefore, the Commission proposed in 1978 that: (1) there be a ban on all ads for children under age eight; (2) a ban on all ads for highly sugared foods for those under eleven be enforced; and (3) there be a requirement for nutritional counter-ads to be paid for by industry.   This stance has been met by derision from the advertising and corporate industries.   In hearings conducted by the Commission, the advertisers and manufacturers argued against the evils of government regulation.   The attorney for Mattel (manufacturer of children's toys) testified that: "Our position, simply stated, is that the proposed ban is unconstitutional, economically injurious and unnecessary." [45]   A spokesman for the National Association of Broadcasters also argued that self-regulation by the industry has worked: "Industry self-regulation has in fact been successful, and now provides the mechanisms for effective regulation of advertising to children." [46]   Also at the hearings, the counsel for the Kellogg Company said that "in an American democratic capitalistic society we must all learn, top to bottom, to care for ourselves.   And the last thing we need in the next twenty years is a national nanny." [47]

These arguments have been countered by others.   A child psychologist agreed with the FTC ban, saying:

"I'm angry. In fact, I'm mad as hell," Dr. Friedlander said. "I'm furious that the most powerful communications system and the most powerfully and persuasive educational device that has ever existed in human history is being used systematically to mislead and lie to children."

He added that children under the age of six, seven, or eight "are absolutely unable to understand and defend themselves against the ulterior motives of our business system." [48]

Syndicated columnist, Ellen Goodman, has said:

Personally, I can't imagine why we should allow advertisers into our homes when they behave like decadent tooth fairies offering our gullible children candy bars and Frankenberrys in return for their molars. But the thing that continues to evade my understanding is how business people have the nerve to bellow against government when they won't address their own faults and hazards. They are the ones, after all, making us choose between nutrition and regulation.[49]

Bill Moyers, after confessing a bias for the necessity of advertising in general, ended his television program with these words:

It's astonishing to me that advertising to young children is even a matter of debate; that high-powered people with enormous skills and resources should have unbridled access to the minds of young children is no less absurd because those who profit from it consider it a sacrosanct right. If the government wanted to shower 20,000 propaganda messages a year on our children [the average number of advertisements seen annually by a child in the U.S.], we would take to the barricades and throw the scoundrels out. Yet the words of an advertising executive are treated as constitutional writ when he tells the FTC: "Children, like everyone else, must learn the marketplace. Even if a child is deceived by an ad at age four, what harm is done? Even if a child perceives children in advertisements as friends and not actors, selling them something, where's the harm? . . ."

In the end, this debate is between two views of human nature. One treats young children as feeling, wondering, and wondrous beings to be handled with care because they're fragile; the other treats them as members of a vast collective to be hustled. We shall know a great deal about our society when we know, in this battle, which view prevails.[50]

The manufacturing, advertising, and selling of known harmful products. Although a number of items fit in this category, we will consider only the example of the tobacco industry. In 1979, fifteen years after the first Surgeon General's warning that smoking is linked to lung cancer and other ills, the Secretary of Health, Education, and Welfare issued the new Surgeon General's report on the health hazards of smoking cigarettes. The report summarized 30,000 previously published scientific studies and provided strong evidence that: (1) smoking is a leading cause of lung cancer and a major factor in heart disease, bronchitis, and emphysema; (2) the babies of mothers who smoked while pregnant were born lighter and displayed slower rates of physical and mental growth than babies born to nonsmokers; (3) two-pack-a-day smokers have a 100 percent greater risk of dying in any given year than nonsmokers; (4) smoking is especially hazardous to workers in certain occupations (asbestos, rubber, textile, uranium, and chemical industries); and (5) smoking kills 346,000 Americans and costs taxpayers eighteen billion dollars annually.[51]

No medical group or scientific group in the world has disputed the conclusion that smoking is very injurious to health, yet the tobacco industry continues to push its products (buttressed, we might add, by government subsidies, such as sixty-five million dollars in fiscal 1977 to administer its tobacco price-support program and to provide crop inspections, grading tobacco research, and market research[52]). The tobacco industry spends 800 million annually promoting its products. The former secretary of HEW, Joseph Califano, has even charged that tobacco companies actually "target" their advertising at teenagers by using attractive models in their campaigns.[53] The tobacco industry has also aimed its advertising at women, resulting, perhaps, in the five-fold increase from 1964 to 1979 in smoking among teenage girls.[54]

In addition to its regular advertising, the tobacco industry has countered the antismoking campaign in several ways, each of which indicates disregard for the health of consumers. First, the industry has refused to accept the evidence against smoking. They argue that the links between smoking and various diseases are merely inferences from statistics. As Bill Dwyer of the Tobacco Institute has put it: "Statistics are like a bikini bathing suit: what they reveal is interesting; what they conceal is vital." [55] Representatives of the industry argue in the media and in speeches before civic groups that there is no conclusive cause-and-effect relationship between smoking and ill health. Smoking, they insist, is a matter of individual choice and not a decision to be made by government.

A second tactic of the tobacco industry has been to shore up its power in Washington, by extensive lobbying efforts and through contributions to the political campaigns of key decision makers. In the 1978 congressional elections, for example, money was given by the Tobacco People's Public Affairs Committee to 157 members of the House and fifteen Senators.

A subtle strategy is the giving or withholding of advertising monies to publications depending on their editorial treatment of the tobacco issue. Accepting cigarette advertising is very lucrative. In an average year, *TV Guide* sells twenty million dollars in cigarette advertising; *Time*,

fifteen million; and *Playboy,* twelve million.[56] A survey in 1978 by the
Columbia Journalism Review found that in the previous seven years not
a single comprehensive article on the dangers of smoking appeared in
any major national magazine accepting cigarette advertising.[57]

Finally, the tobacco companies look for expansion of their market
to overseas, particularly in the developing countries. These countries
do not harass tobacco companies by forcing them to warn users of the
potential dangers. They also present a growing market. Philip Morris,
for example, sells more than 175 brands in 160 countries, and its foreign
sales have grown by eighteen percent annually for the past ten years.[58]
The foreign market also provides the companies with a market for the
high-tar brands that are losing sales in the U.S. The problem with all
this, of course, is that the tobacco firms are promoting the use of a known
health hazard for their own profit.

Dangerous Working Conditions

In a capitalist economy workers represent a cost to profit-seeking
corporations. The lower management that can keep labor costs, the
greater will be their profits. Historically, this has meant that workers
labored for low wages, inferior or nonexistent fringe benefits such as
health care, and in unhealthy conditions. Mines and factories were
often extremely unsafe. The labor movement early in this century gathered momentum because of the abuse experiencd by workers.

After a long and sometimes violent struggle, the unions were successful in raising the wages for workers, adding fringe benefits, and
making the conditions of work safer. But the owners were slow to
change and worker safety was, and continues to be, one of the most
difficult areas. Many owners of mills, mines, and factories continue to
consider the safety of their workers a low-priority item, presumably because of the high cost. The mining industry provides an excellent example of this neglect. Even as late as the 1970s, coal-mining firms have
refused to comply with state and federal safety regulations. ABC News
found, for instance, that the mining companies, when fined for violating
safety regulations, not only refused to make the mines safer but also declined to pay the fines (in 1974 there were some 91,000 unpaid fines
worth some twenty million dollars).[59]

Despite the owners' reluctance to make industry safer, there have
been some improvements. The probabilities of cave-ins, fires, and other
plant disasters are much less now than in the days before unionization.
This does not mean, however, that occupational dangers have been significantly reduced. The dangers today are invisible contaminants such
as nuclear radiation, chemical compounds, dust, and asbestos fibers in
the air. These dangers from invisible contaminants are increasing because the production of synthetic chemicals has increased so dramatically

(1.3 billion pounds in 1940, 96.7 billion pounds in 1960, and 306.6 billion pounds in 1977).[60]

The extent of job-induced illnesses is impossible to ascertain exactly, primarily because for some diseases it takes many years of exposure to affect the skin, lungs, blood chemistry, nervous system, or various organs. The government estimates that about 100,000 Americans die and 390,000 are disabled annually because of occupational diseases. They also estimate that at least twenty percent of all cancer cases are linked to the workplace.[61] Table 4–2 summarizes the dangers that millions of persons face as a result of their occupations.

The following are examples of the specific risks of continued exposure in certain industries:

> *Item:* Workers in the dyestuffs industry (working with aromatic hydrocarbons) have about thirty times the risk of the general population of dying from bladder cancer.[62]

> *Item:* The wives of men who work with vinyl chloride are twice as likely as other women to have miscarriages or stillbirths.[63]

> *Item:* In 1978, Occidental Chemical Company workers handling a pesticide DBCP were found to be sterile as a result of the exposure, substantiating a 1961 study by Dow Chemical which indicated that DBCP caused sterility in rats.[64]

> *Item:* A 1976 government study determined that if 129,000 workers were exposed to the current *legal* level of cotton-dust exposure, over a period of time 23,497 would likely become byssinotics (victims of "brown lung").[65]

> *Item:* Starting with 632 asbestos workers in 1943, one researcher determined each of their fates after twenty years of employment. By 1973, 444 were dead, a rate fifty percent greater than for the average white male. The rate for lung cancer was 700 percent greater than expected and the rate for all types of cancers was four times as great.[66]

> *Item:* Karen Silkwood, a plutonium-plant worker, charged that the plant where she worked, owned by Kerr-McGee Corporation was unsafe and that she was contaminated. After her death in a car crash, her family sued Kerr-McGee. The jury ordered the company to pay Silkwood's estate 10.5 million dollars in damages.[67]

This last case illustrates the disregard of industry for the safety of their employees. During the trial employees testified that they were provided little or no training on the health hazards involved in handling plutonium. They were never told that radiation exposure could induce cancer. Attorneys for Kerr-McGee argued in court, however, that there had been no documented case of plutonium cancer in humans. This

Table 4–2: Ten Suspected Hazards in the Workplace.
(As cited by federal agencies, here are some of the major agents linked to on-the-job diseases.)

Potential Dangers	Diseases That May Result	Workers Exposed
Arsenic	Lung cancer, lymphona	Smelter, chemical, oil-refinery workers; insecticide makers and sprayers — estimated 660,000 exposed
Asbestos	White-lung disease (asbestosis); cancer of lungs and lining of lungs; cancer of other organs	Miners; millers; textile, insulation, and shipyard workers — estimated 1.6 million exposed
Benzene	Leukemia; aplastic anemia	Petrochemical and oil-refinery workers; dye users; distillers; painters; shoemakers — estimated 600,000 exposed
Bischloromethylether (BCME)	Lung cancer	Industrial chemical workers
Coal dust	Black-lung disease	Coal miners — estimated 208,000 exposed
Coke-oven emissions	Cancer of lungs, kidneys	Coke-oven workers — estimated 30,000 exposed
Cotton dust	Brown-lung disease (byssinosis); chronic bronchitis; emphysema	Textile workers — estimated 600,000 exposed
Lead	Kidney disease; anemia; central-nervous-system damage; sterility; birth defects	Metal grinders; lead-smelter workers; lead storage-battery workers — estimated 835,000 exposed
Radiation	Cancer of thyroid, lungs, and bone; leukemia; reproductive effects (spontaneous abortion, genetic damage)	Medical technicians; uranium miners; nuclear-power and atomic workers
Vinyl chloride	Cancer of liver, brain	Plastic-industry workers — estimated 10,000 directly exposed

Source: Occupational Safety and Health Administration; Nuclear Regulatory Commission; U.S. Depts. of Energy, Interior, plus other sources. Reprinted here from *U.S. News and World Report* (Feb. 5, 1979), p. 42. Copyright 1979 U.S. News & World Report, Inc.

was countered by the testimony of Dr. John Gofman, one of the first physicists to isolate plutonium, who said that Ms. Silkwood had an instant "guarantee of cancer based on her exposure." [68]

The record of industry has often been one of ignoring the scientific data or stalling through court actions rather than making their plants safer. Two examples forcefully make this point.

In 1970 an Italian toxicologist reported that long-term intermittent exposure of rats to vinyl chloride in air resulted in the production of several types of cancers.[69] This was the first test on the possible carcinogenicity in the plastics industry. In 1972 the earlier findings were confirmed by a major study supported by British, Belgian, and French firms. Cancers were found at the lowest level tested, fifty parts per million (at that time the permissible exposure level for U.S. workers was 500 ppm). Representatives of U.S. industry were given the full details of these studies in January, 1973, but entered into an agreement with the European consortium not to disclose the information without prior consent. The U.S. organization involved in this agreement, the Manufacturing Chemists Association, failed to disclose the dangers of vinyl chloride despite a request from a government agency for all available data on the toxic effects of vinyl chloride. The data were finally revealed to the government fifteen months later when three workers exposed to vinyl chloride at a B. F. Goodrich plant died of angiosarcoma of the liver. According to a special committee report of the American Association for the Advancement of Science, the Manufacturing Chemists Association had deliberately deceived the government and "because of the suppression of these data, tens of thousands of workers were exposed without warning, for perhaps some two years, to toxic concentrations of vinyl chloride." [70]

The health dangers of asbestos, unlike vinyl chloride, have long been known. The link with asbestosis, a crippling lung disease, was established in 1900 and the relationship between asbestos and lung cancer was first noted in 1935. Studies in subsequent years of asbestos insulation workers have revealed a death rate from lung cancer seven times normal and a death rate from all causes three times that of the general population.[71]

Despite these facts, asbestos workers have been consistently uninformed about the serious health hazards associated with working in that industry. In a Johns-Manville plant, for example, company doctors, when they noted lung disease in workers, never told them that their lung problems were related to asbestos.[72]

Plants have also been lax about meeting government standards for exposure. The maximum exposure level set by the government was set at twelve fibers per cubic meter for plants that had government contracts. An inspection of an asbestos plant in Tyler, Texas, revealed, for instance, that 117 of 138 samples in the plant exceeded the limit. The government fined the owner of the plant, Pittsburgh Corning, a total of 210 dollars for these violations.

When the hazards of working with asbestos became more generally known, the industry reacted by sponsoring research to disprove the dangers of asbestos. One industry study was faulty on at least two counts.

First, it used researchers who had long been consultants to industry and therefore might be suspect for their lack of objectivity. Second, the study examined workers who had worked a relatively short time. Since lung cancer has a latent period of twenty years or so, the use of short-term workers in the study had the effect of "whitewashing" the real situation.[73]

The lack of concern for the safety of workers in the plastics and asbestos industries is typical of other industries as well. Safety regulations for cotton dust have been fought by the textile industry. As usual the claims were that it would cost billions to clean up the mills, jobs would be lost, and prices to consumers would rise dramatically. Similarly, the copper refiners have resisted rigorous safety regulations. For example, a study of mortality among Tacoma smelter workers found the death rate from lung cancer to be between three and four times as high as normal, and ten times as high for workers exposed to the highest toxic concentrations. Moreover, a study found that children within a half mile of the smelter had absorbed as much arsenic as the workers themselves.[74] Despite these findings, the owner of the smelter in Tacoma, ASARCO, led an industry-wide campaign against the government's new standards. Again, the company offered the familiar argument that the costs of compliance would be 100 million dollars, adding fifteen cents to the now seventy-two cents needed to produce a pound of copper.

This raises the critical question — at what point are profits more important than human life? Speaking of the cotton industry, which is representative of the other industries, one observer has argued:

> In a society in which profits did not take precedence over people . . . the finer points of byssinosis [brown lung disease] would have been considered tangential long ago and the road to its prevention would now be clear: Better air filtration systems would have been installed and other capital expenditures made. But in the United States, where society is tuned to a different chord, the present delay over preventive measures, like the oblivion which preceded it, is rooted not in science and technology but in economics and politics — in the callous traditions of the cotton industry and in government's compromising ways.[75]

Finally, we should ask: What is a crime? Is it not when a victim is hurt (physically, emotionally, or financially) by the willful act of another? When 100,000 Americans die annually from occupationally related diseases, is there the possibility of crime? Officially, these deaths and the human suffering induced by willful neglect for worker safety are not considered crimes (see Chapter 1 for the discussion of criminal versus noncriminal deviance). One observer, Joel Swartz, has argued that these deaths should be considered as criminal — as murders.

> By any legitimate criteria corporate executives who willfully make a decision to expose workers to a dangerous substance

which eventually causes the death of some of the workers, should
be considered murderers. Yet no executive has ever served even
a day in jail for such a practice, and most probably are well rewarded for having saved the company money. The regulatory
apparatus that is complicit with such practices should of course
be considered an accomplice.[76]

But the guilt does not stop with corporate executives, as Swartz goes on
to argue:

> In the long run it is not the outright deception, dishonesty and
> cunning of corporate executives, doctors and bureaucrats which
> is responsible for the problem. Rather, the general functioning
> of the system is at the heart of the problem ... the tremendous
> toll in occupational illnesses results from the oppression of one
> class by another. The people who own corporations try to exact
> as much wealth as they can from the workers. Improvements in
> working conditions to eliminate health hazards would eat into the
> profits that could be exacted. ... In particular the asbestos in-
> dustry would rather spend millions of dollars trying to prove that
> asbestos is safe, than spend the money necessary to eliminate ex-
> posures. In oil refineries many of the exposures to chemicals
> result from inadequate maintenance of plant equipment. Mainte-
> nance costs come to 15 percent of total refinery costs, but these
> costs are considered controllable. In other words, skipping on
> maintenance is a good way to cut costs. Only the worker suffers.
> Another reason that the system causes occupational illnesses is
> the pressure it applies for expansion, especially in certain indus-
> tries such as chemicals and plastics. The chemical industry,
> especially, is able to reap high profits by rapidly introducing new
> chemicals. ... Thus demands that chemicals be adequately tested
> before use, and the possibilities that new chemicals found to be
> dangerous might be banned, constitute a tremendous threat to the
> industry. ... The ultimate reason for the problem is the drive of
> corporations to extract as much profit as possible from the work-
> ers. But to continue to function this system requires constant
> efforts by people from corporate executives to scientists to bureau-
> crats. These efforts result in a staggering toll in death and disease
> which should qualify the perpetrators as criminals by any reason-
> able human standards. But the system, functioning the way it is,
> rewards certain criminals very handsomely. The ultimate suc-
> cess in the battle to improve health and safety conditions will
> require getting rid of these criminals, and the system which
> enables them to operate.[77]

COLLECTIVE JEOPARDY

The first part of this chapter focused on the hazards that individuals
face at work or from the products they purchase. In this section the

scope is broadened because here the victims of corporate deviance are not individuals *per se* but the collectivities of people who comprise communities, the society, and even the world. Our discussion will center on two broad areas of this collective jeopardy — the waste of natural resources and ecological damages.[78]

The Waste of Resources

Since the earth's creation billions of years ago, the ecosystem has worked as an interdependent system relatively undisturbed by the impact of human beings. But recent developments have begun to disturb the delicate balance of nature. Explosive population growth (currently the world's population grows by more than 200,000 daily), modern technology, and high rates of consumption have combined to pollute the environment and to deplete resources. We will focus here on the waste of resources.

A most pressing concern for humanity is the accelerated rate of the consumption of nonrenewable resources. Obviously metals and fuels (except for wood and sun) are finite. The greater the number of people, the greater these resources will be consumed. If technology is added to the equation, the result is a further increase in the ratio of resource depletion.

Mineral resources have remained relatively untouched until the last 100 years or so.

> Total mineral production during the last thirty years was greater than that from the beginning of the Bronze Age until World War II. The United States Bureau of Mines estimates that world consumption of aluminum will be twice today's level in nine years, that use of iron will double in a decade and a half, and that demand for zinc will double in 17 years.[79]

The problem is exacerbated further because these resources are not evenly distributed. The indigenous reserves of minerals and fuel of those countries that industrialized first are being exhausted. And these are the very nations where the demand is greatest. Western Europe must now import nearly all of the copper, phosphate, tin, nickel, manganese ore, and chrome ore it uses. The United States, which in 1950 depended on foreign sources for fifty percent or more of four of the thirteen basic minerals, is expected by the year 2000 to rely on imports for at least fifty percent of twelve of these thirteen minerals. Except for coal, the major deposits of raw materials are found in the poor and developing nations of the world, yet because of high technology, most of these resources are consumed by only about one-fourth of the world's population. Because these resources are rapidly diminishing (except for coal), severe shortages and dislocations will occur. The well-endowed countries (e.g., the OPEC cartel) will raise prices and will be able to trade their surpluses for other needed resources. The high-technology countries, and therefore those with the greatest appetite for natural resources, will in the short run not be hurt because they will be able to purchase the necessary resources. In the long term, however, the technological societies will suffer for at least three reasons. First, as the resources are exhausted (and not replaced by adequate synthetics or renewable fuels such as the sun, wind, and tides), these societies will be forced to reduce their productivity, resulting in economic dislocations and dissatisfactions. Second, discontentment will also be found in the resource-rich nations. Although they benefit monetarily, they doubtless will eventually feel exploited as their resources are dissipated. Undoubtedly, these countries will insist on even higher prices for their resources as they near depletion, which will increase the probability of hostile acts by the wealthy nations against the resource-rich nations.

A third source of international unrest brought about by the disproportionate use of limited resources by the wealthy nations will be from the "have-not" nations. The gap between them and the "haves" will continue to widen as the rich get the benefit of more resources, and whatever gains are accomplished by the "have-nots" are cancelled by the rapid population growth. The result from such a situation is the heightened likelihood of hostile outbreaks between the rich and poor nations as the latter become more and more desperate in their need for resources.

The United States is the world's largest per-capita consumer of the world's resources. One example makes the point — the U.S., with only five percent of the world's population, consumes thirty percent of the world's energy resources. The enormous consumption of energy and raw materials by Americans is a huge drain on the American and world storehouses. But, why do we consume so much? Although there are many reasons, we will focus on the major one — the American economic system, a system based on profits, the quest for which is never satiated. Companies must grow. More sales translate into more profits. Sales are increased through advertising, product differentiation, new products, and creative packaging. Advertising creates previously nonexistent demand for products. The introduction of new products makes the old ones obsolete. Product differentiation (many models with different features) is redundant and wasteful but it increases sales. The automobile industry is an excellent illustration of both product differentiation and planned obsolescence. Minor styling changes for each model year, with massive accompanying advertising campaigns, have the effect of making all older cars "obsolete" — at least in the minds of consumers.

Writing in 1960, Vance Packard warned of the waste demanded by our economic system.[80] Progress (through growth in profits) is maximized by consumers who purchase products because they feel the need to replace old ones (because they are used up or because they are outmoded). This "need" is promoted by manufacturers who produce goods that do not last long or who alter styles so that consumers actually dis-

card useable items. These two marketing strategies — creating obsolescence through poor quality and through desirability — produce growing profits. But both strategies are fundamentally based on waste and
this is a societal problem that cannot continue indefinitely.

One type of obsolescence is positive — the introduction of a new
product that outperforms its predecessor. However, even this type can
be orchestrated to increase waste and profit. The technology may exist
for a major breakthrough but the manufacturer or industry may choose
to bring out a series of modifications that lead eventually to the state of
the art. The rationale for this procedure is to saturate the potential
market with the stepped-up technology and then move to the next stage
of development, and so on until the major breakthrough is attained. In
this way, the consumers purchase a number of products rather than
immediately purchasing the ultimate. The history of high-fidelity sound
equipment provides a good illustration of this marketing principle.[81]

The waste of our throw-away age is easy to see. Beverages are
packaged in convenient disposable cans. Meat can be purchased in
disposable aluminum frying pans, which are thrown away after one use.
TV dinners are warmed and eaten in the same containers. We can
purchase disposable cigarette lighters and plastic razors with built-in
blades. These are but a small sample of the products that are quickly
used and destroyed. As another example of resource waste, let's look
at the cost to society of the packaging policies of a single company.
Bruce Hannon, an engineer at the University of Illinois, did an environmental impact study of McDonald's, the hamburger chain, *when that
company was less than half its present size,* and found that: ". . . McDonald's packaging constituted a phenomenal drain on natural resources.
It took the sustained yield of 315 square miles of forest to keep McDonald's supplied with paper packaging for one year." [82] The enormity of
our waste is also seen in the fact that we junk seven million cars annually
as well as ten million tons of iron and steel.[83]

To maximize profits one must minimize costs. Among other things,
this search for profits results in abusing the environment. We will turn
to pollution of the environment shortly, but for now let's consider the
role of the profit motive in raping the land, which is the ultimate waste
of resources.

It is cheaper to extract minerals from the earth by strip mining
than to remove the wealth carefully and restore the land to its original
state. Because the costs of restoration are subtracted from profits,
mining companies have vigorously resisted governmental efforts to curb
the environmental abuses of strip mining. The following is a description of the waste that occurs in the strip-mining process.

> In the flat country of western Kentucky, where thousands
> of acres had already been devastated by strip mining, the coal
> seams lie only thirty to sixty feet beneath the surface. The over-

burden is scraped off and the coal is scooped out. Inevitably such topsoil as the land affords is buried under the towering heaps of subsoil. When the strippers move one, once-level meadows and cornfields have been converted to jumbled heaps of hardpan, barren clay from deep in the earth. This hellish land-scape is slow to support vegetation and years elapse before the yellow waste turns green again. In the meantime, immense quan-tities of dirt have crept into the sluggish streams, have choked them, and brackish ponds have formed to breed millions of mosquitos.

The evil effects of open-cut mining are fantastically mag-nified when practiced in the mountains. Masses of shattered stone, shale, slate, and dirt are cast pellmell down the hillside. The first to go are the thin layer of fertile topsoil and such trees as still find sustenance in it. The uprooted trees are down the slopes by the first cut. Then follows the sterile subsoil, shattered stone, and slate. As the cut extends deeper into the hillside, the process is repeated again and again. Sometimes the "highwall," the perpendicular bank resulting from the cut, rises ninety feet; but a height of forty to sixty feet is more often found. In a single mile, hundreds of tons are displaced.

Each mountain is laced with coal seams. Sometimes a sin-gle ridge contains three to five veins varying in thickness from two-and-a-half to fourteen feet. Since each seam can be stripped, a sloping surface can be converted to a steplike one.

After the coal has been carried away, vast quantities of the shattered mineral are left uncovered. Many seams contain sub-stantial quantities of sulfur, which when wet produces toxic sul-phuric acid. This poison bleeds into the creeks, killing minute vegetation and destroying fish, frogs, and other stream dwellers.[84]

This devastation to the land and its inhabitants is perpetrated by the owners of coal companies for two reasons. Foremost, this type of operation is very profitable. For example, in 1962 a small crew with an auger and a fleet of trucks made a profit of fifteen dollars a minute working a four-to-six-foot seam.[85] Second, the laws have, until recently, allowed the companies complete authority over the land they controlled. The historical bias of the courts toward the coal companies is seen in some of their decisions:

Item: The courts ruled that the rights to mine included the au-thority to cut down surface trees without compensating the owners of the land.

Item: The courts ruled that the companies had the right to divert and pollute all water in or on the lands over which they had mineral rights.

Item: The courts ruled that the companies could build roads where-ever they desired.

Item: When a gob dam (created by dumping refuse from mining into streams) broke during a 1945 storm, causing a flood and tremendous damage in Pike County, Kentucky, the court ruled that the Russell Fork Coal Company was innocent of wrongdoing and negligence because the rain was an act of God.[86]

Summarizing the situation, Caudill has stated: "The companies, which had bought their coal rights at prices ranging from fifty cents to a few dollars an acre, were, in effect, left free to do as they saw fit, restrained only by the shallow consciences of their officials." [87]

✂ Pollution of the Environment

The assault on the environment is the result of an ever-larger population, higher rates of consumption, and an increasing reliance on technology. These are world-wide trends. "Not only are more societies acquiring more efficient tools wherewith to exploit the earth; nearly everywhere, there are increasing numbers to do the exploiting, and befoul the air, water, and land in the process." [88] As an example, let's look at one major consequence of the increased use of technology — heat pollution.

Thermal pollution takes two basic forms: waste heat from the generation of electrical power that raises the temperature of water (affecting fish and plant life in waters), and increases heat in the atmosphere. Obviously, a rapidly expanding population increases the demands for more electricity and more industrial output — thereby adding to the creation of heat. Moreover, the addition of seventy or eighty million people each year (the current world rate) adds heat to the atmosphere just by the metabolism of these bodies.

The consequences of heat pollution are enormous. We know, for example, that the climate of cities differs from the surrounding countryside due to the dissipation of heat from the human activities there. Cities are warmer, cloudier, rainier, and foggier. As urban areas spread, they present great forces for climatic change.

According to one recent estimate, the Boston–Washington megalopolis in the year 2000 will contain fifty-six million people on 11,500 square miles, the dissipation of heat will be equal to 50 percent of the solar energy incident on that surface area in the winter, and 15 percent of the corresponding figure in the summer. If the present global rate of increase in energy consumption — approximately five percent per annum — should persist for another century and a half, man's dissipation then would be equal to ten percent of the solar energy absorbed over the entire surface of the globe, or one-third of the solar energy absorbed over land. Simple calculations suggest a corresponding mean global temperature increase of about 13 degrees Fahrenheit.[89]

If this scenario occurred, the thirteen-degree rise in world temperature would melt the ice at the poles, flooding much of the land surface and causing unbelievable climatological and ecological disruptions.

Another source of heat is the "greenhouse effect" caused by the existence of more carbon dioxide than nature's mechanisms can recycle. Modern technology, through its reliance on the burning of fossil fuels, is the source of great quantities of carbon dioxide. Just like the glass roof of a greenhouse, the molecules of carbon dioxide allow sunlight to reach the earth's surface, but block the escape of heat radiating off the ground. According to the theory, the earth's heat level will rise five degrees Fahrenheit over the next thirty to one hundred years because of this "greenhouse effect." Obviously, coupled with the thermal pollution from other sources, the earth's climate will be changed unless the world's usage of fossil fuels (oil, oil shale, tar sands, and coal) is reduced dramatically and soon.[90]

There is a countervailing force, however, that is believed to have a cooling effect. It, too, comes from pollution: airborne dust — which is increased in every daily activity from suburban driving to farming the soil.

> Periods of global cooling have been recorded over the past two centuries after major volcanic eruptions spewed tons of dust particles into the air. Meteorologist Helmut Landsberg estimates that, along with world population, the amount of dust in the atmosphere has doubled since the 1930s, despite the absence of major volcanic eruptions. Some scientists fear that increased amounts of atmospheric dust may act as insulation, reflecting the sun's rays away from the earth and lowering temperatures.[91]

So, technology creates in its wake two forces, one which screens the sun out and the other which traps the heat in. Both effects are negative for human life as we know it. The exact impact of these forces is not fully understood. Clearly, climate will be affected, but we are unsure of its exact nature. What is known is that modern technology tampers with the climate with negative consequences.

Heat pollution, however, is only one form of pollution and in the short term at least, the least hazardous. Pollution comes in many forms and we are all guilty. Each of us pollutes as we use fossil fuel transportation, burn wood in our fireplaces, use aerosol sprays, kill weeds with pesticides, and throw away junk. Indirectly, we pollute when we use electricity, heat our homes with natural gas, and use the thousands of products created by industry. But what influences our consumer choices? Do we have a choice to travel by mass transit? Do we have a choice to buy products transported by truck or rail (railroads are much less polluting because they are more efficient)? Is soap available instead of detergents? The role of the corporations in limiting our consumer choices is an especially instructive way to understand how a laissez-faire economic system works to the ultimate detriment of people and society.

In a capitalist system companies make decisions based on making profit. This places the environment in jeopardy. Best and Connolly have shown how corporate decision makers choose alternatives that have negative impacts on the ecology.[92] They describe the logic of capitalism in the following:

> Under such circumstances [capitalism] it is quite irrational for any individual producer or consumer to accept the higher costs involved in curtailing various assaults on the environment. Thus a company that purified the water used in production before disposing it into streams would add to its own costs, fail to benefit from the purified water flowing downstream, and weaken its competitive market position with respect to those companies unwilling to institute purified procedures. Since it is reasonable to assume that other companies in a market system will not voluntarily weaken their position in this way, it is irrational for any single company to choose to do so. . . . Thus a range of practices which are desirable from the vantage point of the public are irrational from the vantage point of any particular consumer or producer. And a range of policies which are rational from the vantage point of individual consumers and producers are destructive of the collective interest in preserving nonrenewable productive resources and in maintaining the environment's capacity to assimilate wastes.[93]

Why, for example, does the U.S. depend on an irrational transportation system? If mass transit for commuting replaced the automobile in our urban centers, fifty percent of the fuel now consumed by cars would be saved. Best and Connolly argue that the automobile industry has intervened to suppress a viable mass transit alternative. Three facts buttress their argument. First, in the middle twenties, General Motors, sometimes with Standard Oil and Firestone, purchased control of electric trolley and transit systems in forty-four urban areas. After purchase, the electric-rail systems were dismantled and replaced by diesel-powered bus systems (supplied by General Motors). When the systems were subsequently sold, part of the contract stated that no new equipment could be purchased that used a fuel other than gas. GM favored the diesel bus because its life was twenty-eight percent shorter than its electric counterpart (resulting in more profit for the company). Standard Oil and Firestone obviously benefited from such an arrangement.[94] The result is well known. We are dependent on gasoline for transportation and our cities are smothered in toxic emissions of carbon monoxide, lead, and other deadly chemical combinations from internal-combustion engines.

Other examples come from the substitution of synthetic for organic materials. Decisions by industry displaced soap with synthetic detergents because the profit margin increased from thirty percent of sales to fifty-two percent.[95]   The decision was not made by consumers but by management.   These decisions and others (e.g., the change from wool and cotton to synthetic fibers; plastics substituted for leather, rubber, and wood; and synthetic fertilizers replacing organic fertilizers) have often been incompatible with good ecology because the new chemicals are sometimes toxic and/or nonbiodegradable.   Remember, citizens as voters and consumers were not involved in these decisions to shift from organic to synthetic products.   Rather the decisions were made for them — and, it turns out, against their long-term interests — by companies searching for more lucrative profits.   Barry Commoner has claimed that these new technologies have invariably been more polluting but were introduced nontheless because they yielded higher profits than the older, less polluting displaced technologies.   Moreover, the costs to the consumers are borne in the increased health hazards and in the cost for cleaning up the environment.

> . . . Environmental pollution is connected to the economics of the private enterprise system in two ways.   First, pollution tends to become intensified by the displacement of older productive techniques by new ecologically faulty, but more profitable technologies.   Thus, in these cases, pollution is an unintended concomitant of the natural drive of the economic system to introduce new technologies that increase productivity.   Second, the costs of environmental degradation are chiefly borne not by the producer, but by society as a whole, in the form of "externalities."   A business enterprise that pollutes the environment is therefore being subsidized by society; to this extent, the enterprise, though free, is not wholly private.[96]

Pollution, as we have seen, is a direct consequence of an economic system where the profit motive supersedes the concern for the environment.   This is clearly seen when corporations are unwilling to comply with government regulations and to pay damages for ecological disasters such as oil spills.

Although the government appears passive in its relationship with the business community, there is a strong bias in its action or inaction toward the business community.   This bias is readily seen in the government's relatively cozy relationship with the largest polluters — the corporations.[97]   Ralph Nader, the consumers' advocate, has provided several illustrations of this upside-down effect (i.e., the benefits accrue to the wealthy few):[98]

> *Item:* Who defines violence?   The answer, according to Nader, is that those who define violence are those who perpetuate most of it.   While the government focuses its attention on the violence that occurs from street crimes, it tends to ignore the violence that

emerges from the chemical assault on the environment. Much more is lost in money and health through pollution than crimes of "violence," yet only the latter is defined officially as violence.

Item: Before the recent liberalization of marijuana laws, when an individual in some states could get a jail sentence exceeding ten years for smoking pot, industrialists knowingly smogging a city could be fined just a few hundred dollars a day while they continued.

Item: If you throw a banana peel out of your car window in Yosemite, you will be fined twenty-five dollars, yet the oil companies responsible for the oil spill in Santa Barbara paid nothing.

Item: Why is it a crime for an individual to relieve himself in Puget Sound but a corporation can do it twenty-four hours a day?

Item: Suppose you own a fifteen-room house and rent out rooms to six tenants. You employ several people, such as a cook, gardener, and janitor, and to keep costs down you throw all your garbage and trash out into the street. The city officials do not permit this wanton disregard for the welfare of the city and its citizens. You argue, however, that you must keep your costs down in order to contribute to the employment of some of the city's inhabitants. If forced to pay for garbage collection or recycling of waste materials, your profit would be reduced and you would have to close down, throwing your few employees out of work. Faced with your threat, the city says that you *must* desist. The problem is that your operation is not big enough. If you employed thousands of employees, then the city would very likely allow you to continue your pollution of the environment for fear of what the possibility of thousands added to the unemployment rate would do to the city — a clear case of industrial extortion.

Item: In 1976 Allied Chemical Corporation pleaded no contest to 940 counts of violating federal water-pollution laws by the discharge of the pesticide ingredient Kepone and other chemicals into the James River of Virginia. The Corporation was fined 13.2 million dollars. Allied gave eight million dollars to finance an independent environmental foundation in Virginia to show its good faith. As a result, a federal judge reduced the fine to five million (Allied had asked to have the fine reduced to 1.4 million because it was "contrite and sincere" *). Because Allied was allowed to have the fine reduced by the amount it "voluntarily" gave the foundation, it was allowed a tax write-off of the eight million because it was a contribution (which would not have been possible had the money been paid as a fine).[99]

* The obvious question is: was Allied Chemical "contrite and sincere" when they knowingly polluted the James River until forced to quit?

These examples illustrate that the present laws are minimal in their effect. Moreover, the efforts of the administrative agencies operating under the regulatory laws have been superficial at best. Typically, governmental intervention has had the effect of being but a symbolic "slap on the wrist," and the pollution of the environment has continued virtually unabated. The government, apparently, will not or cannot push the largest and most powerful corporations to do something that is unprofitable. These corporations are not only the largest polluters but they have a vested interest in the status quo. General Motors and Ford, for example, resist the attempts by Congress to make cars less polluting because the necessary devices add to the cost of automobiles and might curb sales. The government has been successful in achieving gradual change but the power of the automobile industry has also been successful in making the government go much slower than the proenvironment lobby wanted.

The government, thus, has enacted laws to curb pollution but they are very mild indeed. Turner has listed the defects in these conservation laws as:

1. The laws are often phrased in ambiguous language, making prosecution difficult.
2. The laws typically mandate weak civil penalties and hardly ever carry criminal penalties.
3. The vast majority of the laws do not attack the sources of pollutants, but rather require treatment of pollutants after they have been created.
4. Many state antipollution laws are enacted with "grandfather clauses" which allow established companies to continue their harmful activities.[100]

The mildness of the pollution laws and their enforcement indicate the power of the powerful to continue their disregard for people and nature in their search for profits. The government could take a much firmer stance if it chose to do so. Suppose, for example, that the situation were reversed:

> Can you possibly reverse this situation and imagine the poor polluting the streams used by the rich, and then not only getting away with it and avoiding arrest, but also being paid by the rich through the government to clean up their own pollution? [101]

In such a case, how would the poor be treated? The answer is obvious. The powerful would punish them severely and immediately curb their illegal behaviors. The implication is: whoever has the power can use it to his or her own benefit, disregarding the masses and nature.

In summary, the United States has a wasteful, inefficient, and vulnerable economy. Our natural environment is being destroyed by pollution and waste. The reasons are several. Foremost, our economic system is exploitive of people and resources. The emphasis is on profit and this means growth and consumption. Thus, short-term goals supersede the detrimental long-term consequences. Second, we are dependent on a technology that is wasteful. Third, the people believe in capitalism, growth, and consumption. Finally, population growth increases the demand for products, energy, and other resources.

CONCLUSION *R* *ᴸᴬᴰ*

The topics of this chapter show conclusively, we believe, the fundamental flaw of capitalism. Corporations are formed to seek and maximize profits. The result is often a blatant disregard for human and humane considerations. To reiterate: the coal companies of West Virginia have acted with glacial slowness to provide safe conditions in their mines, refusing to comply with state and federal safety regulations; corporations direct advertisements at children that deceive in order to manipulate them to consume more sugar-coated products; corporations decide to replace natural products with synthetics, which, while more profitable, are dangerous to the fragile ecology; corporations dump their wastes onto the land and into the air and water, all the time resisting efforts to find ecologically safer alternatives; corporations place dyes, nitrates, and other potentially lethal additives into food; and corporations promote wastefulness in packaging, product differentiation, and planned obsolescence.

It is too simplistic to say that corporations are solely responsible for these dangers to individuals and society. In many cases, consumers insist on convenience rather than safety. They would rather smoke or drink diet cola with saccharin than have the government demand that they quit. Moreover, consumers typically would rather take an unknown risk than pay higher prices for products, which would pay for the cost of cleaning up the pollution. So, too, workers would rather work in an unsafe plant than be unemployed. But for the most part these attitudes are shaped by corporate advertising and by corporate extortion (threatened higher prices and unemployment if changes are enforced). Also the corporations are guilty of efforts to persuade us that the dangers are nonexistent or minimal when the scientific evidence is irrefutable. They also do everything possible to block efforts by the government and consumer groups to thwart their corporate policies. For example, despite studies which estimate that seventy-five to ninety percent of all cancers are environmentally related, corporations have, instead of altering their behavior, counterattacked in two characteristic ways:

> Monsanto Chemical Co.... has embarked on a costly advertising campaign to persuade us that chemical products are essential to our way of life. More than 100 industrial corporations have

banded together to form the American Industrial Health Council, a lobby that is spending more than $1 million a year to combat the stricter carcinogen controls proposed by the Occupational Safety and Health Administration (OSHA).[102]

The probusiness approach argues that risks are inherent in living. The consumer is the ultimate arbiter. He or she may choose. If he or she doesn't buy the dangerous or wasteful products, then the corporations will provide alternative products to suit the wishes of the consumer.[103] Or, the worker in an asbestos plant or a cotton mill can change jobs if he or she feels the current one is unsafe. Companies also argue that it is no business of the government what goes on in the marketplace.

We argue, to the contrary, that the government must provide a watchdog function. We also argue that individuals do not have the options that the corporations suggest. We buy the products that are available. Our attitudes are shaped by advertising. Employees cannot shift from one job to another in the hopes of finding safer conditions, when most of the plants in the industry for which they are trained have similar problems, and when the unemployment rate is high. But more basic, the dangers pointed to in this chapter direct attention to the fundamental irrationality of our economic system. Whenever profits supersede the health of workers and consumers, when corporate decisions encourage enormous waste and pollution, then the economic system is wrong and will ultimately fail.

NOTES

1. National Commission on Product Safety, "Perspectives on Product Safety," in David A. Aaker and George S. Day, eds., *Consumerism: Search for the Consumer Interest* (New York: The Free Press, 1974), pp. 321–322. See also Amitai Etzioni, "Mindless Capitalism, an Unyielding Elite," *Human Behavior* (November, 1975), pp. 11–12; and Ralph Nader, ed., *The Consumer and Corporate Accountability* (New York: Harcourt Brace Jovanovich, 1973), p. 51.

2. "Perspectives on Product Safety," p. 325.

3. *Ibid.,* p. 322.

4. Quoted in Morton Mintz and Jerry S. Cohen, "Crime in the Suites," in Nader, *The Consumer and Corporate Accountability,* p. 79.

5. Ralph Nader, *Unsafe at Any Speed: The Designed-In Dangers of the American Automobile* (New York: Bantam, 1972).

6. Morton Mintz, "Confessions of a GM Engineer," in Nader, *The Consumer and Corporate Accountability,* pp. 301–309. For a similar situation among tire manufacturers, see "Forewarnings of Fatal Flaws," *Time* (June 25, 1979), pp. 58–61.

7. The following is taken from Mark Dowie, "Pinto Madness," in Jerome H. Skolnick and Elliott Currie, eds., *Crisis in American Institutions,* Fourth Edition (Boston: Little, Brown, 1979), pp. 23–40.

8. *Ibid.,* p. 24.

9. *Ibid.,* pp. 30–32.

10. *Ibid.,* p. 30. This is the argument made in Walter Guzzardi, Jr., "The Mindless Pursuit of Safety," *Fortune* 99 (April, 1979), pp. 54–64.

11. Associated Press release (September 14, 1978).

12. Dowie, "Pinto Madness," p. 39.

13. The following is taken from Fred R. Harris, "The Politics of Corporate Power," *Corporate Power in America,* Ralph Nader and Mark J. Green, eds. (New York: Grossman, 1973), pp. 27–29; and "Detroit Fights Airbags," *Dollars and Sense,* no. 38 (July/August, 1978), pp. 6–7.

14. "Detroit Fights Airbags," p. 6.

15. *Ibid.,* p. 7.

16. Upton Sinclair, *The Jungle* (New York: New American Library, 1960). First published in 1905.

17. Charles H. McCaghy, *Deviant Behavior: Crime, Conflict, and Interest Groups* (New York: Macmillan, 1976), p. 215.

18. Harrison Wellford, *Sowing and Wind: A Report from Ralph Nader's Center for Study of Responsive Law on Food Safety and the Chemical Harvest* (New York: Grossman, 1972), p. 69.

19. McCaghy, *Deviant Behavior,* p. 216.

20. Robert Sherrill, *The New York Times Book Review* (March 4, 1973), p. 3, cited in McCaghy, *Deviant Behavior,* p. 216. See also Gene Marine and Judith Van Allen, *Food Pollution: The Violation of Our Inner Ecology* (New York: Holt, Rinehart and Winston, 1972), chapter 2; and Jennifer Cross, *The Supermarket Trap: The Consumer and the Food Industry,* Revised Edition (Bloomington: Indiana University Press, 1976), Chapter 9.

21. The following discussion of additives is taken primarily from Daniel Zwerdling, "Food Pollution," *Ramparts* (June, 1971), reprinted in Richard C. Edwards, Michael Reich, and Thomas E. Weisskopf, eds., *The Capitalist System,* Second Edition (Englewood Cliffs, N.J.: Prentice-Hall, 1978), pp. 19–24. See also Jacqueline Verrett and Jean Carper, *Eating May Be Hazardous to Your Health* (Garden City, N.Y.: Doubleday Anchor Books, 1975).

22. Julie Miller, "Testing for Seeds of Destruction," *The Progressive* (December, 1976), pp. 37–40. See also Richard F. Spark, "Legislating against Cancer," *The New Republic* (June 3, 1978), pp. 16–19.

23. It is even possible that financial ties to huge food corporations may shade the "expert testimony" of nutritionists, as argued by Benjamin Rosenthal, Michael Jacobson, and Marcy Bohm, "Professors on the Take," *The Progressive* 40 (November, 1976), pp. 42–47.

24. Marine and Van Allen, *Food Pollution,* p. 38.

25. Hugh Drummond, "Add Poison for Flavor and Freshness," *Mother Jones* (April, 1977), p. 13.

26. Quoted in Zwerdling, "Food Pollution," p. 20.

27. Jim Hightower, *Eat Your Heart Out: Food Profiteering in America* (New York: Vintage, 1975), pp. 58–59. Copyright © 1975 by Jim Hightower. Reprinted by permission of Crown Publishers.

28. Robert L. Heilbroner et al., *In the Name of Profit* (New York: Warner Paperback Library, 1973), p. 192.

29. U.S. Senate, Select Committee on Nutrition and Human Needs, *Dietary Goals for the United States,* Second Edition (Washington, D.C.: U.S. Government Printing Office, 1977), p. 30; and U.S. Bureau of the Census, *Statistical Abstract of the U.S.: 1979* (Washington, D.C., 1979), p. 127.

30. *Ibid.,* p. 33.

31. *Ibid.,* pp. 31–32.

32. *Ibid.,* p. 32.

33. Ibid., p. 33.

34. *Ibid.*, p. 35.

35. *Ibid.*, p. 19.

36. Hightower, *Eat Your Heart Out*, p. 631.

37. U.S. Senate, *Dietary Goals for the United States*, pp. 35–48.

38. Associated Press release (March 24, 1979).

39. Marilyn Elias, "How to Win Friends and Influence Kids on Television (and Incidentally Sell a Few Toys and Munchies at the Same Time)," *Human Behavior* (April, 1974), p. 17.

40. *Ibid.*, p. 20.

41. *Ibid.* For an extensive review of research, see National Science Foundation, *The Effects of Television* (Washington, D.C.: U.S. Government Printing Office, 1976).

42. Federal Trade Commission, *Staff Report on Television Advertising to Children* (Washington, D.C.: U.S. Government Printing Office, 1978), p. 57.

43. Summarized in U.S. Commission on Civil Rights, *Window Dressing on the Set: An Update* (Washington, D.C.: U.S. Government Printing Office, 1979), p. 49.

44. Elias, "How to Win Friends and Influence Kids on Television," pp. 16–23.

45. Michael Weinstock, quoted in *Broadcasting* 96 (January 22, 1979), p. 25.

46. John Summers, quoted in *Broadcasting* 96 (March 26, 1979), p. 84.

47. Frederick Furth, quoted in "Keep Out of the Reach of Children," *Bill Moyers' Journal,* first aired April 30, 1979, p. 3 of transcript.

48. Bernard Friedlander, quoted in *Broadcasting* 96 (April 2, 1979), p. 64.

49. Ellen Goodman, "Why Allow Decadent Tooth Fairies to Invade Our Homes?" *Rocky Mountain News* (December 5, 1978), p. 61. For an opposite opinion, see Christopher De Muth, "Hands Off Children's TV," *Rocky Mountain News* (April 15, 1979), p. 55.

50. "Keep Out of the Reach of Children," p. 11.

51. See "Slow Motion Suicide," *Newsweek* (January 22, 1979), pp. 83–84; United Press International release (January 12, 1979); and Associated Press release (January 12, 1979).

52. Erik Eckholm, "Four Trillion Cigarettes," *The Progressive* 42 (July, 1978), pp. 26–27.

53. Maitland Zane, "Califano Dares Tobacco Industry," *San Francisco Chronicle* (April 27, 1979), p. 4.

54. Gwenda Blair, "Why Dick Can't Stop Smoking: The Politics Behind Our National Addiction," *Mother Jones* 4 (January, 1979), p. 35.

55. Quoted in *ibid.,* p. 36.

56. *Ibid.,* p. 40.

57. Quoted in *ibid.,* p. 42.

58. Eckholm, "Four Trillion Cigarettes," p. 26. For a discussion of the American tobacco invasion in the Middle East, see "Tobacco Inroads," *Newsweek* (October 2, 1978), p. 106. See also Albert Huebner, "Exporting Cancer," *Rocky Mountain News* (July 1, 1979), p. 60.

59. ABC News special, "West Virginia: Life, Liberty, and the Pursuit of Coal," first shown, 1976.

60. "Is Your Job Dangerous to Your Health?" *U.S. News and World Report* (February 5, 1979), p. 39.

61. *Ibid.*, p. 40. See also Sidney Lens, "Dead on the Job," *The Progressive* (November, 1979), pp. 50–52.

62. Philip Cole and Marlene B. Goldman, "Occupation," *Persons at High*

Risk of Cancer, Joseph F. Fraumeni, Jr., ed. (New York: Academic Press, 1975), p. 171.

63. Dorothy McGhee, "Workplace Hazards: No Women Need Apply," *The Progressive* 41 (October, 1977), p. 25.

64. Daniel Ben-Horin, "The Sterility Scandal," *Mother Jones* 4 (May, 1979), pp. 51–63.

65. Jeanne Schinto, "The Breathless Cotton Workers," *The Progressive* 41 (August, 1977), p. 29.

66. Reported in Samuel S. Epstein, *The Politics of Cancer* (San Francisco: Sierra Club Books, 1978), pp. 84–86. See also Lea Zeldin, "The Asbestos Menace," *The Progressive* (October, 1978), p. 12.

67. Reported in "Silkwood Vindicated," *Newsweek* (May 28, 1979), p. 40.

68. *Ibid.,* pp. 102–106.

69. Epstein, *The Politics of Cancer,* pp. 100–112.

70. J. T. Edsall, "Report of the AAAS Committee on Scientific Freedom and Responsibility," *Science* 188 (1975), pp. 687–693. Reported in Epstein, *The Politics of Cancer,* pp. 103–104.

71. See Richard Doll, *British Journal of Industrial Medicine* 12 (1955), p. 81.

72. The following account is taken primarily from Joel Swartz, "Silent Killers at Work," *Crime and Social Justice* (Spring/Summer, 1975), pp. 15–20.

73. *Ibid.,* p. 16.

74. Roger M. Williams, "Arsenic and Old Factories," *Saturday Review* (January 20, 1979), p. 26.

75. Schinto, "The Breathless Cotton Workers," p. 28. For a description of how the government has "waffled" in this area, see "Brown Lung Compromise," *The Progressive* (August, 1978), p. 13.

76. Swartz, "Silent Killers at Work," p. 18. Reprinted by permission of *Crime and Social Justice,* P.O. Box 4373, Berkeley, CA 94704.

77. *Ibid.,* pp. 19–20. Reprinted by permission of *Crime and Social Justice,* P.O. Box 4373, Berkeley, CA 94704.

78. Portions of this section are taken from D. Stanley Eitzen, *Social Problems* (Boston: Allyn and Bacon, 1980), Chapters 3 and 11.

79. Lester R. Brown, Patricia L. McGrath, and Bruce Stokes, *Twenty-Two Dimensions of the Population Problem,* Worldwatch Paper 5 (Washington, D.C.: Worldwatch Institute, 1976), p. 58.

80. Vance Packard, *The Waste Makers* (New York: David McKay, 1960).

81. *Ibid.,* pp. 55–56.

82. Cited in Max Boas and Steve Chain, *Big Mac: The Unauthorized Story of McDonald's* (New York: New American Library, 1976), p. 74.

83. Paul R. Ehrlich and Anne H. Erhlich, *Population/Resources/Environment: Issues in Human Ecology,* Second Edition (San Francisco: W. H. Freeman, 1972), p. 159.

84. From Harry M. Caudill, *Night Comes to the Cumberlands* (Boston: Little, Brown, an Atlantic Monthly Press Book, 1963), pp. 311–312.

85. *Ibid.,* p. 314.

86. *Ibid.,* pp. 306–324.

87. *Ibid.,* p. 307.

88. Harold Sprout and Margaret Sprout, *The Context of Environmental Politics* (Lexington: The University Press of Kentucky, 1978), p. 17.

89. Paul R. Ehrlich and John P. Holdren, "The Heat Barrier," *Saturday Review* 54 (April 3, 1971), p. 61. See also Lamont C. Cole, "Thermal Pollution," *Bioscience* 19 (November, 1969), pp. 989–992.

90. "Is Energy Use Overheating the World?" *U.S. News and World Report*

(July 25, 1977). See also Stephen H. Schneider and Lynne E. Mesirow, *The Genesis Strategy: Climate and Global Survival* (New York: Delta, 1976); and Brown et al., *Twenty-Two Dimensions of the Population Problem*, pp. 35–37.

91. Brown et al., *Twenty-Two Dimensions of the Population Problem*, pp. 35–36.

92. The following is taken primarily from Michael H. Best and William E. Connolly, "Nature and Its Largest Parasite," *The Capitalist System*, Second Edition, Richard C. Edwards, Michael Reich, and Thomas E. Weisskopf, eds. (Englewood Cliffs, N.J.: Prentice-Hall, 1978), pp. 418–425, an excerpt from their book *The Politicized Economy* (Lexington, Mass.: D. C. Heath, 1976).

93. *Ibid.*, p. 419.

94. *Ibid.*, pp. 420–421.

95. Barry Commoner, "The Economic Meaning of Ecology," *Crisis in American Institutions*, Skolnick and Currie, eds., p. 285. Excerpted from *The Closing Circle* (New York: Alfred A. Knopf, 1971).

96. *Ibid.*, p. 291.

97. See Barry Weisbert, "The Politics of Ecology," *Liberation* (January, 1970), pp. 20–25.

98. All but the final example are taken from two speeches by Ralph Nader at Colorado State University (May, 1970, and November, 1977).

99. Associated Press release (February 2, 1977).

100. Jonathan H. Turner, *Social Problems in America* (New York: Harper & Row, 1977), pp. 419–420.

101. James M. Henslin and Larry T. Reynolds, *Social Problems in American Society*, Second Edition (Boston: Holbrook, 1976), pp. 220–221. See also Michael Parenti, *Power and the Powerless* (New York: St. Martin's, 1978), pp. 19–20.

102. "The Politics of Cancer," *The Progressive* 43 (May, 1979), p. 9.

103. See Guzzardi, "The Mindless Pursuit of Safety," pp. 54–64; and "Diseased Regulation," *Forbes* (February 19, 1979), p. 34.

Chapter 5
National Defense, Multinational Corporations, and Human Rights

This chapter focuses on the international dimensions of deviance by economic and political elites. We will describe the conduct of corporations and the national government that involve price gouging, business-government collusion in fraud, corporate bribery of foreign governments, the sale of known hazards by multinational firms, and the United States' support of repressive regimes.

✗THE MILITARY-INDUSTRIAL COMPLEX

Beginning with the divisive and tragic Vietnam War (1964–1975), a host of incidents has occurred that has heightened public concern regarding the United States' defense and foreign policies. A few specific examples include:

✗ 1. Numerous government investigations, from the 1950s to the 1970s, revealed many unethical, wasteful, and sometimes illegal practices involving Pentagon officials and defense contractors:

Item: In the late 1960s, J. G. McGhee, a civilian fuel inspector working for the Navy, discovered that over 100,000 dollars worth of jet fuel had been fraudulently recorded by Navy officials as having been used. The monies for the fuel were sent to the contractors. When McGhee reported the potential scan-

131

dal to Pentagon officials, he was transferred from Vietnam to Pensacola, Florida. There he was assigned as a laboratory technician, who tested fuel samples. It took a Senate investigation to get McGhee reinstated.[1]

Item: In 1976 Senator William Proxmire (Dem., Wisc.) identified fifty-nine defense officials and high-ranking military personnel who had been entertained by defense contractors at various hunting lodges. It was revealed that the costs of such entertainment, several hundred-thousand dollars, had been added to the costs of defense contracts. One contractor, Northrop, agreed to pay back 2.3 million dollars in fees which were added to contracts for entertainment and illegal campaign contributions.[2]

2. Public concern has also been expressed regarding certain practices of multinational corporations in their overseas business dealings:

Item: By 1979 over 350 major corporations had admitted making illegal or improper payments to foreign governments totaling some 750 million dollars.[3] The Nader organization has compiled a list of some of the largest firms involved (Table 5–1). The table reveals that some companies began making payments shortly after the end of World War II. Moreover,

Table 5–1: Corporations Admitting Illegal or Improper Payments.

Company	Date	Amount	Nature of Payments	Source
Alcoa	1972–74	$4,000,000	foreign payments from secret fund	CiB p. 147
American Home Products	1971–75	$6,462,000	foreign political contributions	SEC
Boeing Co.	1970–75	$70,000,000	foreign commissions	CiB p. 141
Carrier Corp.	1972–75	$2,614,000	foreign commissions	SEC
Chrysler	1971–76	$2,438,000	secret funds abroad; foreign payments	6/77 8K
Cities Service	1971–75	$1,049,400	foreign payments	CEP
Dresser Industries	1971–75	$24,000	payments to foreign officials	SEC
Exxon	1963–75	$56,771,000	foreign political contributions	SEC
FMC	1973–75	$200,000	foreign payments to secure sales	CiB p. 141

Company	Date	Amount	Nature of Payments	Source
Ford Motor Co.	1973–74	$60,000	payments to foreign political parties	CiB p. 144
General Tire & Rubber	1950s–75	$1,349,000	foreign and domestic political payments	SEC
B.F. Goodrich Co.	1971–75	$124,000	foreign commissions	SEC
Goodyear Tire & Rubber	1970–75	$846,000	payments to foreign officials	SEC
Gulf Oil Corp.	1960–73	$6,900,000	foreign political contributions	CiB p. 158
Ingersoll-Rand	1971–75	$797,000	payments acknowledged but not described	CEP
Koppers Co.	1971–75	$1,500,000	foreign payments	CEP
Kraftco Corp.	1969–75	$699,500	foreign payments	SEC
	1972–76	$550	domestic campaign contributions	SEC
3M Co.	1963–72	$545,799	secret fund for domestic political campaign contribs.	SEC
	1975	$52,000	foreign payments	SEC
Reynolds Metals Co.	since 1970	N.A.	undisclosed amounts to foreign political parties	CiB p. 147
R. J. Reynolds Ind.	1968–73	$190,000	payments to presidential and congressional candidates, disguised by diverting royalties	CiB p. 148
	since 1968	$5,500,000	payments to foreign officials and governments, disguised on books as commissions	CiB p. 148
	1971–75	$19,000,000	foreign rebates to shippers by SeaLand, a subsidiary	CiB p. 148
Rockwell Int'l	1971–75	$676,300	foreign payments to secure sales	SEC
Standard Oil Co. of Ind.	1970–75	$1,359,400	foreign payments	SEC
Tenneco Inc.	N.A.	$865,480	foreign payments	SEC
AMAX Inc.	1972–76	$64,877	foreign payments	CEP
Armco Steel Corp.	1971–75	$18,060,000	foreign payments	CEP
Atlantic Richfield	1969–76	$262,000	foreign payments	CEP
Boise Cascade	1971–76	$340,100	foreign payments	CEP
Champion International	1971–75	$537,000	foreign payments	CEP
Clark Equipment	1971–76	$95,000	foreign payments	CEP

Table 5–1 (Continued).

Company	Date	Amount	Nature of Payments	Source
Coca-Cola	N.A.	$300,000	foreign payments	CEP
Dart Industries	1971–76	$126,000	foreign payments	CEP
Dow Chemical	N.A.	$2,500	foreign payments	CEP
Firestone Tire & Rubber	1970–76	$97,000	foreign payments	CEP
GAF Industries	N.A.	N.A.		CEP
General Electric	1972–75	$550,000	foreign payments	CEP
General Foods	1971–76	$162,751	foreign payments	CEP
H. J. Heinz	1971–76	N.A.	foreign payments	CEP
Hercules, Inc.	1971–75	$597,000	foreign payments	CEP
Marcor Inc. (Mobil)	1971–76	$635,517	foreign payments	CEP
Mobil Oil	1970–73	$2,000,000	foreign contributions to Italian political parties	N.A.
Monsanto	1971–76	$533,300	foreign payments	CEP
J. C. Penney	1971–75	$373,000	foreign payments	CEP
Ralston Purina	1970–76	$154,000	foreign payments	CEP
Scott Paper	1971–76	$229,000	foreign payments	CEP
Shell Oil	1969–73	$6,600,000	Royal Dutch Shell and British Petroleum to Italian political parties	N.A.
Stauffer Chemical	1975–76	$7,500	foreign payments	CEP
Weyerhaeuser	1971–76	$1,180,000	foreign payments	CEP
White Motor	1971–76	$1,016,000	foreign payments	CEP
Xerox Corporation	1971–75	$100,000	foreign payments	CEP
United Aircraft	1973–75	$2,040,000	sales fees to foreign government employees or officials	SEC
Westinghouse Electric	N.A.	$323,000	foreign payments	SEC

* Key: SEC — Report of the Securities and Exchange to the U.S. Senate Committee on Banking Housing and Urban Affairs, May 1976; CiB — *Corruption in Business* (New York: Facts on File, 1977); CEP — *The Invisible Hand: Questionable Corporate Payments Overseas (New York: Council on Economic Priorities, 1976)*; 8K or 10K-*Forms filed with SEC on dates indicated.*

Source: Jack Newfield, "Crime in the Suites: Will Congress Go Easy on Corporate Crooks," *The Village Voice* (October 20, 1979), p. 12. Reprinted by permission of *The Village Voice.* Copyright © News Group Publications, Inc., 1979.

some of these same companies were involved in making illegal campaign contributions in the United States as well.

Item: In the 1970s the Interfaith Center on Corporate Responsibility (ICCR) organized an international boycott against the Nestlé Company. Nestlé's sale of baby formula to inhabitants of various poor nations throughout the world was, the ICCR claimed, causing the death of some 10,000 babies per year because the formula was mixed with impure water. Moreover, the people buying the formula were so poor that they could not afford continued purchase of the product, resulting in cases where the formula was so diluted that babies' health was endangered. One tropical health expert, Dr. Derrick Jelliffee, estimates that the sale of such formula by Nestlé and other companies (e.g., Brystol Myers and American Home Products) contributes to some "ten million cases of severe infantile starvation and diarrhea a year" in poor nations.[4]

3. Finally, President Carter placed foreign-policy emphasis on nonsupport by the U.S. of regimes that violate basic human rights. But by late 1979, with the capture of the American embassy in Tehran, columnist Jack Anderson claimed that little had been done to improve the situation. Indeed,

> ... The Iranian crisis is only the latest, and most dramatic, evidence of the enmity the United States has aroused by its support of repressive dictators in the name of anti-communism.... In South America and Africa, we continue to prop up the regimes of generals who beat their countrymen with one hand and rob them with the other.... In Argentina and Chile, we continue to back repressive military regimes to protect U.S. business interests.[5]

The incidents regarding (1) unethical or illegal practices relating to U.S. defense policy, (2) the conduct of multinational corporations abroad, and (3) violations of human rights by nations supported by the United States, are the subject of this chapter. Our thesis is that these deviant acts are caused by the structure of the international political and economic system. That is the unequal relationships between the United States and its allies in Western Europe and Japan, and between the U.S. and the Third World nations of Asia, Africa, and Latin America, has created an environment in which certain types of illegal and objectionable practices tend to flourish. Such practices are often justified or overlooked by the U.S. press because of an ideology which stresses anti-communism, "free enterprise," and the need for a strong national defense. Nevertheless, such practices and their causes, for reasons made clear below, deserve careful examination. Our analysis begins with an inquiry into the nature of the U.S. military establishment.

✓ The Defense Establishment and Its Origins

In 1945, the United States emerged victorious from World War II with its economy and military forces intact. There was at that time a crucial need to help rebuild the war-torn economies of Western Europe. In addition, the communist revolution in China (1949) pointed up the necessity for preventing newly independent Third World nations from entering the communist orbit. Thus, from 1945 to 1975, 170 billion dollars' worth of loans and grants were made by the U.S. to friendly nations all over the world.[6] In return for such aid recipients agreed to adopt the dollar as the standard currency of exchange and to give U.S. firms certain advantageous trade and investment opportunities.

Those nations agreeing to accept U.S. aid were to be protected by a world-wide U.S. military network. By 1969, the United States had "1,517,000 uniformed personnel in 119 countries . . . in 429 major and 2,972 minor military bases"[7] (aside from the substantial commitment in Vietnam at that time). Since World War II, U.S. troops and naval forces have been involved in 215 "shows of force" and have intervened militarily in Korea, Lebanon, the Dominican Republic, and, of course, Vietnam.[8] Militarily, the U.S. has provided what the Douglas Aircraft Company, in a report for the Army Research Office, called the "Pax Americana" (the American peace).[9]

These strategies have resulted in an unprecedented situation. As of 1977, the U.S. had spent, since 1945, an astounding 1,500 billion dollars on defense.[10] The sums spent on defense, together with the nearly worldwide deployment of U.S. military forces, have created a huge permanent military establishment.

In fact, on January 13, 1961, outgoing President Eisenhower, in his farewell address, warned of the consequences of the military-industrial complex. The president said,

> In the councils of government, we must guard against the acquisition of unwarranted influence, whether sought or unsought, by the military-industrial complex. . . .
> We must never let the weight of this combination endanger our liberties or democratic processes. We should take nothing for granted. Only an alert and knowledgeable citizenry can compel the proper meshing of the huge industrial and military machinery of defense with our peaceful methods and goals, so that security and liberty can prosper together.[11]

Despite Eisenhower's warning, the military-industrial complex has continued to increase in both size and influence. Moreover, the nature of the complex is poorly understood by the public. It is not a malevolent conspiracy, as some believe, but an interrelated "community of interests." [12] It is really a "MITLAMP (military-industrial-technological-labor-academic-managerial-political) complex":

1. The military sector of the complex consists of the men and women on active duty whose current allowances make up 30.79 percent of the defense budget. Also included in the military segment are retirees and veterans receiving checks that amounted to close to $12,500,000,000 (fiscal year 1974). Consideration must also be given to the political-economic clout possessed by veterans' organizations such as the American Legion, Amvets, and the Veterans of Foreign Wars. These are the organizations that exercise such political pressures that the Veterans' Administration budget amounted to over $14,-000,000,000 this year.

2. The industrial category consists of over one hundred defense contractors whose economic base is the budget provided by the Federal Government for defense purposes. Retired officers on the payrolls of these companies numbered 3,233 in 1973. . . .

3. The labor segment consists of the five percent of the work force directly involved and sixteen percent indirectly dependent on Pentagon dollars for employment. . . .

4. The academic division is founded on defense-related expenditures taking place on various campuses in the United States. Indeed $2,015,000,000 of the $8,676,000,000 earmarked for research-and-development projects was targeted for expenditures on selected larger college campuses in fiscal year 1974.

5. The managerial grouping consists of the men who "oil the wheels of administrative machinery," the 7.8 percent who are engaged in the managerial functions designed to mobilize and organize the intellectual, scientific, technological, and manpower resources in support of MITLAMP objectives. In addition, another 9 percent are indirectly involved in the operation of the MITLAMP. Excellent examples of this activity are the hard and soft-sell methods formulated by Madison Avenue types to recruit an all-volunteer army.

6. The political segment includes the politicians in Congress who are in harmony with the objectives of the MITLAMP. It should be noted that such men represent states benefiting greatly from MITLAMP expenditures in the form of military installations and defense plants fueled by weapons-systems contracts.[13]

At the apex of the military-industrial complex stand the so-called National Security Managers — a group of politicians, civil servants, and businessmen — who tend to rotate among various posts in the Pentagon, Department of State, Atomic Energy Commission, the FBI, the CIA, the agencies that administer foreign aid and certain national and international police training programs, the White House, and big business. Such people (as was mentioned in Chapter 1) sit on the boards of trustees of the universities who receive the bulk of defense-related research funds, and compose the directors of leading foundations who fund the "think tanks" and elite associations that regularly make policy recommendations to the executive branch of the federal government. This set of relationships is diagrammed in Figure 5–1.

Not surprisingly, the corporations that receive the most financial benefit from defense contracting are the same multinational corporations whose overseas holdings are protected by the military-counterinsurgency umbrella provided by the U.S.'s worldwide military establishment.

As the Chasins have pointed out, "At least 205 firms ranking in the top 500 manufacturing corporations" are "significantly involved in military production." [14] Moreover, "the top 100 corporations monopolize three-fourths of the contracts." [15] With the defense budget hovering near the 130 billion-dollar mark in 1979 and with "half the Defense budget spent on prime military contracts for the development, production, or deployment of weapons," the opportunity for profits is great.[16] These opportunities are enhanced greatly by the practice of letting over fifty percent of defense contracts with no competitive bidding.

In fact, the government's own investigations have revealed surprising patterns of unethical practices. In 1965, the Comptroller General described the following aspects of the military-contract system to a House committee:

1. Excessive prices in relation to available pricing information.
2. Acceptance and payment by the government for defective equipment.
3. Charges to the government for costs applicable to contractors' commercial work.
4. Contractors' use of government-owned facilities for commercial work for extended periods without payment of rent to the government.
5. Duplicate billings to the government.
6. Unreasonable or excessive costs.
7. Excessive progress payments held by contractors without payment of interest thereon.[17]

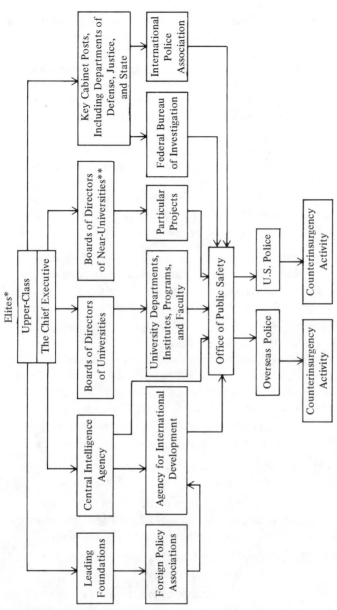

*Includes defense contractors.   **"Think-Tanks" (e.g., Rand Corp).

Figure 5–1. Elites and the Military–Industrial Complex.

Source: John C. Leggett, *Taking State Power* (New York: Harper and Row, 1973), p. 377.   Table title has been changed from the original. Reprinted with permission.

Among these items are thirteen billion dollars in government-owned land, buildings, and equipment which in some cases greatly reduces the need for any capital investments by a contractor.

One of the most notorious defense-contract practices is known as "buying in." Using this device, contractors set very low bids on the costs of weapons systems, but, should the costs rise, as they inevitably do, the government agrees to pay for such increases under a "contract-change notice." [18] Here changes are made by either the Pentagon or the contractors, and in a complex weapons system the number of such notices runs, at times, into the thousands. The practice has resulted in two negative consequences: (1) the so-called cost overrun, where the original price of an item easily multiplies; and (2) the Defense Department's receiving weapons of very questionable quality (in some cases no weapons at all are received). Some examples:

> *Item:* One defense analyst with the Bureau of the Budget, Richard Stubbing, studied thirteen aircraft and missile programs contracted for since 1955 at a cost of more than 40 billion dollars. He found that sixty percent of the electronic components in these systems failed to perform acceptably.

> *Item:* In 1968 the Pentagon stated that in the previous fifteen years, 8.8 billion dollars had been socked into sixty-seven military contracts which were cancelled, either because the Defense Department (DOD) decided it could not use them, or because the projects failed to meet military requirements.

> *Item:* The Minuteman-2 missile's cost went from 3.2 to 7 billion dollars, more than double its original price.

> *Item:* A rescue submarine's costs increased more than 2,700 percent, from three to eighty million dollars.

> *Item:* One system designed to keep track of fuel in Vietnam broke down in 1967, resulting in the inability of the Air Force to account for some twenty-one million dollars' worth of gas and oil.

> *Item:* The Short-Range Attack Missile's cost rose from 301 to 636 million dollars in the twelve months of 1968.

> *Item:* The Navy cancelled a contract for the F-111B when it was declared too heavy to meet its range and altitude requirements, but the government reimbursed the contractor, General Dynamics, to the tune of 216.5 million dollars.

> *Item:* Pentagon efficiency expert, A. E. Fitzgerald, of C-5A fame (see below) testified before the Joint Economic Committee that the Air Force had submitted a figure to the Secretary of Defense on the Mark II "electronic brain" of the F-111 some 229 million

dollars below what it knew its actual costs would be. Fitzgerald said the Air Force officials lied because they did not want to see the project abandoned, and they feared this would happen if its true costs were revealed.[19]

Another practice of the defense-contracting effort is known as "pyramiding profits." Under pyramiding, prime contractors purchase components for systems from subcontractors, who in turn purchase other components from other subcontractors. Each company involved bills the company, to whom it sells, costs plus profits, which is perfectly legal; but taken to an extreme, this system breeds gigantic amounts of profit taking. One example occurred in the 1950s when Western Electric was given the contract for the Nike missile, and, subsequently, the launcher for the missile. Western Electric subcontracted the launcher contract to Douglas Aircraft, who subcontracted to a subsidiary of U.S. Steel. The U.S. Steel affiliate's bill for the transaction, including its profit, was 13.5 million dollars. The Douglas company manufactured the covers that fit over the missile and took a profit of over 1.2 million dollars on the transaction — a return of over 36,000 percent on its original investment. Western Electric based its bill to the government on Douglas' reported costs and profit, 14.7 million dollars. Western Electric's total investment was 14,293 dollars, charged for inspecting equipment on various army bases. Its profit on the transaction amounted to almost one million, a return on investment of over 6,000 percent. The pyramiding arrangement can, then, allow the prime contractor and each subcontractor to add on tremendous profits at each level of the pyramid.[20]

The costs to the government in some defense contracts have reached unbelievable proportions at times. Several years ago the Boeing aircraft corporation delivered eighty-two beds to the Air Force at a cost of 1,080 dollars per bed. Standard Air Force beds were usually purchased for around thirty-eight dollars each.[21]

Undoubtedly, the most famous of all cost overruns is that of the C-5A transport aircraft. The C-5A case demonstrates the excess costs, as well as shoddy quality of goods, sometimes delivered to the Department of Defense. One hundred and fifteen of the Lockheed crafts were contracted for at a cost of 3.2 billion dollars. However, the crafts' costs to the government increased by a whopping sixty-seven percent, to 5.2 billion.

Moreover, the safety and performance record of the C-5A has been a disaster. The plane has been involved in a number of tragic incidents. Following the initial delivery of fifteen C-5As to the government in 1971, it was found that the:

C-5 suffers major technical breakdown once an hour of flight time. The unenviable pilot of the giant jet should anticipate, according to the General Accounting Office, that his landing gear alone will fail once every four hours. One of the planes already accepted by the Air Force and picked at random by the GAO auditors for inspection had 47 major and 149 minor deficiencies. Fourteen of the defects, the GAO reported to Congress, "impair the aircraft's capability to perform all or a portion of six missions" assigned to it.[22]

In May, 1973, the last of eighty-one C-5As were delivered to the Air Force, thirteen months behind schedule. Following the delivery, several additional incidents occurred:

1. In 1973 the Air Force was to supply Israel with emergency material following an Arab invasion, but it discovered that some thirty-six C-5As could not be used because they needed repairs. Ten other of the transports were grounded for lack of parts. Mechanical malfunctions in other C-5As caused twenty-nine flights to be terminated and forty others to be delayed.

2. In 1975 a C-5A leaving Saigon crashed, killing more than 100 Vietnamese orphans bound for the United States.[23]

3. Throughout the 1970s problems of the C-5A continued to escalate. In one six-month period, 3,327 defects were found in the plane's landing gear, and an additional 1.3 billion dollars was needed to strengthen its landing gear. Thus airplanes proven to be faulty, costing twenty-eight million dollars each in 1965, ended up costing sixty-five million by 1970, and, finally eighty-five million by 1979.[24]

The C-5A's history also reveals the miseries bestowed on those who "blow the whistle" on such abuses. Ernest Fitzgerald was the Pentagon efficiency analyst who exposed the initial cost overrun of the C-5A. Once he made the news public, Fitzgerald was transferred to Thailand, where he was placed in charge of overseeing the building of a bowling alley. Subsequently, as part of a "cost-reduction" move his position was abolished and he was fired. It took a congressional investigation to finally get Fitzgerald rehired by the Defense Department. However, during the period that Fitzgerald exposed the plane's cost, the Air Force Office of Special Investigation (OSI) undertook to open his personal mail and tried to uncover information that they could use to discredit him. An OSI report characterized Fitzgerald as "pinchpenny," as evidenced by the fact that he drove an old car, a Rambler.[25]

An additional incident in which Fitzgerald was involved is also instructive. This concerns the Mark II electronic and electrical system of the F-111 fighter. The contract for the system was given to the Autonetics Division of North American Aviation with an initial bid of

750,000 dollars per unit, but with the usual overrun the cost skyrocketed to 4.1 million per unit. In an attempt to hold down costs, Fitzgerald met with the projects director, Major General Zoeckler. After Fitzgerald complained of the program's rising costs, the general replied, "Inefficiency is national policy," necessary for the attainment of such social goals as employment and aid to businesses.[26]

Whether inefficiency is national policy throughout the economy is an open question. That waste and inefficiency often take place in defense contracting is a fact which has dismayed even some members of the defense establishment. A Brookings Institution study concluded that "during the 1950s virtually all large military contracts . . . ultimately involved costs in excess of the original contractual estimates of from 300 to 700 percent." [27] A 1964 study in the *American Economic Review* by economist Walter Adams reported that "a summary of General Accounting Office studies covering May 1963 to May 1964 (exposed) ascertainable waste of 500 million dollars in a 5 percent sample of procurements," and that twelve major weapons systems had exceeded original predictions by 3.2 times on average, ranging from 70 to 700 percent on actual versus predicted costs.[28]

Finally, there are additional reasons why waste and inefficiency are rewarded to such a great extent. These reasons, aside from buying in and cost-plus contracting, include the following:

1. "Goldplating" is the tendency to build into new systems needless levels of technological sophistication. The purchase of exotic features is encouraged by competition between the military services and among the corporations, and is relatively uncontrolled because of military self-regulation in the definition of tactical needs.

2. "Managers without power" cannot effectively supervise contracts. Weapons programs tend to be overseen by middle-ranking military officers who must carry every decision to superiors and who are prevented from developing expertise by frequent job rotation.

3. "Concurrency" is the practice of beginning weapons production before development is complete, to speed deployment and cut lead time. Problems discovered later must be corrected on already produced units, driving up costs.[29]

The situation concerning defense contracting also seems to invite incidents of fraud. For example, the B.F. Goodrich Company was granted a contract to develop the brake assemblies on the Air Force's A7D fighter aircraft in the early 1970s. When the models developed by Goodrich consistently failed to pass their own laboratory tests, Goodrich engineers began falsifying their test data and changing their testing methods so that the brakes would meet Air Force specifications. Upon being tested on the actual aircraft the brakes malfunctioned, causing a number of near crashes. Because of the nature of the doctored test data, Kermit Vandivier, a former Goodrich employee, who later appeared as the government's witness, resigned. In his letter of resignation he described a falsified report which was sent to the Air Force:

> As you are aware, this report contained numerous deliberate and willful misrepresentations which, according to legal counsel, constitute fraud and expose . . . myself and others to charges of conspiracy to defraud. . . .[30]

In the end no charges of fraud were brought against either Goodrich or any of its officials. Goodrich merely announced that it would replace its original brake system with a new and better one.

Other examples of illegal or unethical practices with the Defense Department have included outright bribery. Northrop had, between 1971 and 1974, hired a number of special consultants including military and congressional officials. These seventy-two consultants were paid a total of 5.5 million dollars. Some of the consultants included General John Blandford, former aide to Senator Mendel Rivers, head of the House Armed Services Committee, which oversees the Pentagon's budget in the House of Representatives. (Blandford had also offered his services to Lockheed and Fairchild Industries.) One project for Northrop in which Blandford and Rivers were involved was the development of the Northrop F-5. Never purchased by the Pentagon, the plane was developed by the government and donated to the United States' Asian allies.

In addition, Northrop paid Blandford 40,000–60,000 dollars through another consultant, Frank DeFrancis, for "protection" in dealing with the company's competitors.[31] DeFrancis was paid a total of half a million dollars. Auditors investigating Northrop ruled that payments to DeFrancis were improperly billed to the government by Northrop. Finally, Northrop paid the former head of the Air National Guard, General Wilson, 115,000 dollars in expenses, which auditors documented went for entertainment in Northrop's hunting lodge, "lobbying," and illegal political contributions.

The incidents of corruption, graft, and inefficiency that make defense contracting so profitable continued into the late 1970s. A study by the General Accounting Office in 1978 reported that fifty-five major weapons systems accounted for an increase totaling an amazing eighty-six billion dollars.[32] In late 1978, columnist Jack Anderson reported that within the Defense Department itself there exists staggering amounts of waste and theft in procurement. The Defense Personnel Support Center, which handles contracts for clothing, food, and medical supplies, has become the focus of an investigation by the FBI, the General Accounting Office, the DOD's inspector general, and the Senate Permanent Subcommittee on Investigations. Accounting procedures at the Center were reported so inept that it may be impossible to determine how much inventory has been stolen or is missing.

> The Philadelphia center scandal was touched off by an innocent error by a mail clerk at the facility. Seeing a check for $250,000 to be mailed to P. Morris Co., the clerk sent it off to a legitimate defense supplier, the Philip Morris tobacco company. Philip Morris returned it with a letter explaining that the firm had already been paid once for the order.
>
> Closer examination of the check showed that it was supposed to have been sent to P. Morris Co., a dummy corporation with an answering-service address in Philadelphia. Someone at the support center had been making out duplicate checks which were to be sent to phony contractors and cashed by participants in the scam.
>
> Investigators tracked down some $1.6 million in fake payments which were ready to be mailed out. But the FBI was unable to pinpoint the culprits. Because of the lax accounting procedures, there were hundreds of possible suspects who could have engineered the ripoff.[33] (© 1978 United Feature Syndicate Corp.)

Since some 1.2 billion dollars' worth of orders could not be validated due to the nature of the center's accounting system, thirty professional accountants were sent from Washington to look into the matter. Such waste and theft is, however, only a small portion of the costs of defense to American society.

The Consequences of Defense Policies

By the mid-1970s many economists and social analysts had escalated their criticisms of the social costs of defense. First, there was the Vietnam War with its 150 billion-dollar price tag and its loss of 55,000 American lives. The social costs of Vietnam are something from which American society has yet to recover. By 1968, three and one-half years into the war's escalation, the costs were already prohibitive. Terrence McCarthy calculated that by 1968 the war had:

> reduced the purchasing power of the consumer's dollar by almost 9 percent;
>
> distorted the economy by adding only 1.6 million production workers to manufacturing payrolls compared with 2.3 million to government payrolls;

caused a loss in housing construction of at least 750,000 dwelling units;

raised interest rates to the highest levels in a century;

deepened the poverty of the poor by increasing food prices 10 percent;

raised the interest-bearing federal debt by $23 billion;

produced a $20 billion federal deficit in fiscal 1968 even assuming a tax increase;

rendered impossible required expenditures for renovation of America's decaying cities;

increased the adverse balance of payments insupportably;

cost the nation the gold cover of its dollar;

forced the establishing of a two-tier price for gold throughout the world;

generated the greatest threat of inflation since the Civil War. . . .[34]

Second, according to one study by the Center for Defense Information, "military spending is one of the least effective ways to create jobs." [35] The study, made in 1977, indicated that for every one billion dollars spent on defense, only 45,800 jobs were created. But for every one billion spent on public service employment, 98,000 jobs could have been created. Or, a one billion-dollar investment in nondefense civilian production would have created 53,000 jobs.[36] Although unethical and illegal defense contracting practices have been supported by the American beliefs in "free enterprise" and the need for a strong national defense, ironically neither has been provided by the system.

Third, there is a growing realization that defense spending is a major cause of inflation, robbing consumers of purchasing power. As *The New York Times* has said:

> Virtually all economists agree . . . that military spending tends to be inflationary. This is because it puts money into the hands of workers without expanding the supply of goods they can buy — the consumer market for missiles and the like being somewhat limited — thereby driving up the prices of goods like autos and refrigerators and machine tools.
>
> [Also, arms makers on cost-plus contracts] tend to bid up the prices of resources and skilled labor. This produces a cost-push effect that feeds inflationary pressure throughout the rest of the economy.[37]

Fourth, defense spending continues to absorb over one-half of the money in the federal budget that is not a fixed cost and one-half of the federal research and development funds. This consumes money that could be used for badly needed social programs necessary to provide all Americans with an adequate quality of life. As Melman has said:

> One Polaris sub with missiles costs the country 331 elementary schools, or 6,811 hospital beds, or 13,723 low-rent public housing units. The price of building a colossal military power, and endlessly adding to it, has been the depletion of American society, a process now well advanced in industry, civilian technology . . . education, medical care, and the quality of life.[38]

Fifth, constant military spending for more arms has contributed to international tension between the United States and the Soviet Union, who are locked in an international arms race. More arms make it less likely that either country would survive a full-scale war and thus create more insecurities. The only alternative is to enter into treaties that limit the production of weapons, and this would, of course, diminish the profits that accrue from military spending. In the meantime, the United States had, by mid-1977, produced 30,000 deliverable nuclear warheads, also producing three additional warheads every day. The United States already possesses enough nuclear weaponry to destroy the 218 cities of the Soviet Union with a population of 100,000 or more over 230 times. Should a nuclear war erupt, it is estimated that both the United States and the Soviet Union would lose 95 to 120 million of their citizens, and three-fourths of their respective economies would be destroyed.[39]

Despite these catastrophic potentials, the military-industrial complex continues to spend millions of dollars each year to convince itself and the American public of the dangers of Soviet aggression and of the United States' inferior position in the arms race. General David Shoup, former Commandant of the Marine Corps and head of the Joint Chiefs of Staff, has noted that all service associations (i.e., the Association of the U.S. Army, the Navy League, and the Air Force Association) publish journals that reflect "the party line" within the various services. Defense industries support these "journals" with expensive ads that also lend credence to the anti-Soviet viewpoint. Thus develops an atmosphere among active-duty and retired personnel that allows them to believe their own propaganda, contributing to the creation of what General Shoup has termed a militaristic culture, where force of arms is viewed as an acceptable solution to international problems.[40]

The Defense Department also possesses an immense propaganda apparatus. Its various public-relations divisions employ over 6,000 people who lobby before Congress, make their own movies, aid Hollywood movie makers in making films, sponsor conferences for both defense contractors and civic organizations, and provide speakers to "educate" civic organizations concerning the nature of the communist threat.[41] To date, there has been no effective organization capable of either countering the militaristic view of the world situation or of informing the American people of the international dimensions of deviant behavior (which are masked by the complex's appeals to patriotism and anticommunism).

Moreover, some critics believe that the prevalence of an exaggerated Cold War ideology (i.e., fear of the Russian military threat) sometimes results in the manipulation of public opinion in order to win increased defense funds. As H. R. Rodgers has argued:

> If all else fails, the Pentagon can always use its secret weapon to get its way — the big scare. Despite the fact that the United States already has the nuclear capacity to drop the equivalent of six tons of TNT on every person on earth, the scare campaign always centers on some alleged deficiency in our military capacity. During recent years we have had the bomber gap scare, which led to a considerable increase in defense spending. Only after the funds were committed was it discovered that at the time of the supposed bomber shortage, the United States had 680 bombers and the Soviet Union had between 150 and 200. . . . Recently we have had the missile gap; once again, after the funds were spent, it came to light that the Pentagon had exaggerated Russian missile strength by 30 times.[42]

And most recently there has been a naval gap. The U.S. Navy claimed in 1978 that in the last fifteen years Russia has launched "205 major combatants"[43] compared to 165 for the U.S. Yet subsequent investigations revealed that most of the Soviet's "major warships" were small patrol boats and escort vessels, and that, regarding major surface warships, the U.S. had actually outbuilt Russia 122 units to 57.

In 1976 one national news magazine reported that the Soviet Navy possessed 3,300 ships to America's 478. However, even U.S. admiral Stansfield Turner (later director of the CIA) had to admit that the figures included every "seventy-five foot tugboat and barge, and comparing heaven knows what."[44]

This is not to say that Russia represents no threat to American interests. What there is a genuine need for, however, is an *honest, objective* appraisal of the Soviet threat. This the Pentagon has yet to provide the American public.

Finally, it now appears that there is a good chance that the Pentagon may be experiencing a genuine crisis in preparedness due to its policy of throwing money into costly and sophisticated weapons systems. Recent reports indicate that critical needs exist for such items as ammunition and adequately trained personnel. The problem, again, is a question of priorities:

> There are far too many extremely costly programs in the military budget today. We cannot simultaneously: acquire a vast new arsenal of nuclear weapons; expand costly forces for

defending countries in Europe and Asia; add to substantial forces for rapid intervention everywhere in the world; enlarge a very expensive navy for deployment on all the world's oceans; develop new weapons which are always better than Soviet weapons; and keep existing forces at a high level of readiness and training.[45]

Thus one of the most significant consequences of the practices described above is that they so negatively affect the ability of the U.S. to muster a truly adequate defense capability.

DEVIANCE AND MULTINATIONAL CORPORATIONS

The Structure of the International Economy

Deviant behavior by multinational corporations stems in large part from the structure of the economic relationships between multinational corporations and foreign, especially Third World, nations. What began as a need to rebuild war-torn economies and stimulate trade had, by the 1970s, become an important aspect of the American economy. Thus, during the 1960s American multinational firms invested forty-seven billion dollars overseas, largely in Western Europe and Canada. This created some 3.3 million new jobs overseas. By 1976, U.S.-owned firms were selling more goods overseas (212 billion dollars) than U.S.-based firms were exporting (only 76.6 billion dollars).[46] Thus, *American-owned foreign companies now sell three dollars' worth of goods overseas for each dollar's worth of goods exported overseas from the United States.*

In Asia, Africa, and Latin America (the Third World), U.S. military and foreign aid has created a safe environment for investment by U.S. multinational corporations. Between 1946 and 1976 the U.S. gave 69.197 billion dollars in military aid to the nations of Asia, Africa, and Latin America. During this period, U.S. investments in these areas jumped from 5.7 billion dollars in 1950 to 28.5 billion in 1974.[47] The importance of these investments to industrialized nations is great. They account for two-thirds of the net income received from all foreign investments.[48]

With so much profit and investment potential at stake, both in Western Europe and in the Third World, it is not surprising that a good deal of bribery money for securing contracts and other favors relating to a positive business climate has been spent. But the need for profits and economic growth are only part of the reason for the expansion of U.S. business overseas.

A second reason for the profitability of overseas business activity relates to labor costs. The companies listed in Table 5–2 are firms whose

Table 5–2: Differential Hourly Wage Rates* in Selected Industries.
Underdeveloped Nations vs. U.S.A.

	Average Hourly Rate (*in Dollars*)	
	Underdeveloped Nations	*U.S.A.*
Consumer Electronic Products		
Hong Kong	0.27	3.13
Mexico	0.53	2.31
Taiwan	0.14	2.56
Office-machine Parts		
Hong Kong	0.30	2.92
Taiwan	0.38	3.67
Mexico	0.48	2.97
Semiconductors		
Korea	0.33	3.32
Singapore	0.29	3.36
Jamaica	0.30	2.23
Wearing Apparel		
Mexico	0.53	2.29
British Honduras	0.28	2.11
Costa Rica	0.34	2.28
Honduras	0.45	2.27
Trinidad	0.40	2.49

* Hourly wage rates for a given country and the U.S.A. are for comparable task and skill levels.

Source: Richard L. Barnet and Ronald E. Muller, *Global Reach* (New York: Simon and Schuster, 1974), p. 127. © 1974 by Richard L. Barnet and Ronald E. Muller. Reprinted by permission of Simon and Schuster, a Division of Gulf & Western Corporation.

employees are unionized. Even though only about twenty percent of the labor force is unionized, union members receive higher wages than nonunionized workers. Large corporations in the United States thus face high labor costs, and are, therefore, motivated to find situations where labor costs are less expensive. Table 5–2 reveals that wages in the Third World are very low, compared to the U.S. Wage rates in most industries in the Third World are between two and three dollars *per hour* less than comparable wages in the U.S.

This search for cheap labor has several negative consequences for American society. Specifically, as U.S. business moves abroad, at home "unemployment mounts; the importation of foreign goods increases which results in a flow of dollars abroad; and as our balance of payments deficit increases, the value of the dollar declines relative to other currencies, which increases inflation and causes other economic problems." [49] While none of this is criminal or unethical, it does illustrate that the goals of multinational corporations center around the pursuit of profits and investments and not necessarily around what may be beneficial to the nation as a whole.

Another of the needs of American economic life concerns a dependence on foreign countries, especially poor (Third World) nations, for strategic raw materials. As C. H. Anderson has said: "One half of the sixty-two strategic materials listed by the Department of Defense require 80% to 100% importation, and five-sixths require at least 40%. Three fourths of these materials are taken from underdeveloped areas." [50] One such key ingredient is bauxite. According to Zeitlin, eighty to ninety percent of the bauxite supply comes from foreign sources and its importance is in the making of aluminum, which is used for airplanes, and other material.[51] Probably most important is that the United States is self-sufficient only in a few industrial resources, such as sulphur, magnesium, and coal, and is depleting its supply of these and other resources so rapidly that dependence on foreign sources will probably continue to increase in the future.

Our position is that the nature of the American economy, with its needs for investment outlets, cheap labor, and access to scarce raw materials, has created an environment in which certain types of deviance tend to occur. Regarding multinational corporations, such deviance, in recent years, has centered around illegal payments to foreign governments and the exporting of hazardous goods.

Multinationals and Bribery

According to Sorensen, a bribe is

> a payment voluntarily offered for the purpose of inducing a public official to do or omit something of his (her) lawful duty, or to exercise his (her) official discretion in favor of the payor's request for a contract, concession of privilege on some basis other than the merits.[52]

By the 1970s even the most ardent supporters of America's multinational corporations have admitted that "companies can't condone the practice (of bribery). Responsible executives are right to insist that it shouldn't happen. Many companies have rules prohibiting it. . . . But nearly four years of increasingly sensational disclosures add up to a lot of monkey business." [53] The disclosures of bribery of foreign governments and of American officials reveal a disturbing pattern of corporate secrecy, unaccountability to stockholders, and, in some cases, the undermining of American national security and foreign policy. Corporations insist that bribes are an established custom in many foreign countries and are a necessary part of doing business, but the effect and nature of many of the bribes seem to cast some doubt on this claim. A member of the Securities and Exchange Commission has called the practice of international bribery something of a "national crisis," and an examination of the situation on a case-by-case basis leaves little doubt about the accuracy of the charge.[54]

Lockheed: bribes at the taxpayers' expense? The Lockheed corporation from 1969 to 1975 spent 202 million dollars, paying agents to deliver the money and bribe the government officials in Indonesia, the Philippines, Saudi Arabia, Japan, France, Germany, Turkey, Italy, and the Netherlands. Laundered funds in secret Swiss bank accounts, top secret memos, slush funds, the toppling of governments, and suicides by some of the figures involved characterized the intrigue. Lockheed had been given a 250 million-dollar loan guarantee by the U.S. government in 1971 in an effort to stave off bankruptcy, but Lockheed's connections within the American government run much deeper than being able to secure loans, as some of the incidents in which it has been involved reveal:

1. In October, 1975, a set of papers were made public revealing that Lockheed was aided by the CIA in making bribes to the Indonesian government. When President Sukarno of Indonesia was deposed in a coup, Lockheed asked the American Embassy in Jakarta to have its CIA staff inquire about the relationship of Izaac Dassad, Lockheed's agent, and the new government. The inquiries were made and it was reported that Dassad had a good relationship with the new regime. Subsequently, Lockheed arranged for its agent to deliver bribes to Indonesian Air Force officials involving the status of 300,000 dollars' worth of spare airplane parts and 40 million dollars' worth of plane sales in 1973–1974. The bribes were treated as commissions that amounted to three percent of the price of the planes and five to ten percent of the other contracts (totalling in excess of 1.2 million dollars). In addition, Lockheed's chairman later revealed that many of the bribes were claimed on the company's income tax return as direct business deductions.

2. In Saudi Arabia, Lockheed retained the services of one Adnan N. Khashoggi, president of Triad, the Arab world's first multinational conglomerate. Lockheed paid Mr. Khashoggi a staggering 106 million dollars over a five-year period in "commissions" and bribes. Some of this money went directly "under the table" to Saudi officials and other funds were deposited in secret bank accounts of the officials in Liechtenstein and Switzerland. Through a complicated arrangement with Khashoggi's companies and Lockheed's subsidiaries in Switzerland, Lockheed arranged for taxes on the deals to be paid in Switzerland,

where the tax rate is much lower than in the U.S. And the dummy corporation set up in Switzerland by Lockheed rerouted some of the profits to the U.S., where no profits were claimed because amounts equalling the rerouted profits were deducted as costs for "marketing services" (provided, of course, by Khashoggi's firm. Thus the money moved from the Saudi government, to Lockheed in Switzerland, to Lockheed in California, to Khashoggi in Switzerland. The losers on the deal were taxpayers in both Switzerland and in the U.S.[55]

3. It was established, during a hearing by the Senate Subcommittee on Multinational Corporations, that Lockheed had in some cases paid bribes for contracts where no competition for its products existed. Lockheed virtually admitted that bribery is profitable because the bribes are not only deducted from taxes, but are tacked onto contracts in the form of costs. Moreover, paying bribes where no competition exists means that foreign governments are encouraged to spend money on products like arms, when such money might go for other necessary commodities, like food for a given nation's hungry.

4. In 1976 it was revealed that Lockheed had paid commissions of about seven million dollars to its Japanese agent, Yoshio Kodama, a known right-wing political extremist and convicted war criminal. Kodama was hired to convince a Japanese airline to contract for some 130 Lockheed Tri-Star jets. He had also been instrumental in helping Lockheed obtain a contract from the Japanese government in 1958 for its F-104 fighters. Lockheed succeeded in getting a contract made by the Japanese with Grumann, another American firm, cancelled. In this deal, about 5.6 million dollars in bribes were paid.[56] Talks in 1972 among then Japanese prime minister Tanaka, President Nixon, and Secretary of State Kissinger resulted in the Japanese agreeing to purchase 320 million dollars' worth of American civilian aircraft. Shortly after this meeting, the Japanese airline announced a cancellation of a contract with McDonnell Douglas in favor of a Tri-Star purchase. It is not known if President Nixon and Secretary of State Kissinger played a role in this transaction. Later that year, Prime Minister Tanaka and twenty Japanese industrialists and political officials were sent to jail for their actions relating to the Tri-Star deal.

5. In addition to the Japanese crisis, in 1976 it was revealed that Lockheed had paid some 8 million dollars in commissions and bribes to agents in Turkey, France, Italy, Germany, and Japan, as well as an additional 1.1 million to a highly placed Netherlands official. Moreover, Lockheed paid 12 million dollars to

the West German Christian Social Union, a right-wing political group, to influence a Tri-Star deal there. Files on the transaction mysteriously disappeared from the Defense Ministry, according to a former West German defense minister. In sum, the influence of Lockheed on the international scene has not been beneficial either to American taxpayers or to American foreign policy. As Hougan has claimed:

> Lockheed has invaded the treasury of a dozen nations . . . destabilized the governments of three allies, undermined NATO . . . boosted inflation, and prompted a series of newspaper sensations that appeared to have resulted in suicides as far apart as Tokyo and L.A. (including the suicide of one of its former executives).[57]

By 1976 bribery scandals among U.S. multinational corporations had become almost commonplace. United Brands, Northrop Aviation, Phillips Petroleum, Exxon, Gulf Oil, and Mobil Oil had all been implicated in major episodes of bribery abroad. Exxon, whose slogan relates to building a strong America, was exposed as donating campaign funds (secretly) to the Italian Communist Party. The president of United Brands, Eli Black, leaped forty-four floors to his death in 1975 over revelations that his company had paid the president of the Honduras and other Honduran officials 1.25 million dollars in order to have the tax rate on bananas exported from the Honduras lowered by seventy cents per box.[58] In almost all these cases no one was convicted of a crime. Most of the executives held responsible for these policies were either promoted and given sizeable raises, or were retired with generous pensions and given valuable blocks of stock. Legislation was finally passed in early 1978 that made international bribery illegal and subject to a fine of up to one million dollars. Finally, in June, 1979, Lockheed was convicted of eight felony counts (four of wire fraud and four counts of making false statements) as well as two misdemeanors in concealing its bribes to Prime Minister Tanaka of Japan in 1973–1974. Lockheed was not convicted under the law which outlaws bribery, but was fined 647,000 dollars for concealing such bribes.[59] No Lockheed officials were sent to jail for their crimes. Whether the 1978 law will deter corporations from making further illegal payoffs remains to be seen.

The consequences of bribery by multinationals. It has been noted that bribery by multinationals is now a crime. This is the case not merely because such payments are immoral, but because this practice has resulted in a number of very negative consequences to (1) the corporations themselves, and (2) America's foreign policy and economy. Such consequences result in part because bribes made by multinational corporations are hidden from the stockholders.   Such secrecy within the corporation means that:

1. The prospective investor or stockholder, as well as the government, does not have an accurate financial picture of the corporation, and

2. These practices can be concealed only through various devious means or through improper accounting procedures, both of which endanger the credibility of corporations.[60]

Thus, at home, revelations of corporate bribery have caused distrust among both stockholders and the public at large.

Third, the bribery of foreign officials, especially in countries where it is viewed as unethical or illegal, has endangered American relations with other governments.   This was particularly the case in Japan where the Lockheed scandal helped create the greatest post-World War II crisis in Japanese politics.   Clearly the communists could not have hoped for a more helpful event.

Fourth, bribes by multinationals often endanger the operations of the corporation from an internal standpoint:

In abiding or abetting corruption of public officials, a company gradually corrupts itself.   No organization can remain for long in a state of moral schizophrenia, violating legal or ethical norms abroad while seeking to maintain its institutional integrity at home.   In time, the lower standards accepted as the way of life abroad will corrupt standards of corporate life at home.[61]

Finally, it has been suggested that such bribes not only failed to accomplish the goal of increasing business abroad, but that they may have actually been detrimental to such commerce.   Sorensen has insisted that there

. . . was no gain to our country's balance of payments or economy when U.S. companies paid bribes to win a contract that would otherwise have gone to another U.S. company.   On the contrary, the added cost of these improper contracts to the host country further weakened the market for other U.S. exporters.   The fact that some American companies have succeeded in these countries without the payment of bribes is an indication that U.S. exports will not suffer all that severely from an end to such payments. Those governments desirous of obtaining U.S. technology and quality will unquestionably learn to buy our goods without any special inducement.[62]

Thus bribery by multinationals appears to carry with it a number of ironic and negative consequences for American society as a whole. The same may be said about another deviant practice of some multinational firms, namely the exportation of hazardous products.

The Practice of Corporate Dumping

By the late 1970s a practice known as "corporate dumping" had aroused a good deal of concern among certain public-interest groups and government agencies. The practice involves exporting goods which have either been (1) banned or (2) not approved for sale in the United States. Most often the greatest market for such unsafe products is among the poor of the Third World. This is because hazardous products are often legal in such countries, and because many of the poor in these nations are illiterate, and, therefore, often unaware of the hazards involved with the use of such products.

Examples of the products involved in corporate dumping are growing at a rapid pace. The following are some of these examples:

> An undisclosed number of farmers and over 1,000 water buffalos died suddenly in Egypt after being exposed to leptophos, a chemical pesticide which was never registered for domestic use by the Environmental Protection Agency (EPA) but was exported to at least 30 countries.
>
> After the Dalkon Shield intrauterine device killed at least 17 women in the United States, the manufacturer withdrew it from the domestic market. It was sold overseas after the American recall and is still in common use in some countries.
>
> No one knows how many children may develop cancer since several million children's garments treated with a carcinogenic fire retardant called Tris were shipped overseas after being forced off the domestic market by the Consumer Product Safety Commission (CPSC).
>
> Lomotil, an effective anti-diarrhea medicine sold only by prescription in the U.S. because it is fatal in amounts just slightly over the recommended doses, was sold over the counter in Sudan, in packages proclaiming it was "used by astronauts during Gemini and Apollo space flights" and recommended for use by children as young as 12 months.
>
> Winstrol, a synthetic male hormone, which was found to stunt the growth of American children, is freely available in Brazil, where it is recommended as an appetite stimulant for children.
>
> Depo-Provera, an injectable contraceptive banned for such use in the United States because it caused malignant tumors in beagles and monkeys, is sold by the Upjohn Co. in 70 other countries, where it is widely used in U.S.-sponsored population control programs.
>
> 450,000 baby pacifiers of the type that has caused choking deaths have been exported by at least five manufacturers since a ban was proposed by the CPSC. 120,000 teething rings that did not meet recently established CPSC standards were declared for export and are on sale right now in Australia.[63]

There have been incidents where corporate dumping was aided by government policy. In one instance, the population office of the Agency for International Development (AID) purchased, for distribution in the Third World, hundreds of shoe-boxed-sized cartons of unsterilized Dalkon Shields. The birth-control device, which causes uterine infections, blood poisoning, spontaneous abortion in pregnant women, and perforation of the uterus, was sold to AID at a forty-eight percent discount because of its unsterile condition.[64] The device was distributed in forty-two nations, largely in the Third World. Moreover, insufficient information concerning the use and hazards of the shield accompanied the shipment.

Some companies are dumping workplace hazards, as well as hazardous products in poor nations. One example is the case of asbestos, a cancer causing agent. Thanks to the Occupational Carcinogens Control Act of 1976, fines of 1,000 dollars for violations and 5,000 dollars for repeat violations are provided for U.S. manufacturers who expose workers to carcinogenic agents. However, no such regulations protect workers from contracting cancer from asbestos fibers. On the contrary, Mexican law merely provides a light fine (forty-five to ninety dollars) for failure to warn workers that they are working around a health hazard. As a result, U.S. asbestos makers increasingly locate plants in Mexico and other Third World nations with lax workplace hazard laws (e.g., Brazil) and are now producing large quantities of asbestos there.[65]

Corporate dumping is quite undesirable for two main reasons. First, it poses serious health hazards to the poor and uninformed consumers of the Third World, which, in the long run, contributes to the anti-Americanism of many nonaligned nations. And such anti-Americanism is not infrequently exploited by communist bloc nations. Second, many types of corporate dumping possess a boomerang effect. That is, some of the hazardous products sold abroad by American companies are often used in the manufacture of goods that are exported to the United States and other developed nations.

> The "vast majority" of the nearly one billion pounds of pesticides used each year in the Third World is applied to crops that are then exported *back* to the U.S. and other rich countries. . . . This fact undercuts the industry's main argument defending pesticide dumping. "We see nothing wrong with helping the hungry world eat," is the way a Velsicol Chemical Company executive puts it. Yet, the entire dumping process by-passes the local population's need for food. The example in which DBCP manufactured by Amvac is imported into Central America by Castle & Cooke to grow fruit destined for U.S. dinner tables is a case in point.[66]

The boomerang effect of corporate dumping may represent the breeding ground of still another major scandal regarding the practices of multinational corporations, and certain U.S. government agencies, in the Third World.

We are not suggesting here that deliberate racist and genocidal policies are being practiced by certain corporations and government agencies. What we are suggesting is that corporate dumping may well have such effects on the nonwhite peoples of the world. The same may be said concerning support by corporations and government for regimes which violate human rights.

HUMAN RIGHTS, MULTINATIONALS, AND U.S. FOREIGN POLICY

The United States, under Presidents Ford and Carter, has gone on record as supporting the cause of "human rights" around the world. President Carter, in a United Nations speech of March 17, 1977, pledged to "work with potential adversaries as well as . . . close friends to advance the cause of human rights." [67]   The U.S. is also a party to the International Bill of Rights.   Passed by the U.N. General Assembly in 1948, this document supports a variety of civil and economic rights, and specifically pledges member nations not to subject anyone to "torture or to cruel, inhuman or degrading treatment, or punishment" or to "arbitrary arrest, detention, or exile." [68]   Finally, the United States is also a signatory to the famous Helsinki Agreement of 1975 which contains a detailed human-rights clause.   The clause specifically states that participating nations will "respect human rights and fundamental freedoms, including freedom of thought, conscience, religion, or belief, all without distinctions as to race, sex, language, or religion." [69]   Thus by pronouncement and by legal agreement, the U.S. has firmly committed itself to the cause of human rights.

Unfortunately, there is a mounting body of evidence which indicates that U.S. policy makers have on many occasions either (1) placed in power and/or (2) aided in retaining power some of the world's most repressive dictatorships.   The chief characteristic of such regimes is that they are right-wing (military) dictatorships, and, hence, friendly to the goals of multinational capitalism.   Chomsky and Herman have stated that with the U.S.' support (ranging from foreign aid to military protection), many Third World regimes have done away with democratic practices and instituted brutally repressive measures, including arbitrary imprisonment, torture, death squads, and kidnapping.

In fact, a pattern now exists where U.S. economic and military aid (and aid from U.S.-dominated lending agencies) has been "positively related to investment climate (for U.S. multinationals) and inversely (negatively) related to the maintenance of a democratic order and human rights." [70]   This relationship is described in Table 5–3.   Moreover,

Table 5–3: The Relationship between U.S. Aid, Investment Climate, and Human Rights in Ten Countries.

Country	Strategic Political Dates[1] (1)	Effects on Democracy: Positive (+) or Negative (−) (2)	Increased Use of Torture or Death Squads: Means an (−) (3)	Increase in No. of Political Prisoners: Means an (−) (4)	Improvement in Investment Climate: Tax Laws Eased (+) (5a)	Improvement in Investment Climate: Labor Repressed (+) (5b)	Economic Aid (% Change) (6)	Military Aid (% Change) (7)	(6) + (7) (% Change) (8)	U.S. and Multi-national Credits (% Change) (9)	Total Aid (8) + (9) (% Change) (10)
Brazil	1964	−	−	−	+	+	+ 14	−40	− 7	+ 180	+ 112
Chile	1973	−	−	−	+	+	+558	− 8	+259	+1,079	+ 770
Dominican Republic	1965	−	−	NA	+	+	+ 57	+10	+ 52	+ 305	+ 133
Guatemala	1954	−	−	NA	+	NA	NA	NA	NA	NA	+5,300
Indonesia	1965	−	−	−	+	+	− 81	−79	− 81	+ 653	62
Iran	1953	−	−	−	+	+	NA	NA	NA	NA	+ 900
Philippines	1972	−	−	−	+	+	+204	+67	+143	+ 171	+ 161
South Korea	1972	−	−	−	+	+	− 52	−56	− 55	+ 183	9
Thailand	1973	+	+	NA	−	−	− 63	−64	− 64	+ 218	5
Uruguay	1973	−	−	−	+	+	− 11	+ 9	− 2	+ 32	+ 21

Sources: 1. Information on torture and political prisoners mostly from the *Amnesty International Report on Torture, 1975* and *The Amnesty International Report, 1975–76,* 1976. Supplemented with data from newspaper articles, journals, and books on the specific countries. Data on investment climate largely from articles, journals, and books on the specific countries. 2. Data on aid taken from *U.S. Overseas Loans and Grants and Assistance from International Organizations,* A.I.D., 1972 and 1976 editions, for years 1962–1975. Data previous to 1962 taken from *Historical Statistics of the United States,* Bicentennial Edition, Dept. of Commerce, 1975.
Source: N. Chomsky and E. S. Herman, "U.S. vs. Human Rights in the Third World," *Monthly Review* 29 (July/August, 1977), pp. 30–31. Reprinted by permission.

the decline in aid for South Korea and Chile is somewhat misleading. The decline in South Korea's aid was caused by the end of expenditures for the Vietnam War in which South Korea participated. And the decline in aid for Chile was in fact due to a successful right-wing coup (supported by the CIA) in 1973 and to which high levels of aid had been given before that date. And the U.S., between 1973 and 1978, continued its aid to many of the regimes cited by Chomsky and Herman as well as to others which have been cited by organizations like Amnesty International, the UN Commission on Human Rights, and the International Commission on Human Rights for persistent "torture, assassination, and arbitrary arrest." [71]

Moreover, the Foreign Assistance Act of 1974 provides that the president "shall substantially reduce or terminate security assistance to any government which engages in gross violations of . . . human rights." [72] Under this act, it became illegal (as of July 1, 1975) to provide aid to any law-enforcement organization (e.g., police prisons) of any foreign government. However, under the International Narcotics Control Act, both training and weapons *have* been given to police departments in many foreign countries, including those listed in Table 5–3.

In the cases of Guatemala (1953), Iran (1953), and the Dominican Republic (1965), not to mention South Vietnam, either U.S. troops and/or the American CIA played an active role in actually installing (either through aid or armed forces or both) such regimes.[73] Aside from bringing favorable advantages to multinationals, these regimes have done little to improve the lot of the people over whom they rule. This is especially the case in Latin America.

> *Item:* In Chile (1973), following a U.S. supported coup which overthrew President Allende, a socialist, 45,000 people were arrested, tortured, killed, and/or exiled. Several university facilities were closed down, all left-of-center political parties prohibited, and press censorship rigidly enforced.

> *Item:* Following an invasion by U.S. Marines in 1965, a wave of torture swept the Dominican Republic in 1970. A disappearance or murder was reported every thirty-four hours. Moreover, in 1975 it was reported that the Philip Morris Company had paid over 136,000 dollars in bribes to various Dominican officials in return for favorable tax ruling and other favors.[74]

One of the most significant examples of such support concerns Iran. There the American CIA was responsible for placing the Shah's family in power in 1953 when it assisted in overthrowing leftist Prime Minister Mohammad Mossadeq, in a violent coup. From 1953 until the 1979 Khomeini revolution, the Congress, the U.S. military, the CIA, and private corporate interests all supported the Shah's army and secret police with various types of aid. Under the U.S. Office of Public Safety program, Iran, between 1961 and 1973, received 1.7 billion dollars. This money was used to purchase "police hardware" (e.g., guns, tear-gas grenades, computers, patrol cars, and so on), and to train 179 Iranian police officials at the International Police Academy in Washington, D.C. (and other special U.S. police schools). From 1946 to 1976, Iran received 1.6 billion dollars under a variety of U.S. military-assistance programs. These programs involved outright grants of arms, equipment, and services; credit for the purchasing of U.S. arms; training of Iranian military personnel; and "subsidies" awarded under an act designed to aid threatened pro-U.S. regimes. Between 1950 and 1976, 11,025 Iranian military officers received training under these programs. Iran, aside from dealing with the U.S. government to purchase arms, also purchased them from private concerns. The Bell Helicopter Company helped Iran develop a Sky Cavalry Brigade, operating from helicopters, which was modeled after the U.S. units that fought in Vietnam in this manner.[75] Finally, between 1971 and 1978, the U.S. sold to Iran 15 billion dollars in military supplies,[76] and had stationed in Iran at the moment of the revolution some 40,000 military "advisors," [77] along with an unknown number of CIA agents. In short, the United States had a long history of assistance to the Shah's regime.

In Iran, almost 1,500 people were arrested every month when the Shah was in power. In one day alone (on June 5, 1963), the SAVAK (Iran's secret police) and the Shah's army killed 6,000 Iranian citizens. Amnesty International's report for 1975 indicated that Iranian authorities had arrested and imprisoned between 25,000 and 100,000 political prisoners.[78] The press in Iran was strictly controlled by the police under the Shah's direct orders. Minorities in Iran were not allowed to learn their native languages, and poverty was widespread. Iran was a nation where political stability was maintained by repression — a nation on the brink of massive political turmoil.

Since 1973 Iran was one of a number of nations cited by organizations such as Amnesty International, the International Commission of Jurists, and the United Nations Commission on Human Rights for consistant abuses of human rights.[79] Thus U.S. officials and the press knew full well what was taking place there, yet the government continued to support the Shah with various types of military aid, and the press remained nearly silent on the Shah's abuses.

By mid-1980 the United States had paid a tragic price for its rather blind support of the Shah's regime. In 1979 an anti-American revolution led by Moslem holy man Ayatollah Ruhollah Khomeini, exiled from Iran by the government in 1963, overthrew the Shah's rule. U.S. support for the Shah may also have been partially responsible for the catastrophic increases in oil prices since 1973 (see Chapter 2). A number of sources, including Jack Anderson[80] and CBS's "60 Minutes" have reported that the Shah:

1. was installed in power in the 1950s when the Rockefellers helped arrange the CIA coup that overthrew the Mossadegh;

2. demonstrated his gratitude to the Rockefellers by making heavy deposits of his personal funds in the Rockefeller-owned Chase Manhattan bank;

3. raised Iranian oil prices in 1973–1974 by 470 percent, with the approval of then Secretary of State Henry Kissinger, a Rockefeller associate. (This cost the oil-consuming nations of the West an estimated 95 billion dollars in inflated oil prices.)[81] The price hike was requested by the Shah in part to purchase American-made arms.

4. was admitted into the U.S. for medical care in 1979 when Chase Manhattan president David Rockefeller and Henry Kissinger "organized a pressure campaign to bring the Shah into the United States." [82]   As a result, in November, 1979, militants overran the U.S. Embassy in Tehran, capturing sixty-one American employees following the Shah's admission to the United States for medical treatment. An aborted effort to rescue the hostages in early May, 1980, resulted in the deaths of eight American servicemen. "While the hostages' release was successfully negotiated in January of 1981, in December of 1979 Chase Manhattan filed a $366 million lawsuit against the Iranian government, largest of the over 300 suits filed against the Iranians. The suit is still pending in the Courts." [83]   The Komeini regime has spread anti-American fever throughout the Arab world, and seriously weakened the perception of the strength and consistency of American foreign policy throughout the world.

The American support for the Shah greatly enriched the Chase Manhattan bank, which continues to be the repository for the Shah's sizeable fortune, and the Exxon Oil Company, which is controlled through Rockefeller trust funds and private holdings.[84]   Yet no congressional investigation into these events has been conducted. The consequences suffered in return for U.S. support for the Shah are also indicative of other consequences of supporting regimes which violate human rights.

The Consequences of Support for Repressive Governments

The assessment of the American support for regimes that violate human rights may be made by viewing (1) the conditions of people who live under such regimes, and (2) the effect of such support on U.S. foreign policy.   It must be stressed that the inhabitants of the Third

World often exist under conditions that violate elementary human rights. Thus throughout Asia, Africa, and Latin America:

> An estimated 1.5 billion people are without effective medical care.
>
> Developing countries have an average of 4,000 people per doctor; in some, the ratio goes above 50,000 per doctor.
>
> Half the school-age children are not yet in schools.
>
> 10,000 persons per day in the Third World die from starvation, and another 1.5 billion there suffer from malnutrition.
>
> Unemployment in the Third World is now 30% in most countries.
>
> Per capita income in most Third World nations ranges from less than $250 per year (e.g., Ethiopia, India, Kenya, and Pakistan) to less than $1,600 per year (e.g., Turkey, Mexico, and Chile).
>
> More than 700 million adults are unable to read and write.[85]

To the extent that U.S. support for regimes which violate human rights is based on arms rather than development, U.S. policy becomes a factor in exacerbating these wretched conditions. While it is true that not all Third World peoples live under repressive dictatorships, the vast majority of Third World governments are repressive. Thus, as of 1978, the United States sold 13.6 billion dollars' worth of arms overseas, about half of which went to Third World nations.[86] Such sales help maintain repressive regimes and fuel wars in the Third World, but they do not foster peaceful economic development.

In the India-Pakistan War of 1965, for example, "the Sherman tanks of the Indian Army battled the Patton tanks of the Pakistani Army." [87] These weapons were sold to the two nations with the promise that they would be used to defensively resist communist aggression, yet they helped fight a war between the two noncommunist nations. Such incidents have also taken place between Israel and her Arab neighbors. We are not claiming that U.S. arms sales to nations in conflict are the sole cause of such wars. It is merely that the presence of arms may contribute to the heightening of tensions. In any case, it is thought by many critics that a world where 200 billion dollars a year are spent on arms cannot (or will not) spend funds for projects so desperately needed in the Third World, such as:

> Annual cost for ending world illiteracy in five-year program. Estimate by UNICEF: $1.6 billion.
>
> Annual cost for making "real impact" on the development crisis. Estimate by World Bank Chief Robert McNamara: $15 billion.
>
> Annual cost for investment in land and water needed for poor nations to meet food production targets. Estimate by U.N. Food and Agriculture Organization: $4.5 billion.

> Money needed now by poor countries to maintain essential imports. Estimate by World Bank, Washington: $5.5 billion.

> Cost for solving the crisis of cities and human settlements. Estimate by environment expert Barbara Ward: $25 billion.

> Annual cost for supplying everyone in the poor world with basic maternal health and family planning services. Estimate by food and population expert Lester Brown: $2 billion.[88]

Second, U.S. support for dictatorships in underdeveloped countries, as mentioned, helps create a favorable business climate for multinational firms, but the economic activity of multinationals in such countries is also a hindrance to development. Consider for example the effects of repatriation (return of profits made overseas to the corporation's home base):

> From 1950 to 1970 ... U.S. firms added $1.7 billion to their holdings in four ... countries — Chile, Peru, Bolivia, and Venezuela — primarily to increase production of such export commodities as copper, tin, and oil. But in the same period, these multi-nationals repatriated $11.2 billion to the United States, leaving a net loss to those countries of $9.5 billion.[89]

This net loss often translates into massive indebtedness, with such debts usually owed to multinational banks, governments, and other lending institutions made up largely of members from advanced industrial countries. The results have been very favorable for multinational banks, but devastating to Third World nations:

> From 1965 to 1972 the assets of U.S. banks overseas soared from $9 billion to $90 billion, and by 1976 they had reached $181 billion.

> A mere thirteen of America's 15,000 banks hold two-thirds of all overseas assets, and these monies account for 40% of all deposits and 50% of their profits.

> About $50 billion of such assets are loans to Third World governments, and the total indebtedness of Third World nations to all overseas lending institutions now stands at approximately $200 billion! [90]

This means that certain multinational companies now have an immense stake in preserving certain Third World governments so they may collect their loans and the interest thereon.

Such stakes have sometimes required multinationals to favor foreign-policy measures that are bitterly opposed by the American public. The Panama Canal treaties are a case in point. Thirty-nine percent of the national budget of Panama is spent just to pay the interest on that nation's national debt of 1.8 billion dollars, 77 percent of which is owed to multinational banks. Ronald Steel claims that it was for this, and other reasons favorable to business interests, that multinational firms lobbied hard for the passage of the canal treaties. The treaties assured Panama an income from the canal, plus various foreign-aid payments, which in turn assured Panama's creditors that repayment would continue.[91] The passage of the treaties also meant continued military assistance to the repressive regime of General Torrijos. This despite polls showing a majority of Americans opposed the treaties!

Not only does support for repressive regimes inhibit economic development, and foster unpopular foreign policy measures, but such support often has a detrimental effect on American foreign policy. That is, repressive regimes and American support of them are often quite unpopular with Third World peoples. Such support (as the case of Iran attests) has not infrequently touched off revolutions in such nations which are anti-American, and, often, anticapitalist as well. U.S. support for regimes which violate human rights sometimes has the effect of driving poor nations into the hands of the communists. This has been the case with Cuba, and certain African nations, and may yet be the case with such countries as Nicaragua, the Philippines, and dozens of others. Thus the policy designed to prevent communist influence in developing nations often has precisely the opposite effect.

CONCLUSION

This chapter has examined U.S. defense and foreign policy areas where deviance abounds. These include questionable defense-contracting practices, bribery, the sale of hazardous goods by multinational firms, and U.S. support for Third World regimes that violate human rights. A closer look at these three types of deviance indicates that they are quite interrelated. That is, many of the corporations that do defense contracting with the federal government have also been found guilty of bribery overseas (e.g., Lockheed and Northrop). And many of these same firms are enriched by U.S. arms sales to repressive regimes. Likewise, the needs of the American economic system for cheap labor, raw materials, and investment outlets have contributed immensely to the worldwide deployment of U.S. military forces and U.S. support for dictatorships which are obstensibly anticommunist.

The results of these policies are profitable for major corporations in the short run but may be devastating to the nation and much of the world in the long term. Waste, inefficiency, and cost overruns within the Defense Department threaten to create domestic inflation and a weakened American military capability. Bribery, the sale of hazardous products, and support for repressive regimes often foster resentment toward American corporations and government at home and overseas and further the goals of America's enemies. Such practices also hinder the economic development of the world's poorest and most desperate citizens. In short, nothing less than the future well-being of the United States and much of the world is now at stake in part because of these forms of deviance.

NOTES

1. Senator William Proxmire, *Report from Wasteland: America's Military Industrial Complex* (New York: Praeger, 1970), p. 33.

2. H. R. Rodgers, Jr., *Crisis in Democracy: A Policy Analysis of American Government* (Reading, MA: Addison-Wesley, 1978), p. 142.

3. J. Newfield, "Crime in the Suites: Will Congress Go Easy on Corporate Crooks?" *The Village Voice* (Oct. 29, 1979), p. 12.

4. C. Watson, "Campaign Wins Some Concessions," *Multinational Monitor* 1 (Winter, 1978/1979), p. 12.

5. Jack Anderson, *The Washington Post* (December 30, 1979), p. B–7.

6. S. Lens, "Thirty Years of Escalation," *The Nation* (May 27, 1978), p. 624.

7. H. Magdoff, "Militarism and Imperialism," pp. 421–426, in R. C. Edwards et al., eds., *The Capitalist System* (Englewood Cliffs, N.J.: Prentice-Hall, 1972), p. 425.

8. Lens, "Thirty Years of Escalation," p. 624.

9. M. T. Klare, *War without End: American Planning for the Next Vietnams* (New York: Knopf, 1972), p. 25.

10. R. L. Sivard, "Arms or Alms," *National Catholic Reporter* 24 (April 8, 1977), p. 8.

11. Dwight D. Eisenhower, "Farewell Address," in C. W. Pursell, Jr., ed., *The Military-Industrial Complex* (New York: Harper and Row, 1972), pp. 206–207.

12. Proxmire, *Report from Wasteland,* p. 162.

13. Reprinted from A. Sunseri, "The Military-Industrial Complex in Iowa," pp. 158–170, in B. F. Cooling, ed., *War, Business, and American Society: Historical Perspectives on the Military-Industrial Complex* (Port Washington, N.Y.: Kennikat Press, 1977), pp. 158–159. Used with permission.

14. H. Chasin and B. Chasin, *Power and Ideology* (Cambridge: Schenkman, 1974), p. 167.

15. M. Pilisuk and T. Hayden, "Is There a Military-Industrial Complex which Prevents Peace?" pp. 73–93, in R. Perrucci and M. Pilisuk, eds., *The Triple Revolution Emerging* (Boston: Little, Brown, 1971), p. 77.

16. A. Yarmolinsky, *The Military Establishment* (New York: Harper and Row, 1973), p. 67.

17. D. McDonald, "Militarism in America," *The Center Magazine* 3 (Jan., 1970), pp. 32–53, in Perrucci and Pilisuk, *The Triple Revolution Emerging,* p. 36.

18. *Ibid.,* p. 42.

19. *Ibid.,* p. 42.

20. L. P. Ellsworth, "Defense Procurement: Everyone Feeds at the Trough," *The Monopoly Makers,* M. Green, ed. (New York: Grossman, 1973), pp. 230–232.

21. *Ibid.* See also comment by Congressman Aspin in *The New York Times,* Aug. 29, 1972, cited in S. Melman, *The Permanent War Economy: American Capitalism in Decline* (New York: Simon and Schuster, 1974), p. 44.

22. See Congressional Quarterly, *The Power of the Pentagon* (Washington, D.C.: Congressional Quarterly, Inc., 1972), pp. 88–90.

23. M. Mintz and J. Cohen, *Power Inc.* (New York: Viking Press, 1976), pp. 276–277.

24. See Jack Anderson, "C-5A Costs Up Again," *The Jacksonville Times-Union* (July 26, 1979), p. A–9; and Harold Freeman, *Toward Socialism in America* (Cambridge, MA: Schenkman, 1979), p. 40.

25. Mintz and Cohen, *Power Inc.*

26. A. E. Fitzgerald, *The High Priests of Waste* (New York: W. W. Norton, 1972), p. ix.

27. Walter Adams, "The Military-Industrial Complex and the New Industrial State," *American Economic Review* 58 (May, 1968), pp. 652–655, reprinted in Pursell, *The Military-Industrial Complex*, p. 86.

28. *Ibid.*, p. 86.

29. Steven Rosen, ed., *Testing the Theory of the Military-Industrial Complex* (Lexington, MA: D. C. Heath, 1973), pp. 18–19.

30. Vandivier, Kermit, "Why Should My Conscience Bother Me?" pp. 3–31, in R. Heilbroner, ed., *In the Name of Profit* (New York: Doubleday, 1972), p. 28.

31. Mintz and Cohen, *Power Inc.*, p. 150.

32. T. Coffin, "Conversion, the Answer to Inflation and Recession," *The Washington Spectator* 2 (Feb. 1, 1979), p. 1.

33. Jack Anderson, "Defense Department Procurement Waste, Theft Staggering," *Florida Times-Union* (Nov. 10, 1978).

34. Terence McCarthy, "What the Vietnam War Has Cost," *New University Thought,* Vol. 6, no. 4 (Summer, 1968).

35. *The Defense Monitor* 7 (Sept./Oct. 1977), p. 3.

36. *Ibid.* See also E. Rothchild, "The Arms Boom and How to Stop It," *New York Review of Books* 23 (Jan. 20, 1977), p. 26.

37. Quoted in Coffin, "Conversion," p. 1.

38. S. Melman, *Our Depleted Society* (New York: Holt, Rinehart and Winston, 1965), p. 4.

39. Sivard, "Arms or Alms," p. 1.

40. D. Shoup, "The New American Militarism," *The Atlantic* (1969), reprinted in J. Skolnick and E. Currie, eds., *Crisis in American Institutions* (Boston: Little, Brown, 1973), p. 269. See also W. Fulbright, *The Pentagon Propaganda Machine* (New York: Liveright, 1970).

41. See Col. J. Donovan, *Militarism, U.S.A.* (New York: Scribner, 1970), pp. 191–210; and Fulbright, *The Pentagon Propaganda Machine.*

42. Rodgers, *Crisis in Democracy*, p. 145.

43. G. Ott, "Now It's a 'Naval Gap,'" *The Progressive* 9 (Sept., 1978), p. 22.

44. *Ibid.*

45. Center for Defense Information, *The Defense Monitor* 3 (April, 1980), p. 7.

46. H. Magdoff, "The U.S. Dollar, Petrodollars, and U.S. Imperialism," *Monthly Review* 30 (January, 1979), p. 12.

47. See A. Edward et al., eds., *The Capitalist System,* Second Edition (Englewood Cliffs, N.J.: Prentice-Hall, 1978), p. 478.

48. C. H. Anderson, *The Political Economy of Social Class* (Englewood Cliffs, N.J.: Prentice-Hall, 1974), p. 278; R. Scheer, *America After Nixon* (New York: McGraw-Hill, 1974), pp. 163–164; D. Tiranti, "High Finance and Small People," *The New Internationalist* 69 (Nov., 1979), p. 61.

49. T. Sullivan et al., *Social Problems: Divergent Perspectives* (New York: Wiley, 1980), p. 190.

50. Anderson, *The Political Economy of Social Class,* p. 280.

51. I. Zeitlin, *Capitalism and Imperialism* (Chicago: Markham, 1972), p. 103.

52. T. Sorensen, "Improper Payments Abroad: Perspectives and Proposals," *Foreign Affairs* 54 (July, 1976), p. 722.

53. G. Breckenfeld, "Multinationals at Bay: Coping with the Nation-State," *Saturday Review* (Jan. 24, 1976), pp. 170–176, in P. Wickman, ed., *Readings in Social Problems: Contemporary Perspectives* (New York: Harper and Row), p. 174. Mr. Breckenfeld is on the board of editors of *Fortune Magazine,* a leading business periodical.

54. Mintz and Cohen, *Power Inc.,* p. 153. The following section on multinational and corporate bribery is based heavily on their excellent discussion.

55. J. Hougan, "The Business of Buying Friends," *Harper's* (December, 1976), pp. 130–143, in Dushkin, ed., *Unexplored Deviance* (Conn.: Dushkin, 1978), p. 134.

56. Mintz and Cohen, *Power Inc.*

57. Hougan, "The Business of Buying Friends," p. 130.

58. Mintz and Cohen, *Power Inc.,* p. 147. See H. Maurer, "Bananagate" *The Progressive* 40 (July, 1976), pp. 30–34.

59. "Lockheed Fined $647,000 for Secret Payoffs," *Florida Times-Union* (June 2, 1979), p. B-5.

60. M. Clinard, *Illegal Corporate Behavior* (Washington, D.C.: Law Enforcement Assistance Administration, 1979), p. 200.

61. P. Gabriel, "A Case for Honesty in World Business," *Fortune* (December, 1977), p. 50.

62. Sorensen, "Improper Payments Abroad," p. 729.

63. Mark Dowie, "The Corporate Crime of the Century," *Mother Jones* 9 (November, 1979), pp. 24–25. © *Mother Jones* Magazine.

64. Barbara Ehrenreich et al., "The Charge: Genocide; The Accused: The U.S. Government," *Mother Jones* 9 (November, 1979), p. 28.

65. B. Castleman, "Industries Export Hazards," *Multinational Monitor* 1 (Winter 1978/1979), p. 14.

66. David Weir et al., "The Boomerang Crime," *Mother Jones* 9 (November, 1979), p. 43.

67. J. Cockcroft and E. Cockcroft, *The Nation* (Nov. 18, 1978), p. 523.

68. "The International Bill of Rights," in J. A. Joyce, *The New Politics of Human Rights* (New York: St. Martin's Press, 1978), p. 239.

69. "Excerpts from the final act of the 1975 Helsinki Conference," in J. F. Buncher, *Human Rights and American Diplomacy: 1975–1977* (New York: Facts on File, 1977), p. 12.

70. N. Chomsky and E. S. Herman, "U.S. vs. Human Rights in the Third World," *Monthly Review* 29 (July–Aug., 1977), p. 29.

71. M. Klare, *Supplying Repression: U.S. Support for Authoritarian Regimes Abroad* (Washington, D.C.: Institute for Policy Studies, 1977), p. 8.

72. *Ibid.,* pp. 15–16.

73. *Ibid.,* pp. 25–26.

74. G. MacEoin, "A Continent in Agony: Latin America on the Road to Fascism," *The Progressive* (March, 1979), p. 17.

75. For some interesting assessments, see Richard Falk, "Iran's Home-Grown Revolution," *The Nation* (Feb. 10, 1979), pp. 135–137; A. Cockburn and J. Ridgeway, "The Worst Domino," *The Village Voice* (Feb. 19, 1979), pp. 1,

11–12; W. Laqueur, "Trouble for the Shah," *The New Republic* (Sept. 23, 1978), pp. 18–21; M. Kondracke, "Who Lost Iran," *The New Republic* (Nov. 18, 1978), pp. 9–12; F. Halliday, "Shah's Dreams of Economic Growth Become Nightmares," *In These Times* (Dec. 26–28, 1978), p. 9.

76. Klare, *Supplying Repression,* pp. 20, 33, 36, 41, and 45.

77. Kondracke, "Who Lost Iran," p. 12.

78. R. Baraheni, "Terror in Iran," *New York Review of Books* (October 28, 1976), p. 21. See also *The Los Angeles Times* (Dec. 25, 1979), Part XI, p. 8.

79. Amnesty International, *Report on Torture* (New York: Farrar, Straus, and Giroux, 1975), pp. 227–229.

80. J. Anderson, "Rockefeller-Shah-Kissinger Connection," *The Washington Post* (December 26, 1979), p. D–12.

81. J. Anderson, "Kissinger Cleared Iran's Oil Gouge," *The Washington Post* (December 5, 1979), pp. 13–17.

82. J. Anderson, "Rockefeller-Shah-Kissinger Connection," and "60 Minutes," aired May 4, 1980.

83. *The New York Times* (November 11, 1980), p. 3.

84. J. Anderson, "Kissinger Cast in a Questionable Light," *The Washington Post* (December 10, 1979), p. C-27.

85. See Sivard, "Arms or Alms," p. 9; R. Scheer, *America After Nixon* (New York: McGraw-Hill, 1974), pp. 163–164; and Tiranti, "High Finance and Small People," p. 61.

86. Freeman, *Toward Socialism in America,* p. 46.

87. J. Roebuck and S. C. Weeber, *Political Crime in the United States* (New York: Praeger, 1978), p. 76.

88. *Daily World* in *U.N. Action Pact for World Development* (New York: United Nations Information Division, no date).

89. S. Lens, "The Sinking Dollar and the Gathering Storm," *The Progressive* (May, 1978), p. 23.

90. Tiranti, "High Finance and Small People," p. 5.

91. Ronald Steel, "Beneath the Panama Canal," *The New York Review of Books* 4 (March 23, 1978), p. 12.

Chapter 6
Political Corruption: Continuity and Change

Political corruption is an integral part of American politics.[1] As we will see, Watergate was not an aberration, but just another instance in a long series of political crimes by public officials.

Political corruption is defined as "any illegal or unethical use of governmental authority for personal or political gain."[2] Corruption occurs, then, to accomplish one of two goals — material gain or power. This chapter is divided into two sections, one for each goal. In each case, we will illustrate political corruption at one or more of the various levels of government — community, state, and nation. We should note at the outset, however, that the examples used are just a small sample of the political crimes — known and unknown — that have occurred throughout American history.[3]

MONEY AND POLITICS

Politics and money have always been closely intertwined. Since political campaigns are costly, candidates must either be relatively affluent or accept monies from the wealthy or the special interests. But our concern in this section is with another facet of the money/politics relationship — graft.

Political graft is the illegal act of taking advantage of one's political position to gain money or property. Graft can take several forms. First is the outright bribe, where an individual, group, or corporation offers money to a public official for a favor. Or, the government official may demand money in return for a favor. Such an act is called political extortion.

Second is a subtle form of bribery where the public figure accepts exorbitant lecture fees from organizations or accepts retainers at his law office. A third type occurs when a briber offers the public figure the opportunity to buy securities at a low price and then, when the price goes up, the briber purchases them back at a great profit to the bribee.

A fourth variant is the kickback. This is the practice where contractors, engineering and architectural firms, and others pay back the official responsible for granting a lucrative government contract with a percentage of that contract. We will examine all these forms of graft as we examine the various fields in which they occur.

Fields of Graft

The government, whether city, state, or national, is involved in a number of activities such as law enforcement, the granting of contracts, the use of public funds, the hiring/firing of employees, tax assessment, and land use which are prone to corrupt action.

Purchasing of goods and services. The federal government purchases billions of dollars in goods and services from U.S. business (in 1978 it was eighty-five billion). The money buys an array of goods, such as military hardware, space systems, research projects, musical instruments, desks, clothing, and brooms. The potential for kickbacks is great in all stages of the procurement process, as we found in the General Services Administration (GSA) scandal of 1978.[4] The GSA buys about five billion dollars in goods and services each year. One estimate is that the graft in this one agency costs taxpayers roughly sixty-six million dollars annually. Repair contractors and suppliers have been allowed to bill the government for work never performed and for undelivered materials. One outrageous example of this was when one firm was paid to paint 2.4 million square feet of space in a federal building containing only 1.9 million square feet. Also, store managers have accepted money and other gifts from firms that sell to the government, in return for which the companies were allowed to charge in excess for their merchandise. Also GSA officials deliberately have purchased inferior goods at premium prices for their personal gain. Both the companies and the GSA officials share in the bounty. For example, several contractors pleaded guilty to charges of bribery from 1974 to 1977, with one claiming that he divided 310,000 dollars with GSA employees while doing only 60,000 dollars in legitimate work.[5]

Bidding for contracts is a process especially susceptible to bribery, especially when the bidding is not competitive. Approximately ninety percent of all contracts for new weapons systems are exempt from competitive bidding so that the Defense Department may select the superior system rather than just the most economical one. Unfortunately, this process is especially open to graft.

What does it take to win a defense contract, if it is not being the lowest bidder? The answer is not easy, for there are many possibilities, including superior design, more efficient programs, performance on schedule, and better quality control. Perhaps more important is convincing a few key personnel in the Pentagon, as noted in Chapter 5. A good deal of time and money is spent trying to influence these people, including the practice in industry of hiring former military officers. As Jack Anderson has put it:

> The giant contractors, such as Northrop Corporation and Rockwell International, court Pentagon officials assiduously. The way to many a defense contract has been greased by a mixture of booze, blondes, and barbeques. The brass hats and the industrialists shoot together in duck blinds. They ski together on the Colorado slopes. They drink together and play poker together. And invariably, the tab is picked up by some smiling corporate executive. The relationship is so cozy that many Pentagon officials, upon retirement, go to work for the companies that had come to them for contracts. The last time we counted them, we found 715 former Pentagon bigwigs scattered over the payrolls of the top defense contractors. It's a rare contractor that doesn't employ a few retired generals and admirals who are on a first-name basis with the Pentagon's big brass. Northrop Corporation, for example, has 64 ex-Pentagon officials on the payroll. This may help to explain how Northrop has managed to wangle a whopping $620.3 million in military contracts. Boeing Corporation, which is doing a $1.56 billion business with the Pentagon, has 48 former Pentagon bigwigs on the staff. And Rockwell International, with $732.3 million in defense contracts, has 36 ex-officials in key jobs.[6]

At the local level, competitive bidding is avoided in several ways. "Emergencies" are exempt. So it was that James Marcus, New York City's water commissioner under Mayor John Lindsay, gave an 840,000 dollar contract without bidding to a firm that had agreed to pay a kickback for cleaning a reservoir in the Bronx.[7] Purchases below a specified amount are also not subject to competitive bidding. One creative way to stay below the cutoff in such a situation is to split the contract into smaller parts so that each part can be awarded without bidding.

A common exception to competitive bidding is in the purchase of professional services by engineers, architects, auditors, and others.

While the rationale for this exception is logical — that is, the need for a specialist may mean that there is no competition — the negotiation process is vulnerable to graft. The most celebrated case involving this type of corruption caused Spiro Agnew to resign as vice-president of the United States. Let's briefly look at this interesting and common type of graft.[8]

During the 1960s suburban Baltimore County was growing rapidly. This growth required the creation of new streets, sewers, and bridges, as well as numerous rezoning decisions. Great sums of money were made by those fortunate to receive favorable zoning or contracts from the county. A government investigation revealed that those favorably treated (including contractors, architectural firms, and engineering firms) often kicked back five percent to those responsible for the decision. This practice of kickbacks was not new, but was a time-honored Maryland custom.

Included among those regularly receiving kickbacks was Spiro Agnew. The payoffs began in 1962 when Agnew became Baltimore county executive and continued when he became governor in 1967; as late as 1971, he received a payment in the basement of the White House. He received these payments for all the design jobs in the county, and later as governor he received a percentage of the highway contracts and other engineering contracts. While serving as vice-president the payments continued, amounting to 80,000 dollars during those few years.

During the dark days of the Watergate investigation, the inquiry into Agnew's possible criminal activities became public. The evidence against him was irrefutable and he was forced to plea bargain to reduce the penalty. He was to resign his office, plead no contest to one charge of income-tax evasion, and was given a sentence of three years of unsupervised probation and a fine of 10,000 dollars.

Public funds. A ready source of corruption by those in political power is the use of public monies. Government units at all levels have discretionary powers over money collected, waiting to be spent. The state treasurer, for instance, is custodian over many millions of dollars. Commonly these are deposited in banks to obtain interest for the state. But which banks and at what interest rate? The choice is not a random one and among the criteria used by some officials have been: (1) which banks have given financial support to the candidates and/or party in power; (2) where politicians are shareholders of bank stocks; and (3) which banks will make loans at favorable rates to powerful public officials or to their business associates.

One case of the questionable use of public funds involved Matthew Quay, the State Treasurer of Pennsylvania for thirty years during the late 1800s.[9] Quay demanded political contributions from banks and if they complied he would in return deposit state monies at *no* interest.

This practice deprived the state of the revenue from interest (e.g., 100 million dollars at six percent yields six million dollars in interest), as well as being a form of political extortion.

Public property. Another potential area for corruption is the misuse of public property. Government officials have discretionary powers over public lands. They decide, for example, which ranchers get grazing rights, which lumber companies have the right to timber lands, and what the policies will be on the extraction of minerals and petroleum from lands owned by the government. Fortunes can be made or lost depending on favorable access to these lands. Of course, such a situation is susceptible to bribery and extortion.

Early in American history there were several instances of the improper use of political influence in the disposition of public lands. One example involved a large area of virgin land west of South Carolina known as the Yazoo territory (much of which is now Alabama and Mississippi), which was claimed by the federal government, Georgia, and numerous Indian tribes. In 1794 the Georgia Legislature sold its land (30 million acres) to four companies for 1.5 cents per acre. "The haste of the legislature in concluding such an unprofitable sale was apparently the result of the attentions paid them by the companies which had peddled shares at very low prices to nearly all the legislators." [10] *

The most infamous case involving the fraudulent use of public lands was the Teapot Dome scandal. During the administration of Warren Harding (which along with that of Ulysses S. Grant's is considered among the most corrupt in American history), a scandal broke concerning the leasing of oil lands. In 1921 Secretary of the Interior Albert Fall persuaded President Harding and the Navy Secretary to transfer naval oil reserves from the Navy to his jurisdiction in the Interior Department. When this was accomplished, Fall then transferred the oil reserves at Teapot Dome, Wyoming, and Elk Hills, California, to two private oil producers — Henry Sinclair and E. L. Doheny — for their use. The leases were signed secretly and without competitive bidding. In return, Fall collected 100,000 dollars from Doheny for Elk Hills and 300,000 dollars from Sinclair for Teapot Dome. When the scandal broke, the government cancelled the leases. Fall was sent to prison for a year (the first cabinet officer in American history to be put in prison), but no penalties were given to the two guilty oil companies or their officers.

---

* This quote, plus the quotes on pp. 184, 185, 191, 195, and 199, are reprinted by permission of the publisher from *Political Corruption in America* by George C. S. Benson (Lexington, Mass.: Lexington Books, D. C. Heath and Company, copyright 1978, D. C. Heath and Company).

Tax assessment and collection. The taxation function of government is one that has enormous potential for graft. Tax assessors have
great latitude because many of their decisions are subjective. They are
obvious targets for bribes to reduce assessments. Chicago in the 1920s
had a particularly corrupt tax system. Individual members of the board
of review could raise, lower, or eliminate assessments made by the tax
assessors. Workers in Chicago's political machine "were rewarded by
ridiculously low assessments, a precinct captain's house being assessed
at one-fifteenth the value of a similar house next door." [11]

The situation in Cook County (where Chicago is located) has not
changed much since the 1920s when it comes to taxation. The county
assessor was investigated by the state in 1972 for assessing certain properties on a system subject to manipulation and preference. Upon learning of the pending investigation, the assessor, P. J. Cullerton, "reassessed"
nine high-rise properties in Chicago, adding thirty-four millon dollars to
the city's tax base.[12]

Officials at the federal level are also susceptible to bribes involving
taxation. Internal Revenue Service personnel investigating income tax
evasion could be bribed to "look the other way." So, too, could customs
officials. An additional example of an abusive practice involving taxes
is illustrated by the 1875 Whiskey Ring scandal, which broke during the
Grant administration. Over 350 distillers and government officials were
indicted for defrauding the government of tax revenues. This was accomplished when distillers falsified reports on the amount produced and
bribed government inspectors to verify the fraudulent reports.[13]

Regulation of commercial activities. Government officials are required by law to inspect foods such as grain and meat to ensure that they
are not contaminated and to grade them according to quality. Again,
there are numerous known instances of abuses in these areas as agents
receive bribes to allow questionable items to pass inspection.

Abuses also abound in government efforts to control certain business activities such as gambling and the sale of alcohol. Because these
activities are generally restricted by law, the granting of licences is a
lucrative plum for which people are willing to pay extra. They are also
willing to pay for favorable legislation. In a celebrated 1960 case, Governor Otto Kerner of Illinois was bribed by certain race-track interests
for political favors. The bribe was subtle because it was in the form of
stock. Kerner was offered race-track stock for a fraction of its value.
He paid 15,079 dollars for stock which he later sold for 159,800 dollars
(a profit of 1,050 percent). This was a disguised bribe in return for
Kerner's help in securing legislation favorable to the race track owned
by the donor of the securities.[14] Not so incidentally, the donor, Marjorie
Everett, also contributed 45,000 dollars to Kerner's 1960 campaign and
another 40,000 in 1964. These monies, plus the sweet stock deal, seem

related to some of Governor Kerner's decisions concerning racing:[15] (1) Kerner directed the chair of the Harness Commission to cancel the dates awarded a competitor of Mrs. Everett and to divide them among two other tracks, one owned by Mrs. Everett (when the chairman resisted, he was forced to resign); (2) Kerner was instrumental in getting pari-mutuel taxes on a graduated basis rather than a fixed percentage (saving Mrs. Everett and her co-owners of Washington Park three million dollars between 1966 and 1968); and (3) Kerner signed a bill abolishing the troublesome Harness Commission, giving its duties to the Racing Board, whose membership was expanded with Kerner appointments. Kerner was found guilty in federal court of bribery and conflict of interest in 1973.

Zoning and land use. The areas of zoning, planning, and building codes are highly subject to graft since the decisions can provide or eliminate great financial advantage. The decisions in these areas can choose which individuals or organizations will have a monopoly. Overnight, the decisions can make cheap land valuable or priceless land ordinary. And the decisions can force all construction to be done by certified employees. And so on. The point, as we have shown over and over, is that the government's discretionary powers, while necessary, can be abused by government officials and business people. The problem, of course, is that the decisions are not always made in the public interest but are for sale.

The examples of graft in zoning decisions are plentiful,[16] but we will only present one illustrative case.[17] A small borough in southern New Jersey — Lindenwold — had undergone rapid population growth (it tripled from 1950 to 1970). In this setting a group of speculators was able to make a 2,400 percent gross profit on a tract of sixty-nine acres because of favorable zoning decisions greased by bribes. They purchased the land at public sale for 40,000 dollars. The land was relatively cheap because of strict zoning and a clause that demanded the land be developed within a specified time or revert back to the municipality. The investors then used 30,000 dollars for payoffs to the borough tax assessor and the secretary of the county tax board. This apparently allowed the investors to exceed the deadline without any construction. For another 90,000 dollars, given to the mayor, the tax assessor, and at least one councilman, the owners got the land rezoned for townhouses, making it much more salable than when it was zoned for industry. The land was then sold for one million dollars, which meant a gross profit of 960,000 dollars (or a net profit of 840,000 dollars when the expenses for bribes were deducted). Once again, the political decisions, orchestrated with money, were lucrative to all parties — except the public.

The legislative process. Persons serving in legislatures, municipal councils, or on boards of county commissioners are targets for bribes because their law-making powers are so crucial to the monied interests. There are two special problems in detecting whether bribery occurs in legislatures. The first is that legislators (and candidates for other offices as well) receive campaign contributions. The second is the difficulty in assaying the motivations for how a person votes. Was it because he or he was beholden to those who contributed to the candidate's political campaign or because of a sincere belief that such a vote was in the best interests of the region or nation?

We cannot answer this question with certitude, but the data seem to indicate that money makes a difference. For example, in 1970 dairy farmers had contributed 500,000 dollars to congressional campaigns. They had given money to such powerful congressional figures as Speaker Carl Albert, W. R. Poage (chairman of the House Agricultural Committee), Senators Hubert Humphrey, Edmund Muskie, Gale McGee (chairman of the Agricultural Appropriations Committee), and William Proxmire.[18] These donations paid off, as evidenced by the quick reversal in governmental policy. Within a week of an initial announcement of no support, the House had a bill to increase milk supports (with 116 members as cosponsors) and the Senate had a similar bill (with twenty-nine sponsors). In the meantime, President Nixon's campaign fund was increased by a contribution from the milk producers of 255,000 dollars. At this point, the Department of Agriculture announced the new policy, citing "new evidence" as a reason for its reversal. Describing this process, a president of the local Mid-America Dairy wrote the following to a member:

> . . . on March 23, 1971, along with nine other dairy farmers, I sat in the Cabinet room of the White House, across the table from the President of the United States, and heard him compliment the dairymen on their marvelous work in consolidating and unifying of our industry and our involvement in politics. He said, "You people are my friends and I appreciate it."
>
> Two days later an order came from the U.S. Department of Agriculture increasing the support price of milk to 85 percent of parity, which added from $500 to $700 million to dairy farmers' milk checks. We dairymen cannot afford to overlook this kind of economic benefit. Whether we like it or not, this is the way the system works.[19]

In 1978 the National Association of Realtors contributed 1.1 million dollars to congressional candidates (up from 570,000 dollars in 1976). In June, 1979, this investment paid off as Congress adopted a realtor-backed amendment to pending housing legislation denying the Department of Housing and Urban Development power to issue cease-and-desist orders when it had reasonable cause to believe land developers had engaged in fraud.[20]

We are suggesting the possibility that legislative members, when they accept campaign contributions (or excessive fees for speeches, or proceeds from blocks of tickets to 100-dollar-a-plate dinners), are taking a form of bribe when it is expected that the contributor (individual or group) will somehow benefit from the investment. This is a strong allegation and clearly does not hold in all cases. However, there are some interesting situations where incumbent legislators running unopposed received large contributions. Senator Inoye of Hawaii, in 1972, for example, received 250,000 dollars from special interests to help in his campaign *even though he had no opponent.* The money in this case was given because the contributors expected to gain. In short, as some have alleged, we have the "best Congress money can buy." [21]

A difficult question to answer is what the effects are of receiving campaign contributions or other favors. Will these bias the legislator's actions? Clearly, it is difficult to affirm that the legislator acted because of money, as Amick has argued:

> When people are exercising legislative roles, they have to be given wide latitude. The law can and does forbid them to sell their votes, but it cannot force them to cast those votes in an objective way, or an intelligent way, or a well-informed way. And there is no test that can be designed that will automatically disclose whether a given vote is corrupt; the necessary freedom given to legislators to make honest decisions also makes it easier for them to get away with making dishonest ones.[22]

The relationship between receiving money and favorable decisions by legislators is not always a subtle one, however. A few examples make this point, beginning with the Credit Mobilier scandal.[23] In the late 1860s some of the major stockholders of the Union Pacific Railroad concocted a scheme whereby they would get their company (the railroad) to contract with their construction company (Credit Mobilier). This cozy arrangement allowed the conspirators to charge Union Pacific exorbitant costs. In effect, then, the money that Union Pacific raised through the sale of stocks went to the construction company, which made enormous profits. Concerned over a possible congressional investigation, one member of the conspiracy, who was also a U.S. Representative from Massachusetts, Oakes Ames, gave away or sold Credit Mobilier stocks at very low cost to selected members of Congress. In 1872 the bribes became known and led to the expulsion of Ames and another Congressman, James Brooks. Also implicated were the outgoing vice-president of the U.S. and a future president, James A. Garfield.

Another instance of the outright bribe occurred when the American Bridge Company in 1910 bribed New York legislators to defeat a bill that would have improved the procedure for constructing bridges by requiring a referendum and approval by the state engineer.[24]

There is also the recent example of the efforts by Tongsun Park to purchase favorable legislation. Park, a Korean businessman, gave thirty-one congressional members 850,000 dollars in cash from 1968 to 1975 (in addition to lavish parties and expensive gifts).[25] Park testified, under immunity, that he bribed the Congressman Otto Passman, from Louisiana, to use Passman's influence as the chair of the Foreign Relations Committee to get South Korea to appoint Park as its sole rice agent. This was successful, as Park became that agent and made nine million dollars in commissions during a four-year period.[26]

Finally, from January 1977 to October 1978, fourteen current or former members of the House of Representatives went to prison, faced criminal charges, or were disciplined by their colleagues.[27] The list of charges included: mail fraud, salary kickbacks from aides, accepting bribes, election-law violations, defrauding the government, making false statements to the government, tax evasion, and perjury.

Law enforcement. Formal law-enforcement policy begins with the police. They decide if a law has been broken. They interpret and judge: What behavior is "disorderly"? How much noise is a "public nuisance"? When does a quarrel become a "criminal assault"? When does protest become illegitimate? What constitutes "public drunkenness"? These questions suggest that the police have great decisional latitude. Unlike other aspects of the criminal justice process, the police often deal with their clients in isolation, their decisions not subject to review by higher authorities. As Skolnick has said, "Police work constitutes the most secluded part of an already secluded system and therefore offers the greatest opportunity for arbitrary behavior." [28]

Even after the arrest of defendants, police use their discretionary powers to filter out those whose cases are not worthy of prosecution. A 1960 study of felony cases in California, for example, found that 55,994 defendants out of 98,921 (fifty-six percent) were removed from the felony process by police decisions before formal complaints had been filed.[29]

The police, then, have the power to continue or terminate the criminal-processing process. Thus, the position of the police personnel exposes them to extraordinary pressures. The President's Commission on Law Enforcement and the Administration of Justice noted:

> The violations in which police are involved vary widely in char-
> acter. The most common are improper political influence; ac-
> ceptance of gratuities or bribes in exchange for nonenforcement
> of laws, particularly those relating to gambling, prostitution, and
> liquor offenses, which are often extensively interconnected with
> organized crime; the "fixing" of traffic tickets; minor thefts; and
> occasional burglaries.... Government corruption in the United
> States has troubled historians, political reformers, and the gen-

eral public since the middle of the 19th century. Metropolitan police forces — most of which developed during the late 1800's when government corruption was most prevalent — have often been deeply involved in corruption. The police are particularly susceptible to the forms of corruption that have attracted widest attention — those that involve tolerance or support of organized crime activities. But the police, as one of the largest and most strategic groups in metropolitan government, was also likely targets for political patronage, favoritism, and other kinds of influence that have pervaded local governments dominated by political machines.[30]

The corruption of the police is most likely with the enforcement of "victimless" crimes. Legislatures have typically enacted laws to enforce the morality of the majority — making criminal certain "offensive" acts that may harm the individual who performs them but not others. Laws prohibiting gambling, sex between consenting adults, pornography, liquor, and drug usage create such victimless crimes. Over eighty percent of the police work in the United States has to do with the regulation of private morals. While many police officers are unwilling to accept bribes from murderers and thieves, they may accept them from the perpetrators of victimless crimes. There are at least three reasons for this: (1) they believe these crimes are harmless and impossible to control anyway; (2) there may be strong community pressures against enforcement of such laws; and (3) organized crime, with its threats and enticements, coupled with the former two reasons, encourage the acceptance of bribes.

The following are some examples of police corruption noted by the Knapp Commission for New York City in the early 1970s.[31]

> *Item:* In the five plainclothes divisions where our investigations were concentrated we found a strikingly standardized pattern of corruption. Plainclothesmen, participating in what is known in policy parlance as a "pad," collected regular biweekly or monthly payments amounting to as much as $3,500 from each of the gambling establishments in the area under their jurisdiction, and divided the take in equal shares. The monthly share per man (called the "nut") ranged from $300 and $400 in midtown Manhattan to $1,500 in Harlem. When supervisors were involved they received a share and a half.

> *Item:* Corruption in narcotics enforcement lacked the organization of the gambling pads, but individual payments — known as "scores" — were commonly received and could be staggering in amount. Our investigation . . . revealed a pattern whereby corrupt officers customarily collected scores in substantial amounts from narcotics violators. These scores were either kept by the individual officer or shared with a partner and, perhaps, a superior officer. They ranged from minor shakedowns to payments of

many thousands of dollars, the largest narcotics payoff uncovered in our investigation having been $80,000. According to information developed by the S.I.C. and in recent Federal investigations, the size of this score was by no means unique.

Item: Uniformed patrolmen, particularly those assigned to radio patrol cars, participated in gambling pads more modest in size than those received by plainclothes units and received regular payments from construction sites, bars, grocery stores and other business establishments. These payments were usually made on a regular basis to sector car patrolmen and on a haphazard basis to others. While individual payments to uniformed men were small, mostly under $20, they were often so numerous as to add substantially to a patrolman's income. Other less regular payments to uniformed patrolmen included those made by after-hours bars, bottle clubs, tow trucks, motorists, cab drivers, parking lots, prostitutes and defendants wanting to fix their cases in court.

The organization of power. So far we have focused on public officials, as individuals, who have taken bribes or demanded them from monied interests. More important than these random and sometimes patterned actions are the organizational forms that promote a climate where corruption flourishes. We will examine briefly three of these organizational forms — organized crime, the political machine, and the invisible government.

1. *Organized crime and corruption.* Organized crime is a business seeking profit by supplying illegal goods and services (especially drugs, prostitution, pornography, gambling, and loan sharking), as described in Chapter 3. The profits are enormous for organized crime. Of course, we cannot know the exact figures, but it is estimated that the gross income of organized crime is twice that of all other kinds of illegal activity.[32] The estimated revenues from the organized rackets in 1979 were more than 150 billion dollars (22 billion from gambling, 63 billion from narcotics, 8 billion from pornography and prostitution, and the remaining from such activities as cigarette bootlegging and loan sharking).[33] The net income of organized crime is higher than that of any single legitimate industry.

Several characteristics of organized crime help perpetuate it.[34] First, organized crime supplies illegal goods and services that are in great demand. In other words, one reason for the continued existence of organized crime is that it fills a need. If victimless crimes were decriminalized, organized crime would be left with products and services that could be easily and cheaply supplied from legitimate sources, thereby possibly destroying organized crime's profits and existence.

A second characteristic of organized crime is that it depends on the corruption of police and government officials for survival and continued profitability. Bribery, campaign contributions, delivery of votes, and other favors are used to influence police personnel, government attorneys, judges, media personnel, city-council members, and legislators. Each of the major-crime families has at least one position in their organization entitled "corrupter."

> The person occupying this position bribes, buys, intimidates, threatens, negotiates, and sweet-talks himself into a relationship with police, public officials, and anyone else who might help "family" members maintain immunity from arrest, prosecution, and punishment.... More commonly, one corrupter takes care of one subdivision of government, such as the police or city hall, while another will be assigned a different subdivision, such as the state alcoholic beverage commission. A third corrupter might handle the court system by fixing a judge, a clerk of court, a prosecutor, an assistant prosecutor, a probation officer.[35]

The role of organized crime is a very important source of political corruption at all levels, not just at the level of the police. William Chambliss, in the introduction to his book on corruption in Seattle, Washington, has put it well:

> Money is the oil of our present-day machinery, and elected public officials are the pistons that keep the machine operating. Those who come up with the oil, whatever its source, are in a position to make the machinery run the way they want it to. Crime is an excellent producer of capitalism's oil. Those who want to affect the direction of the machine's output find that the money produced by crime is as effective in helping them get where they want to go as is the money produced in any other way. Those who produce the money from crime thus become the people most likely to control the machine. Crime is not a by-product of an otherwise effectively working political economy: it is a main product of that political economy. Crime is in fact a cornerstone on which the political and economic relations of democratic-capitalist societies are constructed.
>
> In every city of the United States, and in many other countries as well, criminal organizations sell sex and drugs, provide an opportunity to gamble, to watch pornographic films, or to obtain a loan, an abortion, or a special favor. Their profits are a mainstay of the electoral process of America and their business is an important (if unrecorded) part of the gross national product. The business of organized crime in the United States may gross as much as one hundred billion dollars annually — or as little as forty billion — either way the profits are immense, and the proportion of the gross national product represented by money flowing from crime cannot be gainsaid. Few nations in the world have economies that compare with the economic output of criminal activities in the United States.[36]

2. _The political machine_. The political machine became the dominant pattern of government for United States cities in the last part of
the nineteenth century. This type of government is where a clique gets
elected to all the major posts in a city. Once in, the leaders use their
appointing power to fill the municipal boards, thus controlling the decision-making apparatus. To stay in power the political organization actively seeks votes. One technique to get votes is to appoint key persons
from various factions in the community who deliver the votes of their
followers. The other method is to gain the allegiance of voters by providing them with governmental services or public-works projects that
appeal to large voting blocs. The city is also organized so that each
precinct and ward has a machine representative who uses patronage,
bribes, favors, and other techniques to keep the voters in his or her district loyal to the machine.

Political machines have been almost universally corrupt. The pattern of corruption is not limited to the city, however, as typically there
are links to the state and national levels. The corruption of American
cities was typical around the turn of the century.

> The pervasiveness of machine politics and of the accompanying
> corruption in nineteenth-century America is astounding. In his
> _American Commonwealth_ James Bryce estimated that the gov-
> ernment of every American city with more than 200,000 in-
> habitants was corrupt during this last quarter-century. Many
> cities of 50,000 to 200,000 were corrupt, and even several cities
> smaller than 50,000 were riddled with corruption, although on a
> less grandiose scale than, say, New York or San Francisco. The
> findings of the municipal historian Ernest S. Griffith are also
> grim. He noted that from 1870 to 1900 Newark was the only
> large city to remain reasonably honest. The New England towns
> of Cambridge, Worcester, and Springfield were the only medium-
> sized cities he discovered that were consistently uncorrupt. Every
> city he examined in the middle states and all the Southern cities
> except Atlanta, Charleston, and possibly Richmond and Mem-
> phis were persistently or intermittently corrupt. In the West
> only Oakland and in the mid-West only Milwaukee seem to have
> avoided the corrupting tendency of politics in this era.[37]

For an example of graft rampant in one political machine, let's
briefly examine the situation in New York City under the nefarious Boss
Tweed, where the Tweed Ring robbed the city of somewhere between
thirty and two hundred million dollars from 1866 to the mid 1870s.[38]

William March Tweed and two associates gained control of Tammany Hall, New York City's Democratic party organization, in 1863.
The organization under Tweed gained popular support in the city by
providing public works and by actively courting the foreign born (about
one-half of the city's population in 1870). Ward leaders helped their

constituents by finding jobs, fixing minor problems with the law, and remembering families on special occasions. As a result the word captains could deliver the votes in their districts — and power.

Tweed used his power to become wealthy as he and his associates orchestrated the city government to extract money.

> The most accessible and secure source of income was from graft on municipal contracts. Before 1869, city contractors expected to pay 10 percent in graft to the machine. Under Tweed this rapidly rose to 65 percent, of which 25 percent went to Tweed, while the remaining 40 percent was distributed among lesser accomplices. The history of the New York Court House is the most familiar and notorious example of the ring's method of operation. Planned in 1868 at a cost not to exceed $250,000, the Court House under Tweed management eventually absorbed over $8 million of city revenue. Many of the contracts were lent to friends of the ring or to companies owned by the ring's members at inflated prices. The ring collected its 65 percent from the contract on top of the inflated prices. All the costs were passed along to the taxpayers.[39]

As a result of these frauds and others, Boss Tweed and his associates plundered the city. "Of every tax dollar, only fifteen cents went for legitimate uses. The rest went into the pockets of the ring, the overpaid builders, or bribe-welcoming officials." [40]

3. *The invisible government and "legal" graft*. Who really rules a city, a state, or the nation? The obvious answer is that elected officials do, since they make the laws and enforce them. But a strong case can be made that at each level of government there is a permanent alliance of special interests that is more powerful than the elected government. As Newfield and DuBrul have described it:

> We live in a nation where private profit is officially perceived as the maximum good — the engine of all progress. The permanent government . . . at the national level where giant oil companies, defense contractors, and multinational corporations have effectively defined the nation's priorities and allocated its resources through a long series of administrations that have unswervingly agreed with Calvin Coolidge's observation that "the business of America is business." In the early 1960s, John Kennedy quickly learned that a president, no matter how popular, who confronts the combined interests of corporate America is walking into a meat grinder. Faced with the choice between massive public works and social spending, or the "trickle-down" economics of business to cure the Eisenhower recession, he found it expedient, in the face of a carefully orchestrated corporate propaganda campaign, to opt for investment credits for industry and tax cuts that aided the wealthiest segment of society. In dealing with the nation's balance-of-payments problems, he en-

countered the same wall of opposition and finally observed: "It's a ridiculous situation for us to be squeezing down essential public activities in order not to touch private investment and tourist spending — but apparently that's life."

"Life" hasn't changed much in Washington, New York, or hundreds of other cities across the land as we begin the nation's third century. *Corporate power still dominates public need.*[41] (Italics added.)

The material in Chapter 7 will focus on this phenomenon at the national level, so for now let's see how it works at the municipal level, using New York City as the case study. Newfield and DuBrul argue forcefully that a permanent (invisible and unelected) government holds ultimate power over public policy in New York City.[42] It is a government of bankers, brokers, developers, landlords, union leaders, and lawyers. The power of this loose confederation of elites is in their control of institutions, money, property, and even the law-making process. It gets its way no matter who the voters elect as mayor or council members.

> Whenever an assemblyman casts a vote, or when a public-works project is begun, or when a developer gets a zoning variance to build a highrise, or when federal funds come into a district, or when a decision is made to raise the interest rates that the banks charge the city — in all these situations, the real decision-makers are usually off stage, and unknown to the public.[43]

This permanent government makes enormous sums of money through what Newfield and DuBrul call "legal" graft. The money they receive is not "under the table" but rather in the form of finder's fees, title insurance, city contracts, interest-free deposits of the city's funds, zoning variances, insurance premiums, bond-sale commissions, public-relations retainers, real-estate leases, mortgage closings, and legal fees. For example, Robert Moses, head of the New York Port Authority, spent over 4.5 billion dollars on public works for over fifteen years. Much of that money was spent for legal graft. For example, three democratic politicians shared the insurance business from the Triborough Bridge and Tunnel Authority, worth 100,000 dollars annually in commissions. All of the insurance for the 1964 World's Fair was funneled to one insurance agency, providing it with three million in commissions. All of the legal fees for the Fair Corporation were given to the law firm of a former city administrator who had helped draft the legislation exempting the Fair Corporation from the city's Code of Ethics.[44]

Or, when Yankee Stadium was refurbished, Mayor Lindsay used urban-renewal funds, saying that it would cost but twenty-four million dollars, including two million to rehabilitate the streets and shops around the stadium. The stadium was eventually completed at a cost of 101 million (and the two million for the community was never spent), with some contractors doing very well. One outfit — Kinney Systems — was awarded a contract without competitive bidding to build two parking garages and remodel another. They were paid twenty-two million dollars, a management fee from the city, most of the parking fees collected, and a two-million-dollar tax exemption. The city counsel who negotiated the contract in 1972 was, by 1976, working for Kinney systems as a lawyer.[45]

Legal graft occurs in every conceivable area of city activities resulting in money, patronage, and other perquisites. In the case of New York City, the citizens pay multimillions annually for which they receive nothing. Ironically, though, New York's severe fiscal problems are typically blamed on a variety of sources other than the graft perpetuated by the invisible government.

THE CORRUPTION OF POWER

This section describes the illegal and unethical means that various people and organizations use to gain, retain, or enlarge political power. We will focus on four problem areas: the powerful controlling the powerless, the administration of elections, the conduct of campaigns, and the influence of money in elections. The section concludes with an elaboration of the various forms of political corruption manifested in the Watergate-related crimes.

The Powerful Controlling the Powerless

The hallmark of representative democracy is that all of the people have the fundamental right to vote for those who will administer and make the laws. Those in power have often defied this principle of democracy, however, as they have minimized, neutralized, or even negated the voting privileges of the lower classes, minorities, third parties, and the opposition.

The writers of the Constitution, who represented wealth and property, were concerned about the potential power of the masses.[46] Thus, they objected to democracy as we know it today. Their attitude was stated well in the following statement by Alexander Hamilton:

> All communities divide themselves into the few and the many. The first are the rich and the well born, the other the mass of the people. The voice of the people has been said to be the voice of God; and however generally this maxim has been quoted and believed, it is not true in fact. The people are turbulent and changing; they seldom judge or determine right. Give therefore to the first class a distinct, permanent share in the government. They

> will check the unsteadiness of the second and as they cannot receive any advantage by a change, they therefore will ever maintain good government.[47]

Even more blatant was the statement by Governor Morris at the Constitutional Convention:

> The time is not distant when this Country will abound with mechanics and manufacturers [industrial workers] who will receive their bread from their employers. Will such men be the secure and faithful Guardians of liberty? ... Children do not vote. Why? Because they want prudence, because they have no will of their own. The ignorant and the dependent can be as little trusted with the public interest.[48]

As a result of this type of thinking, which by the way was characteristic of the complaints by intellectuals throughout history until the last one hundred years or so,[49] the Constitution was designed to retain the power among the propertied few, while utilizing seemingly democratic principles. The appearance of democracy actually had the effect of fragmenting the power of the masses.

> By separating the executive, legislative and judiciary functions and then providing a system of checks and balances among the various branches, including staggered elections, executive veto, Senate confirmation of appointments and ratification of treaties, and a two-house legislature, they [the Founding Fathers] hoped to dilute the impact of popular sentiments. To the extent that it existed at all, the majoritarian principle was tightly locked into a system of minority vetoes, making swift and sweeping popular actions nearly impossible.[50]

The blatant disregard for the masses, as determined by the Constitution, is seen in the following:[51]

> *Item:* The senators from each state were to be elected by their respective state legislatures (the Seventeenth Amendment, adopted in 1913, finally provided for the direct election of senators).

> *Item:* The election of the president was on the surface to be decided by the voters, but in reality the president was to be selected by an electoral college composed of political leaders. This procedure allowed the upper classes to control the presidential vote regardless of the popular vote. Each state had as many electors as it had senators and representatives. Each political party would select a slate of electors, who would vote for president if their party's candidate carried the state. Interestingly, and indicative of the contempt for the masses, some states allowed their electors to vote for anyone, not necessarily the presidential candidate of their party (five states still retain that right).

The 1876 election illustrates how the electoral college can run counter to the popular will: the winner, Republican Rutherford B. Hayes, received some 250,000 *fewer* votes than his Democratic opponent, Samuel J. Tilden. Two sets of returns arrived from three southern states, each state having one set that showed a Republican plurality and another with a Democratic one. The issue was resolved by a special commission of Congress, which gave all the disputed nineteen electoral votes to Hayes, making him the winner by one electoral vote. A deal was made where the southern Democrats aligned with northern Republicans because Hayes promised that: (1) all remaining federal troops in the three states would be removed; (2) the federal government would subsidize a southern transcontinental railroad; and (3) a southerner would be appointed to the cabinet.[52]

Item: The Supreme Court justices were to be nonelected. They were appointed to life tenure by the president and confirmed by the Senate.

Item: The matter of who was allowed to vote was left to the individual states. This meant, in effect, the disenfranchisement of many voters. All the states disallowed women from voting (changed in 1919 by the passage of the Nineteenth Amendment). All the states denied voting to those held in bondage (changed following the Civil War by the passage of the Fourteenth Amendment). In various states it was common to require that voters own certain amounts and kinds of property.

Other nondemocratic practices occurred throughout the states early in our history, some continuing into the present. One was the limiting of political candidates to the wealthy — candidates had to pass steep property qualifications for holding office. This meant that most voters could not qualify as candidates. "The result was that the gentry, merchants, and professionals monopolized the important offices."[53]

A common practice throughout American history has been for the majority in legislatures (at all levels) to revise political boundaries for their advantage. This tactic, known as "gerrymandering," occurs when the party in power designs the political boundaries to negate the power of the opposition. Assume, for instance, that the Democrats control the state legislature. The boundary lines can be redrawn in order to take Republican strongholds from problematic districts, placing them in nearby strong Democratic districts. The Democratic district is strong enough to absorb the Republicans without losing their advantage, and in the former Republican district, the Democrats have a better chance of gaining control.

Less obvious measures to minimize the effectiveness of the less powerful party have occurred throughout American history. One of the latest was a Democratic proposal in 1978 to cut from 54,600 to 15,000 dollars the maximum amount of money that a political party could give a candidate running for the House of Representatives. The proponents argued for the public that this would begin to reduce the amount of campaign costs. But the opponents argued that this was a ruse by the Democratic party to retain its power in Congress, since the proposal came at a time when the Republicans had raised 18.5 million dollars in campaign money, compared with the Democrats' 5.6 million.[54]

Although the Fourteenth Amendment to the Constitution gave blacks the right to vote following the Civil War, the white majority in the southern states used a variety of tactics to keep them from voting. Most effective was the strategy of intimidation. Blacks who tried to assert their right to vote were often subject to beatings, destruction of property, or even lynching. The more subtle approach, however, was quite effective in eliminating the black vote in the southern states. Through legal means, laws were passed to achieve illegal discrimination. One tactic was the white primary which excluded blacks from the party primary.[55] The Constitution prohibited the states from denying the vote on the basis of race. A political party, however, since it was a private association, *could* discriminate. The Democratic party throughout most of the South chose the option of limiting the primary to whites. Blacks could legally vote in the general election but only for the candidates already selected by whites. And since the Democratic party in the South was supreme, whomever was selected in the primary would be the victor in the general election. This practice was nullified by the Supreme Court in 1944.

Other legal obstacles for blacks in the South were the literacy test and the poll tax, which also have been ruled illegal by the Supreme Court, but only after many decades of denying blacks the right to vote. Both obstacles were designed as two southern suffrage requirements to admit whites to the electorate and exclude blacks (without mentioning race). Let's look briefly at the literacy test because it, and the related requirements, were so blatantly racist.[56]

The object of the literacy test was to allow all adult white males to vote and exclude all blacks. The problem with this test was that many whites would also be excluded because they were also illiterate. The legislators in the various southern states contrived alternatives to the literacy requirements that would allow the illiterate whites to vote. One loophole to accomplish this was the "grandfather clause, which, using Louisiana law as the example, exempted persons from the literacy test who were registered voters in any state on January 1, 1867, or prior thereto, the sons and grandsons of such persons, and male persons of foreign birth naturalized before January 1, 1898." [57]

Another alternative designed to allow illiterate whites to vote was the "understanding" clause. In such an instance a person who could not read any section of the Constitution would qualify as an elector if he could "understand" and give "a reasonable interpretation" of what was read to him. This procedure gave registrars the latitude to decide who could vote, and thus they had the ability to discriminate, which they did uniformly. A similar law in some states authorized registration of illiterates if they were "of good character" and could "understand the duties and obligations of citizenship under a republican form of government."

Election Frauds

Some winners in elections have achieved victory through illegal activities.[58] Violence and intimidation have been used by the supporters of certain candidates to control the vote. Various forms of harassment were used especially prior to 1850 when voting was done orally. This practice allowed bystanders to know how votes were cast and thus intimidate or punish persons who voted contrary to their wishes. In this century, violence has been aimed at southern blacks to keep them from registering, thus ensuring white supremacy.

Most election frauds involving illegal voting, false registration, and bribery have occurred in areas of one-party dominance, especially in cities controlled by a political machine. This has kept the machine in power at the local level, and has delivered votes in state and federal elections to one party, thus increasing the scope of the machine's power.

> In the heyday of machine politics, the use of repeaters and personators — to "vote early and often" — was widespread, from the North Side in Kansas City to the South Side in Chicago, from the Strip in Pittsburgh to South of the Slot in San Francisco. No less important, and generally used in conjunction with these, was the practice of wholesale manipulation of registration lists. The names of aliens (sometimes as the result of illegal naturalization), minors, and nonresidents were added to the registration list, along with fictitious names and the names of reliable nonvoters. In combination, such illegal techniques could yield large numbers of fraudulent votes. In the 1869 election in New York, for example, between 25,000 and 30,000 votes were attributed to repeating, false registration, and illegal naturalization.[59]

These tactics were not limited to the past but have continued to influence elections in the U.S. For example, Harry Truman would not have been elected senator from Missouri without the help of 50,000 fraudulent votes from the Pendergast machine in Kansas City.[60] So too have more recent Democratic victories been predicated on the massive help from Mayor Daley's delivery of the votes in Cook County, Illinois.

Votes have been purchased and continue to be today, especially in poor areas. Money and liquor have been used to bribe voters. It was alleged by the *Los Angeles Times,* for example, that 5,000 dollars was channeled through four black ministers for "street money" to recruit votes during the Carter campaign in the 1976 California primary.[61]

Another form of election fraud is to bypass the manipulation of the voters in favor of forgery and false accounting by election officials. Corrupt election officials can (1) complete ballots when the voter has failed to vote for a particular office, (2) declare ballots for the opposition invalid by deliberately defacing them or marking two preferences for a single office, (3) destroy ballots for the opposition, (4) add pre-marked ballots to the total, and (5) miscount.

One of the most famous recent instances of election fraud involved the election of Lyndon Johnson to the Senate.[62] In 1948 Johnson was running for the Democratic nomination (which meant election in Democratic Texas) against Governor Coke Stevenson. Stevenson won the primary by 71,000 votes but lacked a majority in the crowded field. A runoff was then held with the two top vote getters — Stevenson and Johnson. Stevenson again won — or so everyone thought. Days after the polls had closed, a "correction" of the vote from Duval County gave Johnson 202 more votes than the original count, enough to give him the Democratic nomination by 87 votes. The new vote was orchestrated by George B. Parr, the Democratic boss of the county. It was alleged that "voters" from the graveyard and from Mexico had somehow been recorded for Johnson. Some Chicanos testified that Parr had voted their names without their knowledge. Because of the charges by the defeated candidate of fraud, the Senate voted to investigate the disputed vote. Senate investigators found, however, that the ballots had mysteriously been destroyed. The investigation ended, Johnson became a senator, later the powerful majority leader of the Senate, and finally president of the United States.

The Unfair Conduct of Campaigns

Political campaigns often involve illegal or at least immoral behavior by the competitors and their supporters to achieve the advantage over their opponents.[63] Behavior such as espionage, bribery, sabotage, crowd agitation, lying, innuendo, and the like occur with some regularity. The primary goal of these tactics is to negate the opponent's strengths, which can be done by spreading rumors about his/her character, especially regarding the candidate's sex life and association with communists or criminals. Or, persons in the audience at the opponent's rally may heckle or ask embarrassing questions. Campaign mail has been stolen; billboards have been defaced; public-address systems or the lights for a rally have been sabotaged; and blacks have been hired to pose as workers for the opposition going door-to-door in "red-neck" precincts.

A common tactic, known as "political dynamiting," is to give the voters misinformation about the opposition.[64]   One way to do this is designing, printing, and distributing pamphlets and brochures that blacken the candidate's reputation.   These may be distributed at the last of the campaign so that the victim has no time to respond to the charges.   The techniques here may be blatant, such as those used by Richard Nixon in his early campaigns for office.   He defeated Jerry Voorhis for a House seat in 1946 by stating that Voorhis had been formally endorsed by a labor group (PAC) tainted with known communists (Voorhis, in fact, was a vigorous anticommunist during his four terms in the House and was never endorsed by the PAC).   A newspaper ad placed by Nixon in that campaign proclaimed "A vote for Nixon is a vote against the Communist-dominated PAC with its gigantic slush fund." [65]   Another alleged violation in this campaign was the hiring of workers by Republican headquarters to work at a phone bank asking people at random "Did you know Jerry Voorhis was a Communist?" [66]

In 1950 Nixon was elected to the Senate.   His opponent in that race was Helen Gahagan Douglas, a liberal three-term congresswoman. That election is notorious for Nixon's unethical attacks on Douglas. According to the campaign rhetoric, Douglas was "soft on communism." Moreover, "On 353 times the actress candidate voted exactly the same as Vito Marcantino, the notorious Communist party-line Congressman from New York."   She was called the "pink lady" and described, along with Marcantino, as heroes of the communist movement.   A pamphlet, colored pink, was distributed to thousands of voters.[67]

> On September 9, in San Diego, Nixon stated that "if she [Douglas] had her way, the Communist conspiracy would never have been exposed, and Alger Hiss would still be influencing the foreign policy of the United States." . . .   On November 1, Nixon repeated an earlier charge . . . that Douglas "gave comfort to Soviet tyranny." [68]

The Nixon campaign was aided by favorable treatment in many of California's newspapers.   A cartoon, which appeared in two Hearst papers, the *San Francisco Examiner,* and the *Los Angeles Examiner,* is illustrative of this political help:

> The cartoon, entitled "Rough on Rats," shows Nixon resolutely standing guard with a shotgun in front of a walled farm.   His sleeves are rolled up, and in addition to the shotgun, he carries a net labeled "Communist Control."   Uncle Sam is farming contentedly behind the wall, while rats (labeled variously, "Appeaser," "Professional Pacifist," "Conspirator," "Spy," "Soviet Sympathizer," and "Propagandist") run about.   Hearst cartoons and editorials in those days left very little to the imagination. The editorial under this cartoon, for example, accuses Douglas of favoring "reckless government spending" and "giving away

atomic bomb secrets" and of opposing military assistance programs, Selective Service, the Communist Control Act . . . and
"weeding out poor security risks." [69]

Before we leave the Nixon-Douglas campaign, it must be pointed out that
Nixon's campaign rhetoric was based on falsehood and smears. Ms.
Douglas was not a communist sympathizer. She did vote on the same
side as Marcantino 354 times but so did Nixon 112 times, the gap being
primarily the difference between Republican and Democratic votes on
the various issues. But slander, in this case, was a successful tactic, as
Nixon won fifty-six percent of the vote.

The tactics need not be as blatant as Nixon's, but can be like
Johnson's famous anti-Goldwater television advertisement in 1964: it
never mentioned Goldwater or his "hawk" position but showed a child
amid nature with an atomic mushroom cloud exploding in the distance.

The impact of television in campaigns has been widely used in another way to manipulate opinion. This time the tactic is not directed
at smearing an opponent but by building a particular image of the candidate of choice. Scenes showing his war exploits, or his family, or him
as the rugged horseman, or the lover of nature, or whatever are displayed
without reference to the candidate's positions on the issues. The intent
of these brief ads (generally thirty or sixty seconds long) is strictly to
manipulate the viewers to think positively of the candidate. There is a
debate as to whether this technique is moral or not.

Another borderline technique that has emerged with the growth of
the computer is the use of variable letters. Millions of letters can be
mailed in a political campaign that give "personalized" messages refer-
ring to the recipients' race, ethnicity, religion, children (by name), issues
they favor or oppose (e.g., abortion, busing). The effort is again the
manipulation of the voters by making it appear as if the candidate is
taking a personal interest in his or her concerns. The Nixon campaign
of 1972, for example, had 35,000 different combinations it could employ
for a single letter. This tactic, though legal, subverts the intent of democracy.

Money in Elections

Democracy is a system of government that expresses the will of the
people. In theory, since all persons and groups have a right to contribute to the candidate or party of their choice, all interests and points
of view will be represented. In practice, however, wealthy individuals
and the largest organizations provide the most money and have the
greatest influence on the political process, as we have seen earlier in
this chapter. But money intrudes in a variety of ways to thwart democracy, not just through the voluntary contributions to the few. Let's look

at a few of these, which were not covered in the earlier discussion of the political gift as a form of bribery.

One problem is that political leaders may extort money. There are two victims of this extortion. One set of victims can be the businesses and individuals dependent on the government for contracts, favorable laws, and sympathetic regulation. When confronted with the charge that he had authorized an illegal political contribution of company funds, the chairman of the board of a large corporation replied, "A large part of the money raised from the business community for political purposes is given in fear of what would happen if it were not given." [70] Maurice Stans, the chief fund raiser for Nixon in the 1972 campaign, who raised some sixty million dollars, was especially adept at this form of extortion.

> Stans would approach potential donors threatening that if they did not contribute the desired sum, he would initiate unfavorable pollution action against their corporations. He would take this action, he said, through the Pollution Council he helped establish at the Commerce Department. The scope of Stans' fundraising operations while he was still Nixon's Secretary of Commerce was revealed recently by two oil company executives. They told the Senate Watergate committee that a hundred-thousand-dollar contribution was expected from all large corporations. [71]

The other victims of political extortion are government employees. Although illegal by federal law since 1967, there has been and continues to be, although rarer now, the forced campaign contributions from government employees. The practice has most commonly occurred at the state and local levels, and has been connected to the patronage system. Around 1900, the rate varied from ten percent of one's salary (in Louisiana), to a sliding scale of from three to twelve percent. In 1972 state employees in Indiana paid two percent of their salaries to the party in power. [72]

Closely related to political extortion is the sale of jobs for contributions. This used to be a common practice for postmasterships and other federal positions. Apparently it is still possible for the most prestigious jobs.

> It is clear that the sale of embassies flourished extensively under Richard Nixon, his 1972 campaign reaping $1,324,442 merely from the eight individuals who headed embassies in Western Europe at the time. After this reelection, Nixon made ambassadors of a further eight individuals, each of whom had given no less than $25,000 to the campaign, and in aggregate $706,000. In February, 1974, Herbert Kalmbach, Richard Nixon's personal attorney, pleaded guilty to a charge of promising J. Fife Symington, the ambassador to Trinidad and Tobago during 1969–71, a more prestigious European ambassadorship in return for a

$100,000 contribution to be divided between Republican sena-
torial campaigns and the Committee to Re-elect the President.[73]

Pervasive throughout the money/politics connection is the routine
circumvention of the law.[74]   Candidates and donors commonly exploit
loopholes.   They give less than the amount the law requires must be reported but they give in multiples to a number of committees, each of
which supports the same candidate.   Another ruse is to give money to
others who give the money in their name.   Corporations evade re-
strictions on giving by "laundering" money through other sources or by
contributing to trade associations such as the National Association of
Manufacturers, which, in turn, pass the money on to the candidates of
the original donor.   They may also give bonuses to their employees,
which are then given as individual contributions.   Unions may assess
their members a fee, which is then given to the unions' candidates.   As
noted earlier, some of the largest corporations have given money "under
the table" in a variety of ways to finance their candidates.   A good share
of talent in our largest organizations and in political organizations is devoted to finding ever more creative ways to outwit the letter and the intent of the law for their political and monetary advantage.[75]

Watergate

The Watergate-related crimes, committed by officials of the government, represent the acts of official secrecy and deception taken to the
extreme.[76]   They demonstrate forcefully and fearfully just how far away
from the Democratic ideal the American political system had moved at
the time and how close it was to approaching totalitarianism.   In the
words of David Wise:

> Watergate revealed that under President Nixon a kind of totali-
> tarianism had already come to America, creeping in, not like
> Carl Sandburg's fog, on little cat feet, but in button-down shirts,
> worn by handsome young advertising and public relations men
> carrying neat attaché cases crammed with $100 bills.   Men will-
> ing to perjure themselves to stay on the team, to serve their
> leader.   It came in the guise of "national security," a blanket
> term used to justify the most appalling criminal acts by men de-
> termined to preserve their own political power at any cost.   It
> came in the form of the ladder against the bedroom window,
> miniature transmitters in the ceiling, wiretaps, burglaries, enemies
> lists, tax audits, and psychiatric profiles.
>   It is not easy to write the word totalitarian when reporting
> about America, but if the word jars, or seems overstated, con-
> sider the dictionary definition: "Of or pertaining to a centralized
> government in which those in control grant neither recognition
> nor tolerance to parties of differing opinion."

And that is very close to what happened, for, as we learned from the Watergate investigation, the enormous power of the government of the United States, including the police power and the secret intelligence apparatus, had been turned loose against the people of the United States, at least against those who held differing opinions, against the opposition political party, and the press.[77]

The Watergate investigation revealed a number of criminal and undemocratic actions by President Nixon and his closest advisors. These activities demonstrate how far the U.S. had moved in the direction of a totalitarian government. Let's enumerate a partial list of these acts.[78]

Item: Burglars, financed by funds from the Committee to Reelect the President, broke into and bugged the headquarters of the Democratic party (in the Watergate apartment complex).

Item: These burglars were paid hush money and promised executive clemency to protect the president and his advisors.

Item: Burglars also broke into the office of the psychiatrist of Daniel Ellsberg, the person who leaked the Pentagon Papers to the press. These papers, of course, were instrumental in showing the public how they had been systematically deceived by a series of presidents during the long Vietnam war.

Item: The White House offered the judge in the Ellsberg case, while the trial was in session, the possibility of his being named director of the FBI.

Item: President Nixon's personal attorney solicited money for an illegally formed campaign committee and offered an ambassadorship in return for a campaign contribution.

Item: Money gathered from contributions, some illegally, was systematically laundered (to conceal the donors). Much of this money was kept in cash so when payoffs occurred, the money could not be traced.

Item: President Nixon ordered secret wiretapping of his own aides, several journalists, and even his brother. Additionally, he had secret microphones planted in his offices to record clandestinely every conversation.

Item: The director of the FBI destroyed vital legal evidence at the suggestion of the president's aides.

Item: The attorney general of the U.S., John Mitchell, participated in the preliminary discussions about bugging the Democratic headquarters. He even suggested that one means of gaining information about the Democrats was to establish a floating bordello at the Miami convention of the Democrats.

Item: The president's men participated in a campaign of "dirty tricks" to discredit the various potential Democratic nominees for president. These "tricks" included the publication and distribution of letters, purporting to come from Senator Muskie, claiming that Senator Jackson was a homosexual.

Item: The White House requested tax audits of administration opponents.

Item: The White House used the CIA in an effort to halt the FBI investigation of Watergate.

Item: President Nixon offered aides Robert Halderman and John Erlichman as much as 300,000 dollars from a secret "slush fund" for their legal fees after they were forced to resign.

Item: The president and his advisors, using the cloak of "national security," strongly resisted attempts by the special prosecutor, the courts, and Congress to get the facts in the case.

Item: Various administration officials were found guilty of perjury and withholding information.

Item: When the president, under duress, did provide transcripts of the tapes or other materials, they were edited.

Item: The president, on television and in press releases, lied to the American public over and over again.

This infamous list of discretions comprise a tangled web of activities that posed a significant threat to the United States' democratic political system. All of the efforts were directed at subverting the political process so that the administration in power would stay in power, regardless of the means. There was a systematic effort to discredit enemies of the administration, to weaken the two-party system, and to control the flow of information to citizens.

Although the Nixon administration was guilty of these heinous acts, we should not assume that he was the first American president to be involved in such chicanery. Watergate was no sudden aberration but rather was the end result of practices of government that have been with us in significant ways throughout our history.

CONCLUSION

Politics is probably not as unseemly as it would appear from the description in this chapter, because our task was to focus on the dark side of politics. We have looked at two types of political deviance — the use of political clout for material gain and the unfair means to gain, maintain, or increase political power. In both cases the deviance can be achieved by corrupt individuals or by a corrupt system.   But even when accomplished by individuals, the important sociological point is that the deviance is only possible because the elite occupy positions of power. Because of the duties and powers inherent in their political positions, they are susceptible to the appeals of the monied interests who want to use them, or they are persuaded by the appeal of greater power.

Although political corruption is found in all types of societies and in all types of political and economic systems, the amount of political corruption found in the U.S. is astounding.   Benson, after carefully studying the phenomenon, concluded that:

> Today it is probably fair to say that América has as much cor-
> ruption, both absolutely and proportionately, as any other mod-
> ern constitutional democracy.   There are no international indices
> of corruption, but the available data indicate that corruption here
> is at least as severe and extensive as in other modern democ-
> racies.   American idealism does not appear to be reflected in our
> political ethos.[79]

But why is this high rate of political corruption found in the United States?   The answer is complex and requires an understanding of historical factors, American character, American values, and the political-economic systems.   The rip-off mentality that pervades the economic system is found throughout the social structure, as this chapter has amply demonstrated.   The goal of individual or corporate success supersedes group concerns and therefore any means are used to achieve the goal. The following chapter should provide further insight into this complex societal problem.

NOTES

1. The organization and many of the examples used in this chapter are from two sources: George C. S. Benson, *Political Corruption in America* (Lexington, Mass.: Lexington Books, 1978); and George Amick, *The American Way of Graft* (Princeton, N.J.: The Center for Analysis of Public Issues, 1976).

2. Benson, *Political Corruption in America,* p. xiii.

3. For some excellent reviews of the magnitude of political crimes in America, see: *Ibid;* Amick, *The American Way of Graft;* and Carl J. Friedrich, *The Pathology of Politics* (New York: Harper & Row, 1972).

4. The following is taken from "Another Scandal Breaks Open in Washington," *U.S. News and World Report* (September 11, 1978), p. 82; and "A Sweeping Benefit of the GSA Scandal," *Business Week* (October 2, 1978), pp. 78–86.

5. United Press International release (October 24, 1978).

6. Jack Anderson, "Weapons Makers and Pentagon Brass and Happy Family," *Rocky Mountain News* (February 1, 1976), p. 51.

7. Amick, *The American Way of Graft,* pp. 40–41.

8. The Agnew case is taken primarily from *ibid.,* pp. 42–50; and J. Anthony Lukas, *Nightmare: The Underside of the Nixon Years* (New York: Viking, 1976), Chapter 12.

9. Benson, *Political Corruption in America,* pp. 11 and 127; and Gerald J. McCullough, "Pennsylvania: The Failure of Campaign Reform," *Campaign Money,* Herbert E. Alexander, ed. (New York: Macmillan, 1976), pp. 226–227.

10. Benson, *Political Corruption in America,* p. 69.

11. *Ibid.,* p. 12.

12. Amick, *The American Way of Graft,* pp. 98–99.

13. Benson, *Political Corruption in America,* pp. 81–82.

14. Amick, *The American Way of Graft,* pp. 146–149.

15. *Ibid.,* pp. 109–114.

16. See *ibid.,* pp. 76–94.

17. *Ibid.,* pp. 92–93.

18. Mark J. Green, James M. Fallows, and David R. Zwick, *Who Runs Congress? The President, Big Business, or You?* (New York: Bantam Books, 1972), pp. 25–28.

19. Lukas, *Nightmare,* p. 111.

20. Associated Press release (June 22, 1979).

21. CBS News, "The Best Congress Money Can Buy," first telecast in 1975.

22. Amick, *The American Way of Graft,* p. 77.

23. *Ibid.,* pp. 146–149.

24. Benson, *Political Corruption in America,* p. 13.

25. "Park Talks (a Little)," *Time* (April 17, 1978), p. 20. See also, "FBI Is Pursuing 574 Investigations of Corruption," United Press International release (April 29, 1978).

26. Associated Press release (March 14, 1979).

27. "Congressmen in Hot Water: The List Lengthens," *U.S. News and World Report* (October 23, 1978), p. 35.

28. Jerome H. Skolnick, *Justice without Trial: Law Enforcement in Democratic Society* (New York: John Wiley, 1966), p. 14.

29. Edward L. Barrett, Jr., "Police Practices and the Law — From Arrest to Release or Charge," *California Law Review* 50 (1962), pp. 31–35.

30. President's Commission on Law Enforcement and the Administration of Justice, *The Challenge of Crime in a Free Society,* cited in *Official Deviance,* Jack D. Douglas and John M. Johnson, eds. (Philadelphia: J. B. Lippincott, 1977), pp. 254–255.

31. These three examples are taken from *The Knapp Commission Report on Police Corruption* (New York: George Braziller, 1973), pp. 1–3.

32. *The Challenge of Crime in a Free Society* (Washington: U.S. Government Printing Office, 1967), p. 32.

33. James Cook, "The Invisible Enterprise," *Forbes* 126 (September 29, 1980), p. 60.

34. These characteristics are taken from Charles H. McCaghy, *Deviant Behavior: Crime, Conflict, and Interest Groups* (New York: Macmillan, 1976), pp. 233–235.

35. Donald R. Cressey, *Theft of the Nation: The Structure and Operation of Organized Crime in America* (New York: Harper & Row, 1969), pp. 250–251.

36. Reprinted from William J. Chambliss, *On the Take: From Petty Crooks to Presidents* (Bloomington: Indiana University Press, 1978), pp. 1–2. © 1978 by William J. Chambliss. Reprinted by permission from Indiana University Press.

37. Benson, *Political Corruption in America,* p. 33.

38. The account of the Tweed Ring is taken basically from three sources: *ibid.,* pp. 37–43; Allen Weinstein and R. Jackson Wilson, *Freedom and Crisis* (New

York: Random House, 1974), p. 530; and Gustavus Myers, *The History of Tammany Hall*, Revised Edition (New York: Burt Franklin, 1917), Chapter 13.

39. Benson, *Political Corruption in America*, p. 39.

40. Weinstein and Wilson, *Freedom and Crisis*, p. 530.

41. Jack Newfield and Paul DuBrul, *The Abuse of Power: The Permanent Government and the Fall of New York* (New York: Penguin Books, 1978), pp. 84–85. Copyright © 1977 by Jack Newfield and Paul DuBrul. Reprinted by permission of Viking Penguin Inc. For an elaboration of this thesis of a national power elite, see: C. Wright Mills, *The Power Elite* (New York: Oxford University Press, 1956); G. William Domhoff, *Who Rules America?* (Englewood Cliffs, N.J.: Prentice-Hall, 1967); and Michael Parenti, *Democracy for the Few*, Second Edition (New York: St. Martin's Press, 1977).

42. This material is taken from Newfield and DuBrul, *The Abuse of Power*, pp. 75–108.

43. *Ibid.*, p. 76. From *The Abuse of Power* by Jack Newfield and Paul Du Brul. Copyright © 1977 by Jack Newfield and Paul DuBrul. Reprinted by permission of Viking Penguin Inc.

44. See Robert Caro, *The Power Broker: Robert Moses and the Fall of New York* (New York: Vintage, 1975).

45. Newfield and DuBrul, *The Abuse of Power*, pp. 118–119.

46. For an elaboration of this thesis, see Charles Beard, *An Economic Interpretation of the Constitution of the United States* (New York: Macmillan, 1919).

47. Max Ferrand, ed., *Records of the Federal Convention* (New Haven: Yale University Press, 1927), quoted in Parenti, *Democracy for the Few*, p. 53.

48. Quoted in Parenti, *Democracy for the Few*, p. 57.

49. C. B. Macpherson, *The Real World of Democracy* (New York: Oxford University Press, 1972), Chapter 1.

50. Parenti, *Democracy for the Few*, p. 56.

51. *Ibid.*, pp. 57–58.

52. Weinstein and Wilson, *Freedom and Crisis*, p. 430.

53. Parenti, *Democracy for the Few*, p. 51.

54. Marvin Stone, "More Political Shenanigans," *U.S. News and World Report* (April 10, 1978), p. 96.

55. V. O. Key, Jr., *Southern Politics* (New York: Vintage, 1949), Chapter 29.

56. The following is taken from *ibid.*, Chapter 26.

57. Key, *Southern Politics*, Chapter 26.

58. The following is taken primarily from Benson, *Political Corruption in America*, pp. 170–174.

59. *Ibid.*, p. 171.

60. Victor Lasky, *It Didn't Start with Watergate* (New York: Dial Press, 1977), p. 122.

61. *Los Angeles Times* (August 8, 1976), pp. 1, 24. Reported in Benson, *Political Corruption in America*, p. 172.

62. Lasky, *It Didn't Start with Watergate*, pp. 119–123.

63. This section is taken from Benson, *Political Corruption in America*, pp. 174–176.

64. See Frank H. Jonas, ed., *Political Dynamiting* (Salt Lake City: University of Utah Press, 1970).

65. These examples are taken from Frank Mankiewicz, *Perfectly Clear: Nixon from Whittier to Watergate* (New York: Quadrangle, 1973), p. 39.

66. *Ibid.*, p. 45.

67. These examples are from *ibid.*, pp. 51–52.

68. *Ibid.,* pp. 52–53.

69. *Ibid.,* pp. 54–55.

70. Cited in David W. Adamany and George E. Agree, *Political Money* (Baltimore: Johns Hopkins, 1975), p. 4.

71. Stu Bishop and Bert Knorr, "The Moneymen," *Big Brother and the Holding Company: The World Behind Watergate,* Steve Weissman, ed. (Palo Alto, California: Ramparts Press, 1974), pp. 211–212.

72. Benson, *Political Corruption in America,* p. 177; CBS News, "The Best Congress Money Can Buy."

73. Benson, *Political Corruption in America,* p. 179.

74. *Ibid.,* pp. 181–183.

75. For an elaboration of the reform of the campaign-contributions problem, see: Adamany and Agree, *Political Money;* Herbert E. Alexander, *Money in Politics* (Washington, D.C.: Public Affairs Press, 1972); Alexander, *Campaign Money;* and George Thayer, *Who Shakes the Money Tree? American Campaign Financing Practices from 1789 to the Present* (New York: Simon and Schuster, 1973).

76. This section on Watergate is taken from D. Stanley Eitzen, *Social Problems* (Boston: Allyn and Bacon, 1980), Chapter 2.

77. David Wise, *The Politics of Lying* (New York: Vintage, 1973), pp. x–xi.

78. Cf., *ibid.,* pp. xi–xiv; "The Tangled Web They Wove," *Newsweek* (December 2, 1974), pp. 32–37; "Four Key Convictions in the Watergate Affair," *U.S. News and World Report* (January 13, 1975), pp. 15–17; William A. Dobrovir, Joseph D. Gebhardt, Samuel J. Buffone, and Andra N. Oakes, *The Offenses of Richard Nixon* (New York: Quadrangle, 1973); Theodore H. White, *Breach of Faith: The Fall of Richard Nixon* (New York: Atheneum, 1975); and John Dean, *Blind Ambition* (New York: Simon and Schuster, 1976). For a sociological analysis of Watergate, see Jack D. Douglas, "Watergate: Harbinger of the American Prince," *Official Deviance,* Douglas and Johnson, eds., pp. 112–120.

79. Benson, *Political Corruption in America,* p. 3.

Chapter 7
Political Deviance

Criminologists interested in political crimes have traditionally concentrated on crimes by individuals and organizations against the government — primarily the attempts to change the political system through the violation of criminal statutes. While these political acts are important to understand, the exclusive focus on crimes by people against the government neglects the crimes by the government against the people. The previous chapter along with this one will attempt to right this imbalance by focusing on the deviance of the political elite.[1]

Political deviance is an omnibus concept including a number of practices. Under this rubric are the myriad forms of political corruption noted in Chapter 6. Also included are the consequences of the government's bias toward business that negatively impacts the powerless. This chapter will catalogue additional political acts that are deviant. Specifically, we will examine deviance in the domestic and foreign spheres. Domestically we will consider: (1) the secrecy and deception used by government officials to manipulate public opinion; (2) the abuse of power by government officials and agencies; (3) political prisoners; and (4) official violence as manifested in police brutality and the use of citizens as unwilling guinea pigs. On the international level we will focus on two illegal warlike acts: clandestine intervention and war crimes.

DOMESTIC POLITICAL DEVIANCE

Secrecy, Lying, and Deception

The hallmark of any democracy is consent of the governed based on a reliable flow of information from the government.   There are a number of mechanisms by which this principle is thwarted in American society.*   A common technique to withhold information is the use of "executive privilege" by the president to keep things secret from Congress and the Courts.   The doctrine of executive privilege is the constitutionally questionable belief that the president and his staff cannot be forced to testify and that presidential documents cannot be examined without the president's permission.   The argument given for such immunity is that such information might compromise national security.   Some examples of how this doctrine has been used are:[3]

> *Item:* President Truman refused to turn over to the House Un-American Activities Committee an FBI report on a government scientist.
>
> *Item:* General Maxwell Taylor declined to appear before the House Subcommittee on Defense Appropriations in 1963 to discuss the Bay of Pigs invasion.
>
> *Item:* In 1972 the Securities Exchange Commission refused to give certain information to the House Interstate and Foreign Commerce Subcommittee concerning its investigation of ITT.
>
> *Item:* In 1973 President Nixon refused to surrender the White House tape recordings to Special Prosecutor Archibald Cox.

Another method used to "stonewall" is to designate information as "classified."   The classification of documents is based on the necessity of safeguarding sensitive military and foreign-policy information in the national interest.   One problem with classifying documents as "secret" is defining the category: even while some material is warranted as classified, too much ends up as secret.   Describing the magnitude of this problem, the Chairman of the House Foreign Operations and Government Information Subcommittee said in 1972:

> There are 55,000 arms pumping up and down in Government offices stamping "confidential" on stacks of Government documents; more than 18,000 Government employees are wielding "secret" stamps, and a censorship elite of nearly 3,000 bureaucrats have authority to stamp "top secret" on public records.
> These are not wild estimates.   These numbers were pro-

---

* Our discussion is limited to the federal government, especially the executive branch.   However, attempts by government officials to deceive the public are found at all levels.[2]

vided by the Government agencies, themselves. But even this huge number of Government censors is just the top of the secrecy iceberg.[4]

The classification of sensitive materials can also be used as a ploy to hide materials embarrassing to government officials. An apt example is the attempt by the White House to suppress publication of the Pentagon Papers, which revealed how American involvement in Vietnam had been shaped during several administrations while being shielded from the public. In early 1965, before President Johnson had sent combat troops to Vietnam, the goals of the U.S., as stated in a secret memorandum from the Assistant Secretary of Defense Daniel McNaughton to Secretary Robert McNamara, were:

> 70 percent to avoid a humiliating U.S. defeat (to our reputation as a guarantor),
> 20 percent to keep South Vietnam (and the adjacent territory) from Chinese hands,
> 10 percent to permit the people of South Vietnam a better, freer way of life.[5]

Had the people and Congress been aware of these:

> Would Congress have authorized a major war and more than 50,000 U.S. combat deaths for these goals? Would the American people have supported a war for these goals? And if not, was an American President justified in going to war for them anyway? More importantly, was an American President justified in concealing these goals and our own acts of provocation while he was, in fact, making a unilateral decision to go to war? [6]

Precisely because the people would not have supported the war if they had known about the government's goals, President Nixon, who broadened the war from Johnson's policies, attempted to suppress publication of the Pentagon Papers, which would have revealed our true intentions and behaviors. In addition, the weight of the government's force was brought to the prosecution of those who had leaked the Pentagon Papers (Daniel Ellsberg and Anthony Russo). The government even went so far as to offer the judge in that case the directorship of the FBI, while the case was being heard.[7]

Officials can also deceive the public by the "you did not ask me the right question, so I did not give you the right answer" game.[8] As an example, when Richard Helms was director of the CIA he was asked before Congress if his agency had been involved in Watergate. His reply was "No." Much later, when it became known that the CIA had lent equipment to the Watergate burglars and had concealed the laundering of checks used in the Watergate coverup, Helms was reminded of his previous answer. He explained that he had not been asked the right questions, for he had assumed that the original question meant involvement in the actual break-in at Democratic headquarters.

Although all of the above tactics work to deceive the public, none is more onerous than <u>outright lying by government officials</u>. Examples of this strategy from recent American history are:[9]

Item: In 1954 Secretary of State John Foster Dulles said that Americans were not involved in the coup in Guatemala to depose the regime of leftist President Guzman, even though the operation was financed, organized, and run by the CIA.

Item: In 1960 a U.S. spy plane, flown by a CIA pilot, was shot down over Russia. Although the U.S. had been using U-2 planes to spy on Russia for the preceding four years, our officials denied the incident, saying we had not violated Russian air space.

Item: In 1961 the CIA, under President Kennedy, organized an Invasion of Cuba at the Bay of Pigs. Yet when the Cubans charged in the United Nations that the U.S. was behind the operation, Ambassador Adlai Stevenson responded that no U.S. personnel or government planes were involved.

Item: In 1963, the U.S. supported, but officially denied its involvement, in the coup against South Vietnam President Ngo Dinh Diem.

Item: In 1964 President Johnson used an incident where American ships were allegedly shot at in the Tonkin Gulf to give him a free hand to escalate the war in Vietnam. Congress was deliberately misled by the official representation of the facts.

Item: President Johnson praised our Asian allies for sending "volunteers" to fight in Vietnam when in fact our government had paid Thailand and the Philippines 200 million dollars each if they would make this gesture.

Item: President Nixon and his advisors told the American public that the neutrality of Cambodia had not been violated, when we had already conducted 3,600 bombing missions in a five-year period in that country. To carry out this deception, the death certificates of Americans who died in Cambodia were falsified by our government.

These examples could be multiplied many times over with coverups of the CIA involvement of the takeover of the Allende government in Chile, the attempted whitewashing of the sheep deaths in Utah because of an unintended release of chemicals used in biological warfare, the denial by Attorney General Mitchell that ITT had offered 400,000 dollars to underwrite the 1972 Republican National Convention, and so on.

Coverups, lies, and secrecy by the government certainly run counter to our long-standing philosophical commitment to an open system where the public is included in the decision-making process. In the opinion of Thomas Emerson, Yale law professor, secrecy in a democratic society is a source of illegitimate power for several reasons: (1) where the people are assumed to be the masters and the government the servant, it makes no sense that the master should be denied the information upon which to direct the activities of the servants; (2) each branch of government has its constitutional role to play — for one branch to withhold information from another undermines the whole principle of checks and balances; and (3) it denies the individual due process.[10] Due process demands that the citizen be furnished all the information upon which his destiny rests.

Of course, at times the public must be kept in the dark. The question, though, is when secrecy is legitimate. The burden of proof lies with those imposing the secrecy. The key is whether the intentional tampering with the free flow of public information is more beneficial to the public interest than disclosure.[11] This principle is difficult to operationalize, however, since one can argue that the public interest always is paramount, regardless of the situation. For example, most Americans believed the actions of Daniel Ellsberg were wrong when he disclosed the secrets of the Pentagon Papers. For them the secret leaker was guilty and the secret keepers innocent because the public interest required secrecy in these militarily sensitive matters. Others, in contrast, perceived Ellsberg as a hero, one with courage enough to reveal the errors of the establishment. In this view, the secret keepers were guilty and the secret leaker was honored because public policy in Vietnam was against the public's interest.

As David Wise has bluntly summarized the secrecy problem:

> With its control over information supported by an official system of secrecy and classification, the government has almost unlimited power to misinform the public. It does so for various reasons. The government lies to manipulate public opinion, to generate public support for its policies, and to silence its critics. Ultimately, it lies to stay in power.[12]

Abuse of Power by Government Agencies

Watergate revealed to Americans that their highest leaders had conspired, among other things, to win an election by using such illegal means as dirty tricks, burglary of opponents, and soliciting of campaign funds by threats and bribes. These White House transgressions, which we have examined earlier in some detail, are only one expression of illicit government intervention. In this section we will focus on the deviant actions of government agencies in several key areas.

Many government abuses have occurred under the guise of internal security. Domestic surveillance is one example. Government agencies have a long history of surveillance of its citizens.[13]   The pace quickened in the 1930s and increased further with the communist threat in the 1950s.   Surveillance reached its peak during the height of antiwar and civil-rights protests of the late 1960s and early 1970s.   The FBI's concern with internal security, for example, dates back to 1936 when President Roosevelt asked Director J. Edgar Hoover to investigate domestic communist and fascist organizations in the U.S.[14]   In 1939, as World War II began in Europe, President Roosevelt issued a proclamation that the FBI would be in charge of investigating subversive activities, espionage, sabotage, and that all law-enforcement offices should give the FBI any relevant information on suspected activities.   These directives began a pattern followed by the FBI under the administrations of Presidents Truman, Eisenhower, Kennedy, Johnson, Nixon, Ford, and Carter.

The scope of these abuses by the FBI and other government agencies, such as the CIA, the National Security Agency, and the Internal Revenue Service, is incredible.   In the name of "national security" the following have occurred against American citizens:

Item: From 1967 to 1973 the NSA (National Security Agency) monitored the overseas telephone calls and cables of approximately 1,650 U.S. citizens and organizations, as well as almost 6,000 foreign nationals and groups.[15]

Item: The CIA opened and photographed nearly 250,000 first-class letters in the U.S. between 1953 and 1973.[16]

Item: As director of the CIA, William Colby acknowledged to Congress that his organization had opened the mail of private citizens and accumulated secret files on more than 10,000 Americans.[17]

Item: The FBI over the years conducted about 1,500 break-ins of foreign embassies and missions, mob hangouts, and the headquarters of such organizations as the Ku Klux Klan and the American Communist Party.[18]

Item: The FBI confessed to the Senate Intelligence Committee that it had committed 238 burglaries against fourteen domestic organizations during a twenty-six-year period ending in 1968.[19]

Item: The FBI collected over 500,000 dossiers between 1959 and 1971 on communists, black leaders, student radicals, and feminists.[20]

Item: The husband of an officer in ACTION, a St. Louis civil rights organization, received a handwritten note that said: "Look man, I guess your old lady doesn't get enough at home or she wouldn't be shucking and jiving with our black men in ACTION, you dig? Like, all she wants to integrate is the bedroom and we black sisters ain't gonna take no second best from our men.   So lay it on her man or get her the hell off Newstead (Street)."   The couple soon separated and the local FBI officer wrote to headquarters: "This matrimonial stress and strain should cause her to function much less effectively in ACTION." [21]

Item: In 1972 the FBI paid 7,402 "ghetto informants" to provide information about racial extremists.[22]

Item: In 1970 actress Jean Seberg helped raise money for a militant organization, the Black Panthers. According to documents released by the FBI after the suicide of Ms. Seberg in 1979, the FBI tried to discredit the actress by planting the rumor that the father of her baby was a prominent Black Panther leader. This false story led to a miscarriage and psychotic behavior, and possibly her suicide.[23]

These are but a few examples of government abuses against its citizens. To make the point clearer, we will describe in greater detail two nefarious (but representative) campaigns of the government: (1) the FBI's vendetta against Martin Luther King, Jr.; and (2) the FBI's campaign to nullify the effectiveness of the Socialist Workers Party.

The FBI had a campaign to destroy civil-rights groups. The most infamous of these was the attempt to negate the power of Martin Luther King, Jr. King had been openly critical of the Bureau's ineffectual enforcement of civil-rights laws and this apparently led the director, J. Edgar Hoover, to label King "the most notorious liar in the U.S." and to launch a vendetta against him.[24] From 1957, when King became prominent in the Montgomery Bus Boycott, the FBI monitored King's activities under its vague authority to investigate "subversives." The more powerful King became, the greater the FBI's surveillance of him. King was indexed in the files as a communist and one to be imprisoned in the event of a "national emergency." This charge against King was based on the allegation that two of his associates in the Southern Christian Leadership Conference were communists.

Because Hoover had convinced Attorney General Robert Kennedy of the possible link between King and the communists, Kennedy authorized wiretaps of King's phones, which continued for the next two years. Unknown to Kennedy was that the FBI planned to use the wiretaps to discredit King.

The FBI's efforts to neutralize or even destroy King were intensified with King's increasing popularity as exemplified by his "I Had a Dream" speech before 250,000 in Washington, D.C., in August, 1963. King was thus characterized in an FBI memo as:

> He stands head and shoulders over all other Negro leaders put together when it comes to influencing great masses of Negroes. *We must mark him now . . . as the most* dangerous Negro of the future of this Nation from the standpoint of Communism, the Negro and national security.[25]

The efforts now escalated to include physical and photographic surveillance and the placement of illegal bugs in his living quarters.   Tapes
of conversations in a Washington hotel were used by the FBI to imply
that King engaged in extramarital sexual activities.   The FBI used these
tapes, which may or may not have been altered, to dishonor King.   At
the very time King was receiving great honors, such as the Nobel Peace
Prize, *Time* magazine's "Man of the Year," and numerous honorary degrees, the FBI countered with briefings, distribution of the "tapes" to
newspeople and columnists, and congressional testimony about King's
"communist" activities and "private" behavior.   The FBI even briefed
officials of the National Council of Churches and other church bodies
about King's alleged deviance.

The smear campaign against King reached its zenith when the FBI
mailed the "tapes" to the SCLC offices in Atlanta with a covering letter
suggesting that he commit suicide or face humiliation with the tapes made
public on the eve of the Nobel Award ceremonies in Sweden.

Summing up the sordid affair, Halperin and his associates have
editorialized:

> The FBI had turned its arsenal of surveillance and disruption
> techniques on Martin Luther King and the civil rights movement.
> It was concerned not with Soviet agents nor with criminal activity,
> but with the political and personal activities of a man and a
> movement committee to nonviolence and democracy.   King was
> not the first such target, nor the last.   In the end we are all vic-
> tims, as our political life is distorted and constricted by the FBI,
> a law enforcement agency now policing politics.[26]

This comment is critical of the FBI and justifiably so.   We believe that
the FBI's tactics were illegal, whether King was a communist or not.
But that is a moot point because King was not a communist.   In testimony before a Senate committee, the FBI's assistant deputy director
James Adams was asked by Senator Frank Church if the FBI ever found
that King was a communist.   Replied Adams: "No, we did not." [27]

Another example of an FBI vendetta against a nonexistent threat
involved the Socialist Workers Party, a small, peaceful, and legal political
party.[28]   This party became the target of FBI abuses because it supported
Castro's Cuba and worked for racial integration in the South.   For these
transgressions, the FBI kept the SWP under surveillance for thirty-four
years.   FBI documents have revealed that in one six-and-a-half-year period in the early 1960s the agency burglarized the offices of the party in
ninety-four raids, often with the complicity of the New York City police
department.   Over this period FBI agents photographed 8,700 pages of
party files and compiled dossiers totaling eight million pages.

The FBI tried to destroy the party by sending anonymous letters
to members' employers, working to keep the party's candidates off the

ballot, and by otherwise sabotaging political campaigns. Informants were also used to collect information about the political views of the organization.*

Several points need to be made about these activities of the FBI. Obviously, they were a thorough waste of time and money. As one observer put it: "If they had devoted tens of thousands of man-hours to pursuing true criminals — say, those involved in organized crime — they might have served the public interest as they were meant to." [29] Most important, the FBI's tactics were not only illegal but were directed at an organization that was working legally *within* the system.

> Just as the FBI's illegal assumption of the authority to investigate subversive activities led to illegal methods, the failure of those methods to produce evidence that could be used to take legal action against radical and liberal political movements led to further lawlessness: active efforts to destroy them. In October, 1961, for example, the FBI put into operation its "S.W.P. Disruption Program." The grounds for this program, as a confidential Bureau memorandum described them, were that the Socialist Workers Party had been "openly espousing its line on a local and national basis through running candidates for public office...." The memorandum is astonishingly revealing about the political sophistication of the FBI. If these Socialists were openly espousing their line by running candidates for public office, including the Presidency, these activities obviously weren't illegal. And if their support for the civil-rights movement was subversive, then so was that of many millions of Americans.[30]

Political Prisoners

In 1978, when he was ambassador to the United Nations, Andrew Young commented publicly that the United States was guilty, as were other nations, of having political prisoners. Young's accusation was widely denounced by politicians and editorial writers, many of whom saw such wild statements as reason enough for the ambassador's ouster. Andrew Young, however, was correct.

Let's begin by establishing what is meant by "political" prisoners. They key is that a political prisoner is one who is processed by the criminal-justice system because of his or her political activities.[31] As McConnell has described:

> Socrates, Charles I and Patty Hearst, despite their widely varied times, circumstances and beliefs, shared the common characteristic that at a certain time in their lives they were placed on trial because of behavior found reprehensible by the political elite of

---

* The SWP has sued the FBI (and won) for its violations of the SWP's civil rights.

their day, for activities thought highly prejudicial to the welfare
of the state, and tried in legal proceedings from which a large
political element and an inflamed public opinion could not be
severed. And they were tried, moreover, by bodies seeking to
foster official values or notions of public policy which the victims
repudiated.[32]

Three qualities of the actors are central to our distinction of political prisoners. Our view of political repression begins with the assumption that the law serves the interests of those with the power to make and
enforce them. The law, therefore, is a tool by which the powerful retain
their advantages. They do this by *legally* punishing those who threaten
the status quo.

Second, is that while political criminals, and other criminals may
both pose a threat, the former are considered a direct threat to established political power.*

> If the members of a ruling elite believe a particular individual or
> group to be imminently hostile to the prevailing pattern of value
> distribution, and if they activate the criminal process against him
> (or them) for that reason, what results is a political trial. Addi-
> tionally, if members of the ruling elite feel someone seriously in-
> tends to alter the *way* in which the government distributes those
> values, and if the elite activates the criminal process against them
> for that reason — that, too, constitutes a political trial.[34]

Third, the political criminal does not perceive himself/herself as
a criminal but as one who has violated the law out of a set of convictions
to create a better society. Thus, they see the system and its agents as
criminals and the enemy.

Of course, by our view of political prisoners, acts such as assassinations, treason, mutiny, and conspiracy to overthrow the government are
examples of dissent whose perpetrators will be punished by the legal
system.

Throughout American history groups that were oppressed resorted
to various illegitimate means to secure the rights and privileges that they
believed were rightfully theirs. The revolutionary colonists used acts of
civil disobedience and finally eight years of war to accomplish their goals.

---

* We will consider political crimes only in the narrow sense of crimes
against the establishment. We are sympathetic, however, with the view expressed
by Liazos:

> Only now are we beginning to realize that most prisoners are *political pris-
> oners* — that their criminal actions (whether against individuals, such as
> robbing, or conscious political acts against the state) result largely from
> current social and political conditions, and not the work of "disturbed" and
> "psychotic" personalities.[33]

In this view, then, all prisoners are political in the sense that they became criminals
as a result of struggling against the inequities of society.

Native Americans have fought the intrusions of white settlers and systematic suppression by the United States government. Other groups such as farmers, slaveholders, WASP supremacists, ethnic and racial minorities, and laborers have at times broken the law in efforts to change what they considered an unfair system.[35] While these are extremely important, we will concentrate here on the efforts by dissenters during the Vietnam War to change the government's course and the governmental efforts to silence these critics.

The Vietnam War was never formally declared by Congress.[36] It escalated from presidential decisions and commitments that were camouflaged from the public. In effect, the U.S. had taken a side in an Asian civil war without the consent of the people or, if they had consented as we now know, it was done through the manipulation of events and information by our leaders. Because of the uniqueness of our involvement in this war many young men refused to serve. Some became fugitives from the law by hiding in the U.S. or by fleeing to other countries. Others accepted imprisonment. Some 20,000 Americans of all ages refused to pay all or a part of their taxes because the money would support a war they considered illegal, immoral, and unjust. As a result, they risked harassment by the Internal Revenue Service and possible imprisonment.

At one demonstration before the Oakland induction center in 1965, one David Miller set fire to his draft card saying: "I believe the napalming of villages to be an immoral act. I hope this will be a significant political act, so here goes."[37] He was arrested and later sentenced to two and one-half years in prison. This started a rash of similar protests that the establishment considered a threat to their power. At one rally, the Reverend Sloane Coffin, Dr. Benjamin Spock, and two others announced that they would henceforth counsel young men to refuse to serve in the armed forces as long as the Vietnam War continued. They were arrested for conspiracy and convicted to two years imprisonment for treason.

One of the most infamous political trials of this era involved the Chicago Eight.[38] In 1968, a time of ghetto riots and the assassinations of Martin Luther King, Jr., and Robert Kennedy, Congress passed the "Rap Brown Amendment" (Brown was chairperson of the Student Nonviolent Coordinating Committee — SNCC — at the time), which nearly outlawed interstate travel by political activists. In the summer of that year the Democratic National Convention convened in Chicago. Because Hubert Humphrey, a hawk on Vietnam, was the leading nominee, thousands of youths flooded Chicago bent on protesting the war and venting their anger against what they perceived as an unresponsive political leadership. They protested and the police reacted violently, adding to the volatility of the situation.

Months later when Richard Nixon took office and John Mitchell became attorney general, the federal government issued indictments against individuals felt to be the leaders of the Chicago riots — David

Dellinger, Rennie Davis, Tom Hayden, Abbie Hoffman, Jerry Rubin, Lee Weiner, John Froines, and Bobby Seales — soon to be known collectively as the Chicago Eight. These persons were charged with conspiracy to cross state lines with intent to cause a riot (violating the Rap Brown law). These men represented various kinds of dissent such as radical pacifism, the New Left, political hippies, academic dissent, and black militance. The case was heard in the U.S. District Court in Chicago, Judge Julius Hoffman presiding.

Many knowledgeable observers, including the predecessor of John Mitchell, Ramsey Clark, felt that the trial was a political gesture by the new Nixon administration to demonstrate a no-nonsense policy against dissent. The conspiracy charge made little sense because the actions of the defendants and their constituencies were uncoordinated. Moreover, Bobby Seales, an alleged co-conspirator, knew only one of the other defendants.

This trial was a symbolic showcase for the defendants as well. Because of their disrespect for the system, the defendants refused to accept the traditional role.[39] Instead of allowing the system to keep them quiet while the long judicial process wound down, the defendants acted so that their actions would be headline news. Thus, they continually challenged the judiciary's legitimacy. As Sternberg has characterized their rationale:

> The argument that the court is illegitimate rests on the defendants' analysis and condemnation of the existing situation in the United States. They see themselves as political prisoners trapped by a power structure of laws created by societal groups hostile to their interests. The court is both an agent for these groups and institutions — most significantly, monopoly capitalism, racism, colonialism, the military-industrial complex, and incipient fascism — and also an oppressive power group in its own right. Although defendants may vary somewhat in the rank or order of their targets, all are in agreement that the criminal court's allegiances are squarely with the oppressor groups and directly hostile to the powerless classes in American society.[40]

As a result of their disrespectful behavior toward the court, Judge Hoffman judged the defendants and their lawyers guilty of 159 contempt citations and sentenced them to jail for terms ranging from sixty-eight days to four years and thirteen days. In addition, each defendant was found guilty of inciting a riot, receiving a sentence of five years in prison and a 5,000 dollar fine. All were acquitted of conspiracy charges. Before the sentences were passed, each defendant was allowed to make a final statement. The speech by Tom Hayden captured the essence of the problem from the perspective of the accused:

> Our intention in coming to Chicago was not to incite a riot...
> (It) was to see to it that certain things, that is, the right of every

human being, the right to assemble, the right to protest, can be carried out even where the Government chooses to suspend those rights. It was because we chose to exercise those rights to Chicago . . . that we are here today. . . . We would hardly be notorious characters if they had left us alone in the streets of Chicago last year. . . . It would have been testimony to our failure as organizers. But instead we became the architects, the master minds, and the geniuses of a conspiracy to overthrow the government. We were invented. We were chosen by the government to serve as scapegoats for all that they wanted to prevent happening in the 1970's.[41]

In speaking of his concern for the direction of the government, Daniel Berrigan, himself a political prisoner, has spoken eloquently of the need for dissent:

Indeed it cannot be thought that men and women like ourselves will continue, as though we were automated heroes, to rush for redress from the King of the Blind. The King will have to listen to other voices, over which neither he nor we will indefinitely have control: voices of public violence and chaos. For you cannot set up a court in the Kingdom of the Blind, to condemn those who see; a court presided over by those who would pluck out the eyes of men and call it rehabilitation.[42]

Official Violence

Typically we do not think of governmental actions as violent. Violence is usually viewed as injury to persons or property. We make this distinction because the powerful, through the law-making process and control of communication, actually define what behavior is violent. In this section, however, we want to examine instances of what we have called "official violence." Under this rubric we include those overt acts by the government and those subtle ways the system operates to do harm. Let's consider, for example, the treatment of minorities.[43]

Consider the violence perpetrated against minorities throughout American history according to official government policy. The government supported slavery. The government took land forcibly from the Indians and for a time had an official policy of exterminating them. During World War II Japanese-Americans were relocated in detention camps with great loss of property for them. The law itself has helped to do violence to minority groups.[44] A study of sentences for rape in Florida between 1940 and 1964 found that none of the whites found guilty of raping a black woman was sentenced to death, but fifty-four percent of the blacks found guilty of raping white women were.[45] The system of "justice" works a tremendous hardship on minorities, as seen in the statistics on capital punishment provided by former Attorney General Ramsey Clark:

Racial discrimination is manifest from the bare statistics of capital punishment. Since we began keeping records in 1930, there have been 2,066 Negroes and only 1,751 white persons put to death. Hundreds of thousands of rapes have occurred in America since 1930, yet only 455 men have been executed for rape — and 405 of them were Negroes. There can be no rationalization or justification of such clear discrimination. It is outrageous public murder, illuminating our darkest racism.[46]

The system also injures when reforms that would adequately house, clothe, feed, and provide medical attention are not instituted. A description by Carmichael and Hamilton shows how this phenomenon does violence to minority members:

When white terrorists bomb a black church and kill five black children, that is an act of individual racism, widely deplored by most segments of the society. But when in that same city — Birmingham, Alabama — five hundred black babies die each year because of the lack of proper food, shelter and medical facilities, and thousands more are destroyed and maimed physically, emotionally, and intellectually because of conditions of poverty and discrimination in the black community, that is a function of institutional racism.[47]

Of the many forms of official violence, we will consider two in some detail — police brutality and the use of citizens as unknowing guinea pigs.

Police brutality. What is or is not classified as police brutality depends on one's placement in the hierarchy of power. An act is perceived as violent if it challenges existing arrangements. Thus, what a victimized group may perceive as "police brutality" is viewed by those in power as legitimate because it supports law and order.[48]

The police are legally permitted to carry weapons and use them against citizens. This unique power results occasionally in citizens being killed by their law-enforcement officers. Many more citizens are killed than police in these shootouts (a five-to-one ratio).[49] Also the killings appear to be selective by the social characteristics of the victims. Data from 1952 to 1969, for example, found that very few women are killed by police (.8 percent) and a disproportionately large proportion of non-white males are killed (49.6 percent of all males killed).[50] Put another way, statistically, the shooting deaths of blacks and Chicanos by police is ten to thirteen times higher per 100,000 population than it is for whites.[51] These data lend credence to the charge of "police brutality" that so often emanates from minority communities.

The charge of "police brutality" is often made but seldom punished. One investigation of the deaths of 1,500 citizens killed by police found that only three such incidents resulted in police being punished for their actions.[52]

Three of the most publicized instances of police brutality in recent memory are the Chicago police's treatment of civil-rights demonstrators at the 1968 Democratic convention, the Ohio National Guard's firing of sixty-one shots that killed four college students and wounded nine at Kent State University, and the killing of forty-three inmates at Attica Prison in 1971. Let's examine the Attica incident.

The Attica case is noteworthy because the prisoner revolt at Attica was a result in part of a raised consciousness among the prisoners that they were in jail for political reasons.[53] They tended to think of themselves as political prisoners — as victims rather than criminals — for two reasons: (1) as largely members of black or Spanish ghettos, they were acutely aware of the inequities of society; and (2) they were especially aware of the ways the criminal-justice system singled them out unfairly.

There were other reasons for the inmates' rage but one that stood out was symbolic — the corrections staff did not include one black or Puerto Rican. The all-white staff from rural western New York state was mainly concerned that the inmates "knew their place." This typical attitude clashed with the inmates' view that they were victims rather than criminals, which resulted in a rising level of tension as inmates increasingly refused to adhere to the demands of the corrections officers.

Under these conditions a spontaneous riot occurred after an incident with 1,281 inmates eventually controlling four cellblocks and forty hostages. Negotiations took place over a four-day period with the prisoners demanding twenty-eight prison reforms and amnesty for the uprising. Governor Nelson Rockefeller was convinced that the revolt was led by revolutionaries and he refused to negotiate. As he told the Commission investigating the Attica incident:

> . . . One of the most recent and widely used techniques of modern-day revolutionaries has been the taking of political hostages and using the threat to kill them as blackmail to achieve unconditional demands and to gain wide public attention to further their revolutionary ends. . . . If tolerated, they pose a serious threat to the ability of free government to preserve order and to protect the security of the individual citizens.
>
> Therefore, I firmly believe that a duly elected official sworn to defend the Constitution and the laws of the state and nation would be betraying his trust to the people he serves if he were to sanction or condone such criminal acts by negotiating under such circumstances.[54]

Thus there was a decision to retake the prison by force. The time had come to reassert the sovereignty and power of the state over the rebels. A full-scale assault was launched and in fifteen minutes the State Police had retaken the prison at a cost of thirty-nine deaths and eighty wounded — the bloodiest one-day encounter between Americans since the Civil War, with the exception of the Indian massacres of the late nineteenth century.

The use of citizens as unwilling and unknowing guinea pigs. During the 1950s the U.S. government tested nuclear weapons in Nevada. The prevailing winds spread the fallout especially in the area near St. George, Utah. Following a lag of twenty years or so, we know the results of these experiments to be an abnormally high death rate, especially from an unusually high incidence of cancer. In a sense, the citizens of Nevada, Arizona, and Utah were guinea pigs because they were exposed to radiation during government bomb testing. Scientists at that time felt, however, that if the site chosen for the test was as remote as the Nevada test site was, then the people at a distance were safe.

Whether the exposure to nuclear radiation in the Southwest was a conscious effort by the government to assess the effects of radiation on an unsuspecting population is debatable. The government's guilt is clear, however, in the cases where unknowing citizens were exposed to chemicals at a calculated medical risk. Two examples will illustrate the government's culpability.

A recent declassification of government documents revealed that the American people had been subjects in 239 open-air bacteriological tests conducted by the Army between 1949 and 1969. On one of these tests, San Francisco was blanketed with poisonous bacteria known as serratia, which causes a type of pneumonia that can be fatal. One hospital treated twelve persons for serratia pneumonia and one victim died. The objectives of this and other tests were to investigate the offensive possibilities of biological warfare, to understand the magnitude of defensing against biological warfare, and to gain data on the behavior of biological agents as they are borne downwind.[55]

Another example of the exposure of Americans to potentially dangerous chemicals without their knowledge or consent was the behavioral-control experiments conducted by the government.[56] For thirty-five years various agencies of the government have used tens of thousands of individuals to test several techniques of mind control: hypnosis, electronic brain stimulation, aversive and other behavior-modification therapies, and drugs. Many of the subjects in these experiments were volunteers but many were not. Our interest is in the use of subjects without their consent. We will focus our attention on a government agency that is well known for disregarding the rights of citizens in its quest for national security — the CIA.

Item: In 1953 a CIA scientist slipped LSD into the after-dinner drinks of scientists from the Army Chemical Corps. The drug had an especially adverse effect on one of these persons. He experienced psychotic confusion and two days later leapt to his death from a hotel window. (The CIA kept the facts from the victim's family for twenty-two years.)[57]

Item: The CIA hired prostitutes in San Francisco to give their customers drugs. The behavior of the victims was then observed through two-way mirrors and heard through hidden microphones.[58]

Item: The CIA administered LSD to the borderline underworld — "prostitutes, drug addicts, and other small timers who would be powerless to seek any sort of revenge if they ever found out what the CIA had done to them." [59] "Agents working on the project would randomly choose a victim at a bar or off the street and, with no prior consent or medical pre-screening, would take the individual back to a safe house and administer the drug. For many of the unsuspecting victims, the result was days or even weeks of hospitalization and mental stress." [60]

These examples demonstrate the arrogance of an agency of government that is willing to victimize some of its citizens to accomplish an edge in its battle against the country's enemies. Some would argue that this behavior, so contrary to life in a free society, makes them the enemy.

INTERNATIONAL CRIMES

Crimes by the government are not limited to those directed at its citizens. War is an obvious example of the willful attempt by a government to harm citizens of another country. Other acts by government short of war are also harmful to others — like trade embargos, arms sales, colonial arrangements, and the like. In this section we will discuss two other types of crimes perpetrated by the American government against others — intervention in their domestic affairs and war crimes.

American Intervention in the Domestic Affairs of Other Nations

What would be the response of our political leaders and citizens if: Foreigners assassinated the president? Foreign agents tried to influence the outcome of an election? Or a foreign power supported with money and weapons one side in a domestic dispute? Obviously we would not tolerate these attempts by outsiders to affect our domestic affairs. Such acts would be interpreted as imperialistic acts of war. The irony, of course, is that we have and continue to perpetrate such acts on other countries as part of our foreign policy.

The number of clandestine acts of intervention by the U.S. government is legion. Evidence from Senate investigating committees has shown, for example, that over a twenty-year period one government agency — the CIA — was involved in over 900 foreign interventions, including paramilitary operations, surreptitious manipulation of foreign governments, and assassinations.[61] We will limit our discussion here to several of the more well-known cases of CIA involvement in the domestic affairs of other nations.

Chile. The U.S., primarily through the CIA, has been actively involved in orchestrating the internal politics of Chile for a number of years.[62] The government's concern was to protect American business interests, primarily those of ITT. ITT feared the rise of revolutionary parties because they would likely expropriate foreign holdings. In 1966 an election was held and the U.S. gave the moderate candidate Eduardo Frei twenty million dollars in direct campaign contributions. After Frei's victory, Chile expanded its telephone system, giving the contract to ITT even though a Swedish company had a lower bid.

In the 1970 elections the CIA and ITT feared the election of the socialist candidate Salvador Allende because he had pledged to seize the company's 150 million-dollar Chilean property. The CIA spent some thirteen million dollars to block Allende's election, including 350,000 dollars to bribe members of the Chilean Congress, who cast electoral votes, to vote against Allende.* Despite these efforts Allende was elected. After Allende's victory the CIA plotted his overthrow. The strategy was to create economic chaos in the country, which would lead the Chilean army to pull a coup. Some of these efforts were: (1) the CIA spent eight million dollars on economic sabotage; (2) U.S. banks boycotted Chile; (3) rumors were spread that Chile's copper supplies were far greater than they were in reality in a deliberate campaign to weaken the price of copper, Chile's major product; (4) U.S. companies refused to supply repair parts for machines; and (5) the U.S. played an important role in the creation of an extensive black market in goods and dollars. These efforts were successful, as Allende was assassinated in 1973 amidst right-wing violence and a military takeover.

The ruling military regime that followed Allende completely changed domestic and foreign policy. Most important to ITT and the U.S. was the adoption of a program of unconditional support for U.S. policies and business interests in Chile.

Iran. The U.S. has had a long-term special interest in Iran because of that country's vast supplies of oil and its proximity to Russia. U.S. involvement in the internal affairs of Iran began in the early 1950s when

---

* The extent of ITT's involvement in the 1970 election has not been made public because the government has refused to prosecute for fear that such a trial would expose CIA secrets.

Prime Minister Mohammed Mossadegh moved to nationalize U.S. oil companies, as we noted in Chapter 5. The CIA engineered a coup that ousted Mossadegh and restored the Shah to power. Over the next twenty-five years, despite the Shah's rule becoming increasingly tyrannical, the U.S. supported the Shah's government, especially with military aid. The Shah in turn was a trusted ally faithfully supporting U.S. interests in the Persian Gulf area, supplying oil, and remaining staunchly anticommunist.[63]

CIA murder plots. In 1975, the Senate Select Committee on Intelligence reported on the activities of the CIA over a thirteen-year period. The publication of this report occurred over the objections of President Ford and CIA Director William Colby. The reason for their fears was obvious — the government was embarrassed for citizens to find out that the CIA was actively involved in assassination plots and coups against foreign governments.[64]

> *Item:* Between 1960 and 1965 the CIA initiated at least eight plots to assassinate Fidel Castro, Prime Minister of Cuba. The unsuccessful attempts included applying instantly lethal botulinium toxin to a box of Castro's cigars, hiring the Mafia to poison him, and presenting him a gift of a wet suit (for skin diving) treated with a fungus.
>
> *Item:* The committee found strong evidence that CIA officials had planned the assassination of Congolese (Zaire) leader Patrice Lumumba and that President Eisenhower had ordered his death.
>
> *Item:* The U.S. was implicated in the assassinations of Dominican dictator Rafael Trujillo, South Vietnam's President Ngo Dinh Diem, and General Rene Schneider of Chile.

The CIA's actions are contrary to American principles in fundamental ways. Aside from supporting regimes notorious for their violation of human rights (see Chapter 5), the U.S., which achieved its independence claiming the people's right to self-determination, is now actively involved in manipulating foreign governments to achieve its will. The infusion of money in foreign elections, the use of propaganda, assassination attempts, and the like are all contrary to the guiding principle of the Monroe Doctrine — the self-determination of peoples — which we invoke readily when other nations intrude in the affairs of state in any Western Hemisphere nation.

War Crimes

There are three interpretations of war crimes. One is that crimes in war are illogical — war is hell and anything goes. The only crime, from this position, is to lose. A second view is that war crimes are acts for which the victors punish the losers. The winners denounce the atrocities committed by the enemy while justifying their own conduct. Thus, the Germans and Japanese were tried for war crimes at the conclusion of World War II, but the U.S. was not, even though it had used atomic bombs to destroy two cities and most of their inhabitants. (Even if one assumes that the bombing of Hiroshima was necessary to bring an early end to the war, a debatable assumption, the bombing of Nagasaki two days later was clearly an unnecessary waste of life.)

A third view of war crimes is one that applies a standard of morality to war that is applicable to winners and losers alike. As the Chief U.S. Prosecutor at Nuremberg, Robert Jackson, said:

> If certain acts in violation of treaties are crimes, they are crimes whether the United States does them or whether Germany does them, and we are not prepared to lay down a rule of criminal conduct against others which we would be unwilling to have invoked against us.[65]

We will apply this last approach to our understanding of war crimes. As we use the concept, nations throughout history have been guilty of war crimes including the U.S. (in our case, some examples are the conquering of the Indians,[66] and our 1900 counterinsurgency campaign in the Philippines).[67] Since the government, the media, and the schools always point out the heinous acts of our enemies throughout history, we will focus on the war crimes perpetrated by the U.S., limiting the discussion to the Vietnam experience. The principle we will apply is the definition of war crimes established by the Nuremberg tribunal (Principle VI, b):

> Violations of the laws or customs of war which include, but are not limited to, murder, ill-treatment or deportation to slave-labor or for any other purpose of civilian population of or in occupied territory, murder or ill-treatment of prisoners of war or persons on the seas, killing of hostages, plunder of public or private property, wanton destruction of cities, towns, or villages, or devastation not justified by military necessity.[68]

The Vietnam War provides many examples of American actions in violation of this principle.

Indiscriminate shelling and bombing of civilians. The National Liberation Front was difficult to fight because they were everywhere. We often could not distinguish allies from enemies. Thus, in strategic terms, the entire geographical area of Vietnam was the enemy. As Roebuck and Weeber have observed: "In order to 'save' Vietnam from Communism, it was therefore necessary to destroy the entire country." [69] Thus, civilian villages were bombed in the enemy region of North Vietnam and in South Vietnam as well. The amount of firepower was unparalleled in history.

> From 315,000 tons of air ordnance dropped in Southeast Asia
> in 1965, the quantity by January–October, 1969, the peak year
> of the war, reached 1,388,000 tons. Over that period, 4,580,000
> tons were dropped on Southeast Asia, or six and one-half times
> that employed in Korea. To this we must add ground munitions,
> which rose from 577,000 tons in 1966 to 1,278,000 tons in the
> first eleven months of 1969.[70]

A most significant bomb used by the U.S. was napalm. This is a jelly-like, inflammable mixture packed into canisters and dropped from aircraft. The mixture of benzene, gasoline, and polystyrene is a highly incendiary fluid that clings. It is an antipersonnel weapon that causes deep and persistent burning.

> Napalm is probably the most horrible anti-personnel weapon ever
> invented. The point of a weapon in war is to put an enemy out
> of action, and that is most readily and permanently accomplished
> by killing him; but civilized nations have tried not to induce more
> suffering than is necessary to accomplish this end. Napalm, in its
> means of action, in its capacity to maim permanently and to in-
> duce slow death, is a particularly horrifying weapon. That its
> use in Vietnam has involved many civilians — peasant families in
> undefended villages — has magnified the horror.[71]

Ground attacks on villages and civilians. The most celebrated and infamous incident of the war was the March, 1968, massacre at Song My (also known as My Lai). Under orders from their superiors, American soldiers slaughtered over 500 civilians.[72] The troops had been told to destroy all structures and render the place uninhabitable. They killed every inhabitant, regardless of age or sex, and despite this no opposition or hostile behavior was encountered.

In Operation Cedar Falls, 30,000 American troops were assigned the task of destroying all villages in a forty-square-mile area. In this and other operations, groups of soldiers, known as "Zippo squads" burned village after village.

> The intensely cultivated flat lands south of the Vaico Oriental
> River about 20 miles from Saigon are prime "scorched earth"
> targets. U.S. paratroopers from the 173rd Airborne Brigade be-
> gan operating there last weekend.
> They burned to the ground every hut they saw. Sampans
> were sunk and bullock carts were smashed. The 173rd laid their
> base camp among the blackened frames of burned houses. Within
> two miles of the camp not a house was left standing. . . .
> Every house found by the 173rd was burned to the ground.
> Every cooking utensil was smashed, every banana tree severed,

every mattress slashed.... Thousands of ducks and chickens were slaughtered.... Dozens of pigs, water buffalo and cows were destroyed. A twenty-mile stretch along the Vaico Oriental was left scorched and barren.[73]

Ecocide. A variation on the "scorched earth" policy just noted was the use of anti-crop chemicals. The Air Force sprayed defoliants on 100,000 acres in 1964 and 1,500,000 acres in 1969. Herbicides were used to destroy foliage that hid the enemy and crops that fed the Vietcong soldiers and their civilian supporters. The results of this campaign were devastating in a number of ways: (1) timber, a major crop in South Vietnam, was destroyed and replaced by bamboo, generally considered a nuisance; (2) the mangroves in swamp lands were killed, negatively affecting shellfish and migratory fish, major sources of protein for the Vietnamese; (3) vast areas of soil eroded; and (4) toxic substances such as 2,4,5T were ingested by humans and animals, which may lead to birth abnormalities.[74] Gaston has summarized this catastrophe of American strategy as:

> After the end of World War II, and as a result of the Nuremberg trials, we justly condemned the willful destruction of an entire people and its culture, calling this crime against humanity *geno-cide*. It seems to me that the willful and permanent destruction of environment in which a people can live in a manner of their own choosing ought similarly to be designated as a crime against humanity, to be designated by the term *ecocide....* At the present time, the United States stands alone as possibly having committed ecocide against another country, Vietnam, through its massive use of chemical defoliants and herbicides.[75]

In addition to ecocide, the American conduct in Vietnam killed a sizable portion of the population. The population of entire villages was killed. Thousands were killed in bombings. The enormity of this is seen in data supplied by the Senate Subcommittee on Refugees. It estimated that from 1965 to 1969 over a million refugees were killed and two million were wounded by the U.S. Armed Services.[76]

In sum, America's strategy in the Vietnam civil war shattered the whole society from its ecology to village life, and to life itself. Daniel Ellsberg has called this violent destruction of a patterned society **socio-cide.**[77] Most certainly that qualifies as the ultimate war crime.

CONCLUSION

We have catalogued many overt and horrifying forms of political deviance in this chapter. The ultimate irony of this is that in a country that takes pride in calling itself a free and open society, we have government organizations that in the name of national security operate to make society anything but free and open. To protect the national interest means to punish dissent and to manipulate foreign governments. Somehow the FBI, the CIA, and other agencies have believed that it is necessary to break the law in order to protect the system. In so doing, their actions reap the very results they wish to abolish. As Harris has said, quoting Supreme Court Justice Louis Brandeis:

> For to break some laws in order to enforce other laws is not to fight anarchy and terrorism but to create them. "In a government of laws, existence of the government will be imperiled if it fails to observe the law scrupulously. . . . Our government is the potent, the omnipresent teacher. For good or for ill, it teaches the whole people by its example. Crime is contagious. If the government becomes a lawbreaker, it breeds contempt for the law; it invites every man to become a law unto himself; it invites anarchy. To declare that in the administration of the criminal law the end justifies the means — to declare that the government may commit crimes in order to secure the conviction of a private criminal — would bring terrible retribution." [78]

NOTES

1. For other books that emphasize the government as deviant, see especially: Julian Roebuck and Stanley C. Weeber, *Political Crime in the United States: Analyzing Crime by and against Government* (New York: Praeger, 1978); Alan Wolfe, *The Seamy Side of Democracy: Repression in America,* Second Edition (New York: Longman, 1978); David Wise, *The American Police State: The Government against the People* (New York: Vintage, 1978); and Charles E. Reasons, *The Criminologist: Crime and the Criminal* (Pacific Palisades, California: Goodyear, 1974).

2. For examples of coverups, secrecy, and the like at other levels see: Seymour M. Hersh, *Cover-Up* (New York: Random House, 1972); Peter K. Manning, "The Police: Mandate, Strategies, and Appearances," *Criminal Justice in America: A Critical Understanding,* Richard Quinney, ed. (Boston: Little, Brown, 1974), pp. 170–200; and Mike Royko, *Boss: Richard J. Daley of Chicago* (New York: E. P. Dutton, 1971).

3. Norman Dorsen and John H. F. Shattuck, "Executive Privilege: The President Won't Tell," *None of Your Business: Government Secrecy in America,* Norman Dorsen and Stephen Gillers, eds. (New York: Viking, 1974), pp. 27–60.

4. Cited in William G. Phillips, "The Government's Classification System," in Dorsen and Shattuck, *None of Your Business,* p. 71.

5. Cited in Paul N. McCloskey, Jr., *Truth and Untruth: Political Deceit in America* (New York: Simon and Schuster, 1972), p. 54.

6. *Ibid.*

7. Michael Parenti, *Democracy for the Few,* Third Edition (New York: St. Martin's Press, 1980), p. 157.

8. Anthony Lewis, "Introduction," in Dorsen and Shattuck, *None of Your Business,* pp. 3–24.

9. These examples are taken from David Wise, *The Politics of Lying: Government Deception, Secrecy, and Power* (New York: Random House Vintage Books, 1973).

10. Thomas I. Emerson, "The Danger of State Secrecy," *The Nation* 218 (March 30, 1974), pp. 395–399. See also, Arthur S. Miller, "Watergate and Beyond: The Issue of Secrecy," *The Progressive* 37 (December, 1973), pp. 15–19.

11. Itzhak Galnoor, "The Politics of Public Information," *Society* 16 (May/June, 1979), pp. 20–30.

12. Wise, *The Politics of Lying*, p. 40.

13. For a history of the government's monitoring of its citizens, see Alan Wolfe, "Political Repression and the Liberal Democratic State," *Monthly Review* 23 (December, 1971), pp. 18–38; Donald B. Davis, "Internal Security in Historical Perspective: From the Revolution to World War II," *Surveillance and Espionage in a Free Society*, Richard H. Blum, ed. (New York: Praeger, 1972), pp. 3–19; "It's Official: Government Snooping Has Been Going On for 50 Years," *U.S. News and World Report* (May 24, 1976), p. 65; and Select Committee to Study Governmental Operations with Respect to Intelligence Activities, U.S. Senate, *Intelligence Activities and the Rights of Americans: Book II*, Report 94-755 (April 26, 1976), pp. 1–20, found in *Corporate and Governmental Deviance*, M. David Ermann and Richard J. Lundman, eds. (New York: Oxford University Press, 1978), pp. 151–173.

14. This brief history of the FBI is taken from Richard Harris, "Crime in the FBI," *The New Yorker* (August 8, 1977), pp. 30–42.

15. "Project Minaret," *Newsweek* (November 10, 1975), pp. 31–32.

16. U.S. Senate, *Intelligence Activities*, in Ermann and Lundman, *Corporate and Governmental Deviance*, p. 156. Also see "Who's Chipping Away at Your Privacy," *U.S. News and World Report* (March 31, 1975), p. 18.

17. *Ibid.*

18. "The FBI's 'Black-Bag Boys,'" *Newsweek* (July 28, 1975), pp. 18, 21.

19. Associated Press release (March 29, 1979).

20. United Press International release (November 19, 1975).

21. "Tales of the FBI," *Newsweek* (December 1, 1975), p. 36.

22. "Curbing the Spooks," *The Progressive* 42 (November, 1978), pp. 10–11.

23. "The FBI vs. Jean Seberg," *Time* (September 24, 1979), p. 25.

24. The following account is taken from several sources: Morton H. Halperin et al., *The Lawless State: The Crimes of the U.S. Intelligence Agencies* (New York: Penguin, 1976), pp. 61–89; "The Truth about Hoover," *Time* (December 22, 1975), pp. 14–21; "Tales of the FBI," and "The Crusade to Topple King," *Time* (December 1, 1975), pp. 11–12.

25. Final Report of the Select Committee to Study Governmental Relations with Respect to Intelligence Activities, U.S. Senate, *Supplementary Detailed Staff Reports on Intelligence Activities and the Rights of Americans: Book III*, "Dr. Martin Luther King, Jr., Case Study" (Washington, D.C.: U.S. Government Printing Office, 1976), pp. 107–198, cited in Halperin et al., *The Lawless State*, p. 78.

26. Halperin et al., *The Lawless State*, p. 89.

27. Quoted in "The Crusade to Topple King," p. 11.

28. The evidence presented on the FBI's campaign against the SWP is taken from Harris, "Crime in the FBI"; Associated Press release (March 29, 1976); and "Monitoring Repression," *The Progressive* 41 (January, 1977), p. 7.

29. Harris, "Crime in the FBI," p. 40.

30. *Ibid.*, p. 40.

31. Charles Goodell, *Political Prisoners in America* (New York: Random House, 1973), pp. 3–13.

32. W. H. McConnell, "Political Trials East and West," *The Sociology of*

Law: A Conflict Perspective, Charles E. Reasons and Robert M. Rich, eds. (Toronto: Butterworth, 1978), p. 333.

33. Alexander Liazos, "The Poverty of the Sociology of Deviance: Nuts, Sluts, and Preverts," *Social Problems* 20 (Summer, 1972), p. 108.

34. Theodore Becker, ed., *Political Trials* (Indianapolis: Bobbs-Merrill, 1971), pp. xi–xii.

35. See D. Stanley Eitzen, *In Conflict and Order: Understanding Society* (Boston: Allyn and Bacon, 1978), pp. 62–66; Richard E. Rubenstein, *Rebels in Eden: Mass Political Violence in the United States* (Boston: Little, Brown, 1970); and Goodell, *Political Prisoners in America.*

36. Much of this account is taken from Goodell, *Political Prisoners in America,* pp. 126–159.

37. Quoted in *ibid.,* p. 130.

38. The following account is taken primarily from David J. Danelski, "The Chicago Conspiracy Trial," in Becker, *Political Trials,* pp. 134–180. We have taken this case as representative of many others from the same time period. For other illustrations of the existence of political trials and political prisoners, see the account of the vendetta against the Black Panthers, Tom Hayden, *Trial* (New York: Holt, Rinehart and Winston, 1970); the trials of the Berrigans, Daniel Berrigan, *The Trial of the Catonsville Nine* (Boston: Beacon Press, 1970); and the trial of the Wilmington 10, Jack Anderson, "U.S. Is Cited for Human Rights Violations," *Rocky Mountain News* (December 11, 1978), p. 61. For general statements on political criminals see: Judith Frutig, "Political Trials: What Impact on America?" *Christian Science Monitor* (August 27, 1976), pp. 16–17; Goodell, *Political Prisoners in America;* and Becker, *Political Trials.*

39. See David Sternberg, "The New Radical-Criminal Trials: A Step Toward a Class-for-Itself in the American Proletariat?" in Quinney, *Criminal Justice in America,* pp. 274–294.

40. *Ibid.,* p. 281.

41. Quoted in Danelski, "The Chicago Conspiracy Trial," p. 177.

42. Berrigan, *The Trial of the Catonsville Nine,* pp. x–xii.

43. The following is taken from Eitzen, *In Conflict and Order,* pp. 321–322.

44. See Haywood Burns, "Black People and the Tyranny of American Law," in Reasons and Rich, *The Sociology of Law,* pp. 353–365.

45. Florida Civil Liberties Union, *Rape: Selective Electrocution Based on Race* (Miami, 1964).

46. Ramsey Clark, *Crime in America: Observations on Its Nature, Causes, Prevention and Control* (New York: Simon and Schuster, 1970), p. 335.

47. Stokely Carmichael and Charles V. Hamilton, *Black Power: The Politics of Liberation in America* (New York: Random House, 1967), p. 4.

48. See Jerome Skolnick, *The Politics of Protest* (New York: Ballantine Books, 1969), pp. 3–8.

49. Arthur L. Kobler, "Police Homicide in a Democracy," *The Journal of Social Issues* 31 (Winter, 1975), pp. 163–184.

50. U.S. Public Health Service data, quoted in *ibid.,* p. 164.

51. Paul T. Takagi, "Abuse of Authority Is a Very Explosive Situation," *U.S. News and World Report* (August 27, 1979), p. 29.

52. Kobler, "Police Homicide in a Democracy," p. 166.

53. The following is taken from the New York State Special Commission on Attica, *Attica: The Official Report* (New York: Bantam, 1972), excerpted in Jack D. Douglas and John M. Johnson, *Official Deviance* (Philadelphia: J. B. Lippincott, 1977), pp. 186–194.

54. Quoted in *ibid.,* p. 193.

55. Norman Cousins, "How the U.S. Used Its Citizens as Guinea Pigs,"

Saturday Review (November 10, 1979), p. 10. See also United Press International release (December 4, 1979).

56. See W. H. Bowart, *Operation Mind Control: Our Government's War against Its Own People* (New York: Dell, 1978); and John Marks, "Sex, Drugs, and the CIA," *Saturday Review* (February 3, 1979), pp. 12–16.

57. Bowart, *Operation Mind Control,* pp. 87–91.

58. Marks, "Sex, Drugs, and the CIA," pp. 12–16.

59. Marks, "Sex, Drugs, and the CIA," p. 14.

60. Halperin et al., *The Lawless State,* p. 52.

61. Roebuck and Weeber, *Political Crime in the United States,* p. 82.

62. The CIA involvement in Chile is documented from several accounts: *ibid.,* pp. 83–86; Adam Schesch and Patricia Garrett, "The Case of Chile," *Uncloaking the CIA,* Howard Frazier, ed. (New York: The Free Press, 1978), pp. 36–54; Hortensia Bussi de Allende, "The Facts about Chile," in Frazier, *Uncloaking the CIA,* pp. 55–68; Jack Anderson, "Evidence Strong CIA, ITT Behind Chile Coup," *Rocky Mountain News* (September 27, 1974), p. 66; Associated Press release (March 8, 1979); Thomas Powers, "Inside the Department of Dirty Tricks," *The Atlantic* 244 (August, 1979), pp. 45–57; and James F. Petras, "Chile: Crime, Class Consciousness and the Bourgeosie," in Reasons and Rich, *The Sociology of Law,* pp. 413–427.

63. Parenti, *Democracy for the Few,* p. 174.

64. The following list is taken from "CIA Murder Plots — Weighing the Damage to U.S.," *U.S. News and World Report* (December 1, 1975), pp. 13–15; and "The CIA's Hit List," *Newsweek* (December 1, 1975), pp. 28–32.

65. Quoted in Erwin Knoll and Judith Nies McFadden, eds., *War Crimes and the American Conscience* (New York: Holt, Rinehart and Winston, 1970), p. 1.

66. See Bruce Johansen and Roberto Maestas, *Wasi'chu: The Continuing Indian Wars* (New York: Monthly Review Press, 1979); and Dee Brown, *Bury My Heart at Wounded Knee: An Indian History of the American West* (New York: Bantam, 1972).

67. See Stuart C. Miller, "Our My Lai of 1900: Americans in the Philippine Insurrection," *Trans-action* 7 (September, 1970), pp. 19–28; and Telford Taylor, *Nuremberg and Vietnam: An American Tragedy* (New York: Bantam, 1971), pp. 173–174.

68. Cited in Knoll and McFadden, *War Crimes,* p. 183. See also William Thomas Mallison, "Political Crimes in the International Law of War: Concepts and Consequences," in *Crime and the International Scene: An Inter-American Focus,* Freda Adler and G. O. W. Mueller, eds. (San Juan, Puerto Rico: North-South Center Press, 1972), pp. 96–107.

69. Roebuck and Weeber, *Political Crime in the United States,* p. 70.

70. Gabriel Kolko, quoted in Knoll and McFadden, *War Crimes,* p. 57.

71. George Wald, in *ibid.,* p. 73.

72. See Taylor, *Nuremberg and Vietnam,* pp. 122–153; and Richard A. Falk, "Song My: War Crimes and Individual Responsibility," *Trans-action* 7 (January, 1970), pp. 33–40.

73. Associated Press release, quoted in Edward S. Herman, *Atrocities in Vietnam: Myths and Realities* (Philadelphia: Pilgrim Press, 1970), p. 84.

74. Arthur W. Gaston, quoted in Knoll and McFadden, *War Crimes,* pp. 69–72.

75. *Ibid.,* p. 71.

76. Roebuck and Weeber, *Political Crimes in the United States,* p. 71.

77. Quoted in Knoll and McFadden, *War Crimes,* p. 82.

78. Harris, "Crime in the FBI," p. 35.

Epilogue
The Economy and Elite Deviance: A Proposal to Transform Society

As long as there are social problems in American society such as the various forms of elite deviance described throughout this book, we cannot be content with the status quo. The dominant theme of this book is that the source of these problems is the structure of society. It follows, then, that any solution should require the system to be changed fundamentally. We believe that changing the basis for the existing system — the capitalist economy — is the key.

The economy must be changed so that people, rather than profit, are paramount. The economy must be changed to achieve a reasonably equitable distribution of goods and services. While absolute equality is Utopian, the economic system *can* be changed to eliminate the "upside-down effect" where the few benefit at the expense of the many, and where jobs for all are guaranteed with a living wage along with the assurance of adequate housing, food, and medical care. There is no excuse for a society to allow some of its citizens to live in squalor, to be poorly fed, to have inadequate medical attention, and to be the objects of contempt from other citizens. A final change needed for our economic system is greater regulation of business activity in accord with central planning to achieve societal objectives and meet the needs of a future characterized by shortages, ecological threats, and worldwide population pressures.

In this epilogue we propose an economic system that makes the most sense to us — economic democracy. We will outline the assumptions and programmatic details of this economic form as a way to generate dialogue and debate about alternatives to the present system. Other proposals may also help to solve the problems endemic to contemporary America. We should, however, be aware that all social systems, regardless of their economic and political underpinnings, will have social problems. Utopia literally means nowhere. We do not assume that the system we propose will be perfect. There will be unanticipated problems. But the fear of unknown problems should not deter our willingness to work for the transformation of society to reduce or even eradicate current problems. Also, we reject the proposition that just because Utopia is impossible to attain, we should not try to approximate perfection.

We believe that the effect to change society to eliminate current problems is the highest calling for patriots. What follows is our plan for change. We challenge you to work your way through it, find the flaws, and propose alternative planks to the platform or entire new schemes to achieve the goal of "a more perfect Union."

ECONOMIC DEMOCRACY

Basic Assumptions

Let's begin by enumerating the assumptions that must guide the search for the possible solution to the elite deviance that plagues contemporary American society. Foremost is the assumption that these problems will be alleviated only through changing the structure of society, not altering "problem persons." This assumption does not deny that some individuals are pathological and need personal attention. But attending to these individuals only attacks the symptoms of the problem rather than attacking the disease itself. The basic premise is that elite deviance is endemic to our social system.[1]

A second guiding assumption for the solution of elite deviance is that the system must be *fundamentally* changed. Cosmetic changes or even genuine reforms are likely to fail because they are based on the political-economic base that is the source of many social problems. As Parenti has observed: "As long as we look for solutions within the very system that causes the problems, we will continue to produce cosmetic, band-aid programs. The end result is shameful public poverty and shameless private wealth."[2]

In short, the economic system (state-supported capitalism) is the source for many of our elite-deviance problems. This is because capitalism and the government in a capitalistic society have no fundamental commitment to remedying social ills.[3] Instead of a commitment to a more equitable distribution of resources, capitalism promotes competition with the "victors" widening the gap over the "losers." Tax reforms are instituted to encourage profits rather than solve unemployment and low wages. Inflation rather than unemployment is viewed as the culprit. Suburbanites may work in the city but they do everything possible to avoid paying taxes that will help the city eliminate its fiscal woes. The current wave of reducing taxes, government services, and government intervention, while aimed at government waste, also reflects the lack of humane concern for those less fortunate, which characterizes capitalists.[4] Capitalism and the highly competitive individuals it engenders create this me-first mentality. In the words of Michael Parenti:

> . . . Contrary to the view of liberal critics, the nation's immense
> social problems are not irrational offshoots of a basically rational
> system, to be solved by replacing the existing corporate and po-
> litical decision-makers with persons who would be better inten-
> tioned and more socially aware. Rather, the problems are
> rational outcomes of a basically irrational system, a system struc-
> tured not for the satisfaction of human need but the multiplication
> of human greed.[5]

A third assumption is that the magnitude of the United States' current social problems will be magnified further by the conditions of the future, unless the politico-economic structure is changed significantly. International tensions in the future will be heightened by scarcity, pollution, and the ever-increasing gap between the rich and the poor nations. Domestically, the future holds similar problems as well as increased unemployment, deeper economic cycles, urban blight, and problems of racism, ageism, and sexism. Will societies propelled by the profit motive increase or lessen these international and domestic problems? While capitalism was instrumental in bringing the United States to its present level of affluence and power (at the expense of labor, minorities, and the Third World), the organization and needs of capitalism are not appropriate for a world of scarcity, overpopulation, ecological disasters, and vast inequities. The future does not hold promise unless: competition gives way to cooperation; individual choice is superseded by the needs of society; uncoordinated efforts are supplanted by *democratic* (not bureaucratic) planning; and economic advantages are spread more evenly throughout society.

The final assumption posited here is that any attempt to make significant changes in society will be resisted by those holding disproportionate resources and power under the current organization of society. Those who benefit by the present arrangements quite naturally favor stability, law and order, and other practices that guarantee their advantages. On the other side are those who favor change because they are disadvantaged under the existing system. Thus, the basic problem of implementing change is that ". . . those who have the interest in fundamental change have not the power, while those who have the power have not the interest." [6] We assume that the changes will only occur with the emergence of a mass political movement that is a coalition of the poor, the disadvantaged blue-collar worker, and the increasingly impoverished middle class. The formation becomes all the more probable as the current economy and polity become less effective at meeting contemporary problems described in the following quote from Michael Harrington:

> The economy has become a sickening, uncontrollable roller coaster; cities rot, and the black, the Spanish-speaking, the poor, women, the young and the old are the special victims of our collective failures. The corporations arrogantly propose to deal with these crises by holding down wages, cutting social spending and legislating increased profits. The threat of nuclear war persists and the anti-environmentalists are on the offensive.[7]

The General Principles of Economic Democracy

Given these assumptions, which we believe reflect reality, what is the best solution? As a prologue for further discussion and realizing that one cannot foresee all the possible angles, let us elaborate on the features of the political-economic form for American society that would make the necessary structural changes to alleviate numerous problems endemic to the current politico-economic system — economic democracy (also called "democratic socialism").

The form of socialism characterized here is the ideal — what socialism is supposed to be and how it is supposed to work. It is important to start with the ideal form of socialism because the closer a social system approximates it, the greater is the promise of solving many of the problems native to capitalism.

The three fundamental themes of economic democracy are democratism, egalitarianism, and efficiency.[8] Authentic socialism *must be* democratic. Representatives must be answerable and responsive to the wishes of the public they serve. This means that public officials, whether in the political or economic spheres, must be accountable for their actions. Elite deviance is above all a problem of the lack of what Mintz and Cohen have called "accountability."

> Unaccountability pervades American life — not merely the Presidency, not merely the rest of government, but all public and private institutions that exert substantial power over us and, inevitably, over future generations.... Accountability, if it means anything, means that those who wield power have to answer in another place and give reasons for decisions that are taken...." [9]

The problem for present-day American society is that the democratic goal of the people having the ultimate power is not realized. As Parenti has charged, " 'Democracy,' as it is practiced by institutional oligarchs, consists of allowing others the opportunity to *say* what they want while the oligarchs, commanding all institutional resources, continue to *do* what they want." [10]

The democratic socialism proposed here is *not* the socialism found in Cuba, China, Poland, or Russia. Those nations claim to be socialistic but are totalitarian, and, therefore, run counter to this fundamental aspect of socialism. The key to differentiation between authentic and spurious socialism is to determine who is making the decisions and whose interests are being served.[11] Democratic relations must also be found throughout the social structure: in government, at work, at school, and in the community. Along with the election of officials responsive to public opinion and the disappearance of authoritarian relations, democracy entails the full extension of civic freedoms to protect individuals and groups from the arbitrariness of officials.

The second principle of democratic socialism is egalitarianism. The goal is equality: equality of opportunity for the self-fulfillment of all; equality rather than hierarchy in making decisions; and equality in sharing the benefits of society. Thus, there is a fundamental commitment in socialism to achieving a rough equality by leveling out the gross inequities in income, property, and opportunities. This means, of course, that arbitrary distinctions by sex, age, race, ethnicity, or whatever, no longer serve as criteria for oppression or for tracking certain categories of persons into limited opportunities.[12] A major question for socialism is whether the goal is equality of opportunity or equality of outcomes. The former is a necessity of socialism while the latter is probably impossible to attain in complex societies. The key is a leveling of the advantages so that all receive the necessities (food, clothing, medical care, living wages, sick pay, retirement benefits, and shelter) but an absolute equality of outcomes is very likely an unattainable goal given unequal endowments, motivations, and the like. Moreover, the efforts to approximate this goal would require the imposition of the tightest straightjacket on society and thus is very likely destined to fail.

A third feature of democratic socialism is efficiency. This refers to the organization of the society to provide, at the least possible individual and collective cost, the best conditions to meet the material needs of the citizens. Production of necessary goods must be assured, as well as the distribution of the goods produced, and the services offered must be planned and managed. But this is true of all types of economies. The key method to accomplish economic efficiency for socialism is the substitution of public for private ownership of the means of production. The people own the basic industries, financial institutions, agriculture, utilities, transportation, and communication companies. The goal is serving the public, not making profit as is the case in capitalism. Socialism, compared to capitalism, will likely have lower prices, greater availability of necessary goods and services, better coordination of economic endeavors, and better central planning to achieve societal goals (such as protecting the environment, combating pollution, saving natural resources, and developing new technologies). A proposal by former President Gerald Ford, former Vice-President Nelson Rockefeller, and Senator Henry Jackson provides an example of a fundamental difference between the present state-supported capitalism and socialism. They proposed that the taxpayers subsidize the huge developmental costs of new energy technologies (e.g., refining of shale oil, gasification of coal) and, once perfected, to *turn over the benefits to private corporations*. This tactic allows private corporations to let the public take all the risks and then take over the enterprise for their own profit at the expense of the public. If the socialist principle were applied, the people would collectively take the risks and then reap the benefits.[13]

A fundamental argument of the socialist credo is that private corporations work in opposition to human needs. In the search for profit, private corporations have withheld supplies, such as oil, to contrive shortages, colluded with "competitors" to keep prices abnormally high, encouraged extraordinary and wasteful military expenditures, polluted the environment, and encouraged wasteful consumptive patterns. Moreover, capitalism encourages unemployment. As Harrington has argued, ". . . Sustained full employment is a threat to corporations. For when there is full employment, the labor market tightens up, unions become more combative, and wages tend to rise at the expense of profits." [14]

To summarize, democratic socialism or economic democracy is a politico-economic form of organization dedicated to: full human equality, cooperation, participatory democracy, and meeting human needs. Admittedly, these goals are idealistic. But the closer American society approaches them, the magnitude of social problems such as poverty, racism, sexism, exploitation, unemployment, and human misery will be minimized. To the degree that they are achieved, elite deviance is reduced.

The Planks of a Democratic-Socialist Platform

A number of fundamental changes must be made to bring about democratic socialism. Let's begin with the central problem of capitalism — corporate control of the economy for private gain.

The large corporations reorganized to meet public needs. The major corporations present the primary obstacles to social justice. The primacy of profit means that these huge organizations resist social goals. They are not concerned with their role in unemployment, pollution, and the perpetuation of poverty. The curbing of pollution reduces profits. High labor costs at home "force" the company officials to move their operations overseas or to another part of the country where costs are lower. "Competing" corporations in a shared monopoly continue to raise prices even during economic downturns, which contributes to the problem of stagflation. The greed of corporate officials and owners inclines them to use and abuse natural resources without regard for conservation. This greed also encourages them to produce and market unsafe and unhealthy products.

In sum, whereas once economic activity was the result of many decisions made by individual entrepreneurs and the heads of small businesses, now a handful of corporations have virtual control over the marketplace. The decisions by the boards of directors and the management personnel of these huge corporations — determined solely by the profit motive — affects employment and production, consumption patterns, wages and prices, the extent of foreign trade, the rate of natural resource depletion, and the like.

Economic democracy requires that the decisions made by corporations are in the *public* interest. The public's interest will not be primary unless there is democracy within these corporations and the boards of directors are composed of owners *and* representatives of the workers and the public. Representatives of the workers are important to democratize the workplace and to improve the morale and the material conditions of the workers. The public also must be represented on the boards so that the decisions of the organizations will take into account the larger public issues of pollution, use of natural resources, plant location, prices, and product safety. These moves from economic oligarchy to industrial democracy represent a monumental shift from the present arrangements.

There are a number of ways to achieve economic democracy. All major corporations could be required to have a certain proportion of public and employee representatives on their boards of directors as a condition for doing business in interstate commerce.[15] Another procedure would be that every year the corporation would add a number of worker and public representatives depending on the profits of the previous year. This would mean, in effect, that after fifteen or twenty years the corporation would be controlled by the workers and public representatives. A final example of how industrial democracy could be accomplished would be for the government to insist that with each subsidy given to the company a proportion of the company's stock be given to the workers and the public. Thus, in return for tax breaks, low-interest loans, loan guarantees, and the like, the owners of the corporation would lose some of their control. As an example, in 1980 the government agreed to prop up the ailing Chrysler Corporation with loan guarantees of 1.5 billion dollars. Under a plan to bring about democratic socialism, the government could have agreed to this proposal in return for a percentage of Chrysler's stock, say thirty percent. Such a plan would give the public a return for its risk capital.

The goal of all these proposals is the social management of the corporations for the public good. There is some interesting evidence which indicates that the American public is in favor of such measures. A poll by Hart Research Associates of 1,209 American adults, during the week of July 25, 1975 (commissioned by the Peoples' Bicentennial Commission), revealed the following related alternatives to our present economic system:

> 66% of the American public feel that it would do "more good than harm" to develop a program in which employees own a majority of the company's stock, while only 25% feel that it would do "more harm than good."
>
> 74% of the public feel that it would do "more good than harm" to institute a plan whereby consumers in local communities are represented on the boards of companies that operate in their local region, while only 17% feel that it would do "more harm than good."
>
> 50% of the public feel that employee owned and controlled companies — ones where the people who work in the company select the management, set policies and share in the profits — would improve the condition of the economy. 14% say that such an arrangement would worsen the economy's condition. 29% feel the institution of employee ownership and control of companies would not make much difference in terms of the country's economic condition.
>
> 44% of the public believe there is "a great possibility" or "some possibility" that our country will have employee owned and controlled companies within the next 10 years, while 49% feel there is "little possibility" or "no possibility."
>
> 56% of the public would "probably support" or "definitely support" a candidate for President who favored employee ownership and control of U.S. companies, while only 26% said they would "probably not support" or "definitely not support" such a candidate. 18% volunteered that their presidential decision would be based on other factors or were not sure.
>
> 67% of the public feel there has been "too little discussion" about employee ownership and control of U.S. companies, while only 10% feel there has been "too much," and just 9% feel that there has been "about the right amount." [16]

These data indicate that a majority of the American public favors the basic structure of economic democracy and would support a mass democratic movement designed to move the U.S. in this direction.

One question raised about socialism involves individualism, as we know it. A socialist society is generally perceived as one where the group smothers the individual personality and where people are prohibited from using individual "initiative" to start their own businesses. Neither assumption needs be true. One plan to promote individualism is to nationalize only those companies that possess, or are soon likely to possess, a great amount of assets (e.g., 100 million dollars). Small companies could still be owned by groups or individuals. Large apartment complexes, supermarkets, and department stores could be purchased by government and run cooperatively by local community groups.

Certain industries owned by the government to ensure that certain basic services are provided at a fair price. We propose that the utilities, owners and processors of natural resources, transportation, banks, and credit institutions should be nationalized to ensure the adequacy of services, to plan for the social good, and to minimize business cycles. The irony of the capitalist system stems in part from its bouts with economic crises: inflation, unemployment, depression, and the like. In order to end the vicious swings of business cycles and to provide rationally for the needs of all, economic planning is a necessity. Community needs, regional needs, and national needs would all be balanced against each other at succeeding levels of government. But this planning, like all other decisions in this regard, would be made democratically by boards of elected representatives at each governmental level. There are already many such bodies in existence today, but their roles are largely advisory. Thus we do not see ourselves merely "adding another layer of bureaucracy" with this proposal. Rather, we propose to provide a democratic mechanism that would make the most humane and rational use of human and natural resources.

Such planning would also apply to wages, prices, monetary supplies, and interest rates. Presently, these decisions are already "planned" in substantial part by business-dominated groups such as the Federal Reserve Board. The question of economic planning, in the estimation of many, is not if it will be done, but *who* will do it — big business or the people. For people to have a democratic voice in economic matters requires a democratization of banking and credit as well as production.

Finally, we would nationalize all major defense contractors whose prime client is the government. These companies are currently subsidized by the government. They take no risks but can make enormous profits. The nationalization of these companies would reduce Pentagon waste significantly, increase efficiency, and eliminate the current sham of these companies making a profit at public expense with no risk.[17]

A democratic government. Government control, governmental planning, and the nationalization of industries will not accomplish socialist goals unless accompanied by true democracy.

Where the government owns or directs the means of production, the crucial question is: Who owns the government? There is only one way for the majority to "own" the government: through a political democracy which allows them to change its policies and personnel and which assures minorities, not only civil liber-

ties to try and become a majority, but technical and financial
means to exercise that liberty as well. So democracy is thus not
simply central to the political structure of socialism; it is the
guarantee, the only guarantee, of the people's economic and social power.[18]

Hidden in this quote are two important points. The first is that the lack
of democracy found in the communist countries means that they are *not*
socialist. Second, if democracy at the national level is missing under
socialism, then we will likely repeat a fundamental problem of contemporary American society — the collusion of the government with the
economic elite.

A progressive income-tax, without loopholes.   One of the perennial
issues in American politics is the structure of the income-tax laws. In
the 1976 election President Carter termed such laws "a disgrace to the
human race." We have examined many of the loopholes that make for
this disgrace, but little has been done to correct this situation. We believe that little will continue to be done until a mass democratic movement brings about changes in such laws. Again, the tax system is a key
mechanism by which the rich retain their wealth, and numerous studies[19]
reveal that the middle class and the poor pay a higher percentage of their
incomes in taxes than do the rich.

The problem socialists face concerning tax reform is that the average person is taught that socialist reforms mean heavier taxes for the
nonwealthy, but this need not necessarily be the case. What is being
proposed here is no less than a truly progressive income tax, one which
would require those of most means to pay the highest *percentage* of their
incomes in taxes. Thus, 100 percent of the money *over* a certain amount
(to be determined democratically) would be taxed. Under the current
system, a number of millionaires pay no income taxes. Under the proposed system, such people would still be comfortable but would pay
their "fair share."

**A one-hundred percent inheritance tax above a certain level, com-
bined with methods to eliminate those tactics used to circumvent the
inheritance tax.**   We have seen that the foundation of the power and
wealth of elites rests in part on the special tax advantages they have been
granted. The heart of these advantages is the ability to transfer their
wealth from one generation to the next via inheritance and tax-exempt
foundations. This proposal would not end inheritance altogether, but
would prohibit the amassing of *huge fortunes* that make elite rule possible. One recent study[20] shows that fifty percent of American families
(if they had to pay all their debts at once) would have less than 3,000
dollars to leave to their children. Contrast this with a net worth of 100
million dollars that is possessed by upper-class families, and you have
some idea of the necessity for this provision.

As to the amount a given individual or family would be allowed to inherit, such a decision would be made democratically.   The monies raised by the imposition of such taxes would go to pay for the various social projects and programs deemed necessary for a decent standard of living for all.   Such standards are already regularly set by the federal government and are not difficult to determine.

A program for progressive redistribution of income through: (a) cradle-to-grave insurance, paid for entirely from income and inheritance taxes; (b) guaranteed full employment; and (c) a guaranteed annual income approximately equivalent to trade-union wages.   The goal of this plank is to eliminate misery associated with poverty.   All citizens would, under this proposal, be guaranteed adequate housing, an acceptable standard of health care, and a sufficient standard of living.   As the Democratic Socialist Organizing Committee has stated: "Socialist democracy, we believe, would make it increasingly possible for the free provision of the necessities of life.   That should be done as soon as possible with medicine; eventually, it should extend to housing, food and clothing." [21]

The societal commitment to full employment is crucial.   The typical criticism of full employment concerns the incentive to work.   Socialists are often accused of favoring measures that would reward people for not working, but this proposal might not be for the "able-bodied" who "refused" to work.   This proposal would be coupled with one which makes it a legal requirement for American society to provide full employment.   The wages and programs mentioned above would go to those unable to work as well as to all who did work.   Not everyone would earn the same amount of money, but the great inequalities of income that plague this society would be reduced.

In addition, there would be no need for "welfare" from the state to those who were unemployed because there would be no unemployment.   As for those who refused to work, we believe that there are very few such people in society.   Studies demonstrate that those on "welfare" who are able to work constitute less than twenty-five percent of welfare recipients.   The studies done concerning various groups of poor show that they are virtually unanimous in demonstrating a willingness and need to engage in useful labor.[22]   The problem with capitalism is that it has always required a pool of cheap labor to exploit, and it has created unemployment during economic crises.   We believe that a decent wage and fringe benefits, together with full employment, are the most rational and humane ways of guaranteeing a decent standard of living for all.

A vastly expanded program of social construction — mass transit, schools, low-cost housing, parks, hospitals, alternative energy sources, and the like.   In providing full employment, there are always questions about the kind of work people will do.   Will such jobs be meaningful, and will they be undertaken voluntarily?   We believe that there is a great deal of work that urgently needs to be done but which has a low priority due to the profit motive that dominates American capitalism. The need for low-cost housing is immense, with inflation placing the cost of homes beyond even families at the median income level. Moreover, four out of ten American families live in apartments. Many people, especially those of modest means, would like a house but cannot afford one. Aside from housing, there are energy needs which can be urgently met by converting to power from the sun, wind, and tides, a step that would provide millions of new jobs.[23] Employment in construction and related trades is often erratic because of weather and market conditions. This industry contains many who would prefer steady work at a decent standard of living. We believe that in providing full employment there are enough unmet and important needs in this nation to provide everyone who wants one a freely chosen position.

Aside from social construction, we envision more teachers for special education and a reduction in class sizes at all levels of education. We also foresee the creation of many jobs for people who wish to represent community interests at all levels of government.

National indicator planning that uses monetary, import, resource allocation, and other controls to direct production into more useful channels and is charged particularly with redistributing income and wealth in favor of the lower classes. Unlike the current system where private, profit-maximizing corporations are the planners of the economy, we propose a system where the primary goal of economic activity is the public good. The present system requires that government policy making benefits the corporations. These "trickle-down" solutions disproportionately benefit the elite and are therefore not only unfair but inefficient.[24] For example, the government is faced periodically with the problem of finding a way to stimulate the economy during an economic downturn. The socialist solution would be to spend federal monies through unemployment insurance, government jobs, and housing subsidies. In this way the funds go directly to those most hurt by shortages, unemployment, inadequate housing, and the like. The capitalist response, on the other hand, is to advocate subsidies directly to business, which, they claim, will help the economy by encouraging companies to hire more workers, add to their inventories, and build new plants. To provide subsidies to businesses rather than directly to needy individuals is based on the (faulty, we contend) assumption that private profit maximizes the public good.

A national ecological plan to mesh with the overall economic plan. As discussed earlier, we live in an age in which the environment is threatened daily by hazardous chemicals, nuclear waste, and a host of air and water pollutants. We believe that decisions concerning nuclear power and the dumping of hazardous materials should be made by the people who will be most affected by such events. We have provided ample evidence that the pollution problem in America is primarily a problem involving the priorities of capitalism, namely, profit. We believe that only a system which does *not* depend on profit, economic growth, and the continuous use (and depletion) of resources can practice conservation. Such conservation, we feel, must be carefully planned in a way which balances human needs with environmental quality. Again, we feel that this is best accomplished through the widest democratic participation.

Michael Lerner has written about the economic and ecological planning in a democratic socialist state. He envisions each home being equipped with a voting device that is attached to the phone or television set.* After issues had been debated in the media and at community meetings, the wishes of the public could be recorded and presented to elected public officials at local, regional, and national levels (each of whom would face a recall election anytime ten percent of the registered voters signed a petition to that effect). In addition, groups would also have the power to put a given issue on the political agenda:

> Signatures of 1 percent of the voting population in the relevant area would give the group the right to (1) write its own proposal to be put directly to the people, and (2) air its views on the media (it would be given more time than any single position normally is, on the grounds that its view had not previously been given exposure in the usual debates on relevant issues).[25]

Lerner has further suggested that there would be an elected executive branch at all levels, but their decisions could easily be put to the voters for approval. In Lerner's scheme the planning required for production and ecology, while complex, would be democratic:

> ... Each work unit and each consumer entity would submit its ideas and desires to a community board which would try to adjust them into a coherent whole, then resubmit the adjustments back to the populace for approval. Thereafter, they would be submitted to a regional board that took all the ideas and tried to develop a regional plan, which itself would be sent to a national board, which would try to adjust the regional plans. The last step would be to send that plan back to everyone for approval.[26]

Lerner has argued that planning which is equally complex is *already done* by the Department of Defense and other governmental units. However, the people consulted now are the heads of corporate boards, not working-class people. The decisions made by such boards reflect, of course, the wishes of the decision makers.

---

* Cable television in Columbus, Ohio, currently provides an interactive system where individuals can instantaneously record their preferences in a central computer.

Lerner has argued that it would be necessary to vote on the components as well as the totality of plans, and that one aspect of any plan would be the economy of the local community in which it is generated.

> Every community must have enough resources to experiment with education, housing, creativity, etc. The regional and national plans should deal with the minimum necessary number of issues: e.g., where to build new cities, how to solve general ecological problems, how to arrange transportation between localities, foreign trade, taxation, and long-term financing. The regional and national plans would have as one key task the allocation and redistribution of resources in such a way as to guarantee that no one area suffers because it does not have adequate natural resources or because a main source of its economic strength (e.g., car manufacturing or mining) is shut down for reasons of preserving the ecology. But since the idea of giving each community a large sum initially for discretionary planning is key to this conception, the national plan is likely to be less complicated than the present federal budget in an unplanned economy, because so much that is now decided nationally will be decided at the local level.[27]

Such planning would be oriented toward overcoming some of the root causes of certain types of elite deviance. Goods, instead of being based on planned obsolescence, would be designed to last as long as possible. This would eliminate much waste, pollution, and save energy.

A tax policy that would discourage private investment by U.S. corporations overseas and stringent measures to curb, then liquidate, the great multinational corporation. We suggest that the United States does not need a multinational empire. Rather its best hope lies in the promotion of a peaceful, stable, and prosperous world. We believe that this is best accomplished by policies designed to end the poverty, famine, and political instability in the Third World. They are also designed to end the unpopular opinion concerning "ugly Americans," and "Yankee imperialism" in much of the Third World. In addition, these policies will return many jobs to the U.S. that have been exported by multinationals in recent years. This cannot be accomplished overnight and will require a transition period to minimize the disruption of the American economy. We do, however, believe such a conversion is both possible and prudent.

The Implementation of Economic Democracy

Now that we have characterized how economic democracy ought to work, let's deal with some of the practical problems and questions that always seem to arise in any serious discussion of how it might be implemented. To begin, the essence of socialism is a cooperative spirit among the people, yet it is commonly believed that people are naturally sinful, aggressive, and self-seeking. In this perspective, competition is natural and long-range cooperation is impossible. If this postulate is accurate, then the goal of socialism will always elude human societies. The question, then, is whether human beings in groups are capable of long-range cooperative relationships where the needs of the group supersede the needs of the individual. The American experience is so competitive that we easily assume that competition is natural. Virtually all aspects of American life, whether in school or the job, in organizations, or in activities such as sports, music, and dating, are highly competitive. However, there is ample evidence from anthropological studies to show that societies like the Zuni have individuals who are group centered. The members of these societies *never* attempt to outdo anyone in their society and they accept the sacrifice for the accomplishment of group goals as "natural." [28] The conclusion from data like this is that people in societies can be taught to be competitive or cooperative. There is no necessary obstacle to the possibility that Americans could be taught from infancy to work for group goals rather than individual achievement at the expense of others. In short, human nature is really *social* nature shaped by the society in which the individual is imbedded.

In a related issue, it is often argued that socialism runs contrary to human nature because one's needs are met by society whether he or she works or not. The assumption is that massive inequalities are necessary to motivate citizens to work and avoid a class of lazy welfare recipients. Motivation in socialist countries could be achieved in several ways without using the repressive tactics of a totalitarian regime. The first is to socialize citizens to work for the good of the community. Evidence from the many experiments with communes shows that the successful ones developed an ideology that the members of the community shared. In a group sharing a common ideology, informal sanctions could be used to achieve conformity among potential deviants.

All societies have members who vary in talent, achievement, and motivation. The problem for a socialist society is how to reward excellence. This could be done in nonmaterial satisfactions such as honors or responsible community functions or in some extra material benefits. The exta material benefits must be kept in check within a socialist economy, however, so that the private accumulation of wealth is confined within tolerable limits. The permissible maximum, for example, could be twice the median income with the guaranteed minimum being one-half the median income. Such a plan would allow everyone the necessities and the personal choice to work for some additional benefits.[29]

Another motivational problem is how to get people to do society's "dirty work." After all, if all of one's basic needs are met, why should one do dangerous jobs or menial ones? Capitalist countries accomplish this problem of job allocation by, in the case of hazardous jobs, paying extra monies or, in the case of demeaning work, having an underclass (usually minorities) whose opportunities are so limited there is little choice but to do society's dirty work. A socialist country could see that these necessary tasks were done by either appealing to persons on ideological grounds to give a period of time for these societal duties or by conscripting youth to do the necessary work of society as a kind of societal tax that they owe as citizens. Just as in the time of war, able-bodied persons (male and female) would owe, say, two years of service to their society.

A problem that plagues all existing socialist systems (but is not limited to them) is massive bureaucratization. The more that the economy is controlled by the government, the greater the problem of inflated statism, which translates into the twin problems of centralized power and inefficiency. The problem of inefficiency can be addressed through the constant monitoring of procedures and administrators, with the people affected having the power to redress grievances and change inadequate procedures.

The other problem emanating from excessive bureaucratization — centralized power — is especially crucial, for if it is not solved, then the goal of democratic socialism is unachievable. This is the problem of the so-called socialist countries with totalitarian regimes. The group that took power tends to stay in power and sees its goals as those needed by the society. This illustrates the strong organizational tendency labeled the "Iron Law of Oligarchy" by Robert Michels.[30] While this probability plagues social organizations, under certain conditions it does not occur — i.e., where democracy prevails.[31] By definition, a democracy exists where at least two political parties regularly compete for office, and control alternates periodically. The chances of this happening are maximized when: (1) the citizens have a strong interest, concern, and commitment to the society; (2) the subunits (communities, states) are relatively autonomous units forming a federation; (3) the leaders get few special prerequisites of office making them little different from the masses in material rewards; and (4) dissent and innovation are allowed.[32] Admittedly, the problem of the emergence of a self-serving power elite is an especially dangerous problem for socialist countries. Therefore, these societies must institutionalize forms of democratic control at all levels using the insights provided above. The key is to have power at once concentrated and dispersed. The citizens must be ever diligent to counter oligarchic tendencies and there must be constitutional avenues for the control of the controllers.

Another practical problem facing any socialist society is the high cost of providing for the minimal benefits to all members. The semi-socialist countries of Western Europe have extremely high taxes to level material differences and to provide the necessary services. Also, it is charged, societies will experience ruinous inflation if they increase expenditures for social services.   There are at least two basic ways that money can be raised in the United States for increasing social programs without too great an adjustment.   One source of money would come from paring the inflated military budget.   The question is how much the 150 billion-dollar budget could be reduced without endangering the safety of the society.   This question quickly divides liberals and conservatives, but we believe that it is safe to say that if objective observers (i.e., those outside the military, those in business without military contracts, and those public officials outside districts with huge military expenditures) examined military expenditures carefully, they would find numerous military bases that should be closed, redundancy in weapons systems, too many highly paid officers, and a too-expensive pension system.   Obviously, the savings if the appropriate cuts in the military budget were made could be deployed elsewhere to meet the social needs of the society.

A second and even more lucrative source of monies to finance increased social programs would be to eliminate the tax expenditures (about 120 billion dollars).   These are monies that the government could collect but chooses not to.   Most of these tax breaks go to the upper middle and upper classes.   "There are enormous savings to be made in these areas simply by following in fact the principle we now honor in the breech: that those best able to pay should bear their share of the tax burden." [33]

Finally, there is the question upon which all else hinges: how is economic democracy to come about in American society?   If the corporate rich are the powerful and they control the governmental apparatus including the ability to repress dissent, the media, and the universities, how are the fundamental changes in the structure necessary for democratic socialism to occur?   Who will be included in a social movement bent on making these social changes?   The obvious candidates are those most oppressed by capitalism — the poor, minorities, women, aged, and the working class (including white and blue-collar workers).   These categories, however, have historically failed to cooperate in a common venture to change the system.   They have not developed the class consciousness Marx envisioned because of racial antipathies and other prejudices, because of their own self-doubt, and because they believe in the viability of the current politico-economic system.   They tend to believe that the opportunities available in society will eventually pay off for them or their children.   They believe that capitalism is responsible for our greatness and will meet the challenges of the future successfully.   In short, persons in these social categories have not seen that they are oppressed.   Ironically, they accept the system that works to their disadvantage.   Thus, they adhere to beliefs damaging to their interests, or what Marx termed "false consciousness."

The key to developing the needed awareness of a common oppression among society's have-nots lies most likely in the increasing inability of state-supported capitalism to meet the needs of its citizens. The following is a partial list of the problems that the present system faces:

1. Capitalism has provided for people's consumption needs (created in part by advertising), yet these cannot continue to escalate as material resources and energy decrease in supply.

2. The number of capitalists continues to decline, reducing the proportion of natural defenders of capitalism to an ever smaller minority. "Two hundred years ago, over three-fourths of white families owned land, tools, or other productive property; this figure has fallen to about a third and, even among this group, a tiny minority owns the lion's share of all productive property." [34]

3. Capitalism has a fundamental problem with employment. Under capitalism people can sell their labor only if someone can make a profit. Machines continue to replace human workers (especially unskilled and semiskilled workers). At the upper levels, there is the escalating problem of underemployment, as too many educated persons are seeking too few jobs for which they qualify.

4. Inflation has made it extremely difficult for the small entrepreneur to compete. The cost of new equipment and supplies continues to rise above the capacity of these persons to purchase them, making their operations less efficient and more costly. Inflation also has made home ownership and other badges of affluence harder and harder to attain for those at the median income level and below.

5. Because of compounding economic woes, many corporations have sought special help from the government in the form of tax breaks, gifts, and guaranteed loans. Lockheed, Chrysler, Penn Central, Amtrak, and others have pled for and received such bailouts. As Harrington has noted, the nation should stop nationalizing the losses of these companies and privatizing the profits.[35] More and more of the public are reacting negatively toward such largesse at their expense.

6. Similarly, the people are becoming more aware that they are being asked to pay through taxes for the development of technologies (communications satellites, solar batteries, the production of oil shale, etc.), which are then turned over to the corporations for their benefit, and at additional expense to the consumer.

7. The plight of the underclass in American society appears hopeless with millions in the newest generation uneducated, un-

skilled, and angry. The present society holds no hope for these persons.

8. There is an increasing awareness that society cannot fulfill its promises implied in "The American Dream" as inflation makes home ownership more difficult and educational attainment no longer translates automatically into an equivalent job.

9. The public is becoming more and more aware of the corporate elite's intransigence to curb their abuses such as pollution, supplying hazardous goods, and monopolistic practices.

10. The current efforts to limit social services (e.g., California's Proposition 13), will increase the militancy of the disadvantaged.

These factors, and the list is not exhaustive, suggest the strong possibility that increasing numbers of Americans will begin to recognize that capitalism works against their interests and that there is a better way. This ever larger group must be led by a self-conscious group bent on revolutionary change. They must provide the organization to increase the numbers and provide the tactics to achieve the goals. But must revolutionary change be accomplished through violence? Violence has been used to bring about socialism in a number of countries but in most cases the revolutionary cadre, when successful, has become itself a repressive power elite, contrary to the goals of economic democracy.

A nation could accomplish such democracy through a slow process involving constitutional changes and the eventual control of a political party or parties committed to the principles of democratic socialism. A strategy along these lines for the United States has been called the "revolution-in-stages" by Sidney Lens.[36] Rather than a single lunge for power, the effort is for a protracted struggle to change the ratio of power.

> ... Those who orient on a phased transformation do whatever is possible "within" the system,* such as lobbying, but concentrate their main energies "outside" the system, on strikes, demonstrations, civil disobedience, vigils — acts of resistance and defiance. They also function within the trade union movement as a left wing, seeking to reshape it and make it more militant. But the orientation of strategy is toward gaining *institutional* changes, one at a time and under the old order — until it is transformed. Thus the party that radicals build need not be so close-knit, nor does it have to be primarily an instrument for workingclass goals. It can be, and probably will be in America, an amalgam of antiwar coalitions, left-wing unionists, black, Chicano, Puerto Rican, and Indian organizations, radicalized consumer movements that will

* See Appendices A and B for groups to join and ways to affect the media.

emerge from Ralph Nader's crusade or from such forces as the
Citizens Action Program in Chicago, and others not yet existing.
If the purpose is to win institutional changes over a period of
time rather than prepare for a single lunge, the radical party can
be broader and looser than the Leninist parties of the past. . . .
What distinguishes the revolution-in-stages is the transformation
of institutions is more even-paced and goes on intensely even
while the old classes are in the saddle. It is an ongoing process to
eradicate the private profit factor in the political economy and
to eviscerate those institutions (such as the military, the judicial
system, the government structure) which enhance it.[37]

Some might consider this gradual approach naive, but we believe
that the use of force will be counterproductive, not only in the senseless
killing but because it will also drive away many potential converts from
the socialist position. The movement requires the broad-based support
of those who choose to belong rather than those who are coerced to
belong, if it is to work according to the principles of economic democracy.

We believe that economic democracy is the only answer to solving
the social problems and elite deviance that plague American society.
Without the structural changes concomitant to socialism, the present
downward spiral will be accentuated by future contingencies. As Michael Harrington, National Chairman of the Democratic Socialist Organizing Committee, has argued, ". . . the socialism defined here does
not pretend to be the name of the future: It is simply our only hope." [38]

NOTES

1. For the elaboration of this point, see James M. Henslin, "Social Problems and Systemic Origins," *Social Problems in American Society,* Second Edition,
James M. Henslin and Larry T. Reynolds, eds. (Boston: Holbrook, 1976), pp.
375–381; William Ryan, *Blaming the Victim,* Second Edition (New York: Pantheon, 1977); and Michael Parenti, *Power and the Powerless* (New York: St.
Martin's, 1978).

2. Michael Parenti, *Democracy for the Few,* Third Edition (New York: St.
Martin's, 1980), p. 314.

3. *Ibid.*

4. Cf. Vernon E. Jordan, Jr., "The New Minimalism," *Newsweek* (August
14, 1978), p. 13.

5. Parenti, *Democracy for the Few,* p. 314.

6. *Ibid.,* p. 312.

7. Michael Harrington, cited in "We Are Socialists of the Democratic
Left," statement of principles, Democratic Socialist Organizing Committee (1978),
p. 2. For an elaboration on this theme, see Michael Harrington, *Decade of Decision* (New York: Simon and Schuster, 1980).

8. Ralph Miliband, "The Future of Socialism in England," *The Socialist Register 1977* (London: Merlin, 1977), pp. 38–50. See also Samuel Bowles and Herbert Gintis, *Schooling in Capitalist America: Educational Reforms and the Contradictions of Economic Life* (New York: Basic Books, 1976), Chapter 11.

9. M. Mintz and J. Cohen, *Power Inc.* (New York: Viking, 1976), p. iii.

10. Parenti, *Power and the Powerless,* p. 203.

11. Michael Harrington, *Socialism* (New York: Saturday Review Press, 1979), pp. 8–9.

12. Richard C. Edwards, Michael Reich, and Thomas E. Weisskopf, eds., *The Capitalist System,* Second Edition (Englewood Cliffs, N.J.: Prentice-Hall, 1978), p. 517.

13. Miliband, "The Future of Socialism," pp. 42–43.

14. Michael Harrington, "How to Reshape America's Economy," *Dissent* 23 (Spring, 1976), p. 122.

15. *Ibid.*

16. John Woodmansee et al., *The World of a Giant Corporation* (Seattle: North Country Press, 1975), pp. 70–71. Used with permission of People's Business Commission.

17. Harrington, "How to Reshape America's Economy," p. 22.

18. Harrington, "We Are Socialists of the Democratic Left," p. 3.

19. See, for example, R. Parker, *The Myth of the Middle Class* (New York: Liveright, 1972); Phillip Stern, *The Rape of the Taxpayer* (New York: Random House, 1973); J. Turner and C. Starnes, *Inequality: Privilege and Power in America* (California: Goodyear, 1976).

20. M. Zeitlin, "Who Runs America? The Same Old Gang," *The Progressive* (June 1978), pp. 14–19.

21. Harrington, "We Are Socialists of the Democratic Left," p. 2.

22. See C. H. Anderson and J. R. Gibson, *Toward a New Sociology,* Third Edition (Homewood, Ill.: Dorsey Press, 1978), pp. 170–176 for a detailed review of such studies.

23. See the "program for economic conversion" designed to shift America toward a peacetime economy. The program is available from SANE, Washington, D.C.

24. Michael Harrington, "The Socialist Case," *The Center Magazine* (July/August, 1976).

25. Michael Lerner, *The New Socialist Revolution* (New York: Dell, 1973), p. 535 in M. Edwards et al., eds., *The Capitalist System,* Second Edition (Englewood Cliffs, N.J.: Prentice-Hall, 1978).

26. *Ibid.,* p. 536.

27. *Ibid.,* p. 536.

28. Cf. Ruth Benedict, *Patterns of Culture* (New York: Mentor Books, 1934).

29. Cf. Henry Pachter, "Freedom, Authority, Participation," *Dissent* 25 (Summer 1978), p. 296.

30. Robert Michels, *Political Parties,* Eden and Cedar Paul (trans.), (New York: The Free Press, 1966). See also Max Weber, *The Theory of Social and Economic Organization* (Glencoe, Illinois: The Free Press, 1947).

31. Cf. Seymour Martin Lipset, Martin Trow, and James C. Coleman, *Union Democracy: The Internal Politics of the International Typographers Union* (Garden City, New York: Doubleday Anchor, 1962).

32. Anthony M. Orum, *Introduction to Political Sociology: The Social Anatomy of the Body Politic* (Englewood Cliffs, N.J.: Prentice-Hall, 1978), pp. 259–260.

33. Harrington, "How to Reshape America's Economy," p. 122. See also Robert M. Brandon et al., *Tax Politics* (New York: Pantheon, 1976).

34. Samuel Bowles and Herbert Gintis, "Socialist Revolution in the United States: Goals and Means," in Edwards et al., *The Capitalist System,* p. 524.

35. Harrington, "The Socialist Case," p. 66.

36. Sidney Lens, *The Promise and Pitfalls of Revolution* (Philadelphia: A Pilgrim Press Book, 1974). See also Sidney Lens, "For a Revolution-in-Stages," *The Progressive* 4 (April 1974), pp. 38–39.

37. *Ibid.,* pp. 254–255.

38. Harrington, *Socialism,* p. 10.

Appendix A
A Catalog of Community Groups

Typology of Grassroots Groups. (Table to be read across two pages.)

Type of Group	Location	Age	Origin		Constituency	
I. *Direct-action* *groups* A. Multi-issue	Headquarters	Date of Origin	Historic Antecedents	Rural or Urban	Class*	Race
Statewide						
GROWTH (Grassroots Organizations with/without Tom Hayden)	Los Angeles, CA	1975	Antiwar movement	Urban & suburban	Working & middle class	Mostly white
IPAC (Illinois Public Interest Council)	Chicago, IL	1975	AFL-CIO & new left	Rural & urban	Working class	Mixed
PACC (People's Alliance for A Cooperative Commonwealth)	Chapel Hill, NC	1975	NAM (New American Movement)	Urban	Low & moderate income	Mixed
Citywide						
CAP (Citizen Action Project)	Chicago, IL	1969– 1970	Organizer training (Alinsky School) & ecology movement	Urban	Low & middle income	60% whi 30% Bla 10% His panic
COPS (Community Organizations for Public Service)	Phoenix, AZ	1974	Organizer training (Alinsky School-IAF)	Urban	Working & lower middle class	Chicano
Metropolitan Phoenix Indian Coalition	Phoenix, AZ	1975	Civil rights	Urban	Low	America Indian
Neighborhood						
AMO (Adams Morgan Organization)	Washington, D.C.	1972	Civil and social action groups	Urban	Low & moderate income	Black, white, Hispanic
COPO (Coalition of Peninsula Organizations)	Baltimore, MD	1976	Organizer training, federated community, direct action	Urban	Working class	Mostly white
GO (Guadelupe Organization)	Guadelupe, AZ	1964	Catholic church, social work	Rural style in city	Low	Yaqui Indian & Chicano

Source: Janice E. Pearlman, "Grassrooting the System," *Social Policy* 2 (Sept./Oct., 1976), 13–17. Published by Social Policy Corp., New York, New York 10036. Copyright 1976 by So Policy Corporation.

Size	Funding	Issues *	Media Profile
Membership			
35 chapters, 15 new ones planned	Hayden campaign, direct contributions	Local neighborhood issues	Low profile
New group. 100 groups expected at founding convention	Canvassing, ad book	Housing, taxes, utilities, crime, economic justice	Medium profile; growing coverage
New group	Contributions	Neighborhood preservation, consumer protection, taxes, senior citizens, environmental issues	Low profile; very little media
8,000 members at peak, 35 neighborhood groups, 50 senior groups	Canvassing, dues, foundations	Pollution, tax reform, municipal services, redlining/greenlining, Crosstown Corridor Highway	High profile; good media relations
40,000. 300 groups	Churches, dues	Zoning, water rates, voter registration, neighborhood improvement	Medium profile; fair media
19 groups. 400 people at Spring Convention	Foundations, contributions	Intertribal cooperation, links between on- and off-reservation Indians. Indians empowerment, immediate needs	Low profile; very little media
4,000. 200 active	Fundraising	Housing & neighborhood revitalization, antispeculation, recreation, environment	Low profile; high locally
36 member organizations	Dues, fundraising, contributions, United Fund	Neighborhood issues with particular emphasis on housing, taxes, transportation	Low profile
425 now. 550 at peak	Foundations, churches	Incorporation referendum, neighborhood improvement (street lights, drainage ditches, roads, etc.), land use	Low profile

* The class base and issues are noted in the vocabulary of the groups themselves.
** Abbreviations: NWRO — National Welfare Rights Organization; SDS — Students for a mocratic Society; SNCC — Student Nonviolent Coordinating Committee.

	Type of Group	Location	Age	Origin		Constituency	
	I. *Direct-action groups* A. Multi-issue	Headquarters	Date of Origin	Historic Antecedents	Rural or Urban	Class*	Race
Multistate	NPA (National People's Action)	Chicago, IL	1973	Organizer training	Urban	Low & moderate income	Mostly white
	ACORN (Assoc. of Community Organizations for Reform Now)	Little Rock, AR	1970	NWRO **	Urban & rural	Low & moderate	70% whit
	NASP (National Assoc. of the Southern Poor)	Petersburg, VA	1968	Civil Rights, British parliamentary democracy; Jeffersonian democracy	Mostly rural	Poor	Black
Statewide	Massachusetts Fair Share	Boston, MA	1973	NWRO SDS	Urban & suburban	Low & moderate	Mostly white
	CAL (Citizen Action League)	San Francisco, CA	1974	SNCC SDS NWRO Alinsky tradition	Urban	Low & middle income	Mostly white
	Carolina Action	Durham, NC	1973	NWRO ACORN Organizer training	Urban & rural	Low & moderate income	Black & white
	MAC (Maryland Action Coalition)	Baltimore, MD	1975	Organizer training	Urban	Working class	White

	Size	Funding	Issues*	Media Profile
ff	Membership			
-30	39 states, 104 urban areas, 11,000+ members	Churches, foundations, business, direct mail	Housing and neighborhood revitalization, redlining, S & L disclosures, variable-rate mortgages	High profile; uses the media
-40	6,000 member families, 5 states (AR, SD, TX, MS, LA), 14 offices	Dues, foundations	Lifeline utility rates, generic drugs, Quorum Court, Wilbur Mills Exp. White Bluff Power Plant, tax assessments	Medium profile; work with local media
	45,000. 900 active "conferences," 18 counties & 3 cities in VA, 9 counties in NC	Churches, foundations, direct mail	Racial discrimination, welfare and food stamps, municipal services, schools (curriculum, expulsions, suspensions), Black land loss, agricultural co-ops, tobacco allotment	Low profile; avoids media
	600–1000. 8 affiliate groups around Boston	Canvassing, churches, foundations, fundraising	Utility rates, tax reform, telephone rates, homeowner insurance, housing abandonment	High profile; good media relations
ganizers	620–1000. 3 chapters (S.F., San Mateo, L.A.)	Foundations, membership dues, churches, canvassing, fund-raising	Utility rates, tax assessments, tenant organizing, child care, crime, nursing homes	High profile; works with media
	700–1000. Durham, Raleigh, Greensboro	Dues, canvassing, churches	Lifeline fair share utility rates, property taxes, telephone rates, senior citizen bus service, city council, neighborhood revitalization	Low profile; wants more coverage
	Just beginning	Canvassing	Utilities, taxes	Low profile

	Type of Group	*Location*	*Age*	*Origin*		*Constituency*	
	I. *Direct-action groups* B. Single-issue	Headquarters	Date of Origin	Historic Antecedents	Rural or Urban	Class*	Race
Multistate	Carolina Brown Lung	Greenville, SC	1974	Black lung, United Mine Workers, Welfare rights	Rural & urban	Lower working class	White
Multistate	Minority Peoples' Coalition on the Tennessee-Tombigbee Waterway	Epes, AL	1975	Civil rights, Federation of Southern Co-ops	Rural	Low	Black
Citywide	WE (Women Employed)	Chicago, IL	1973	Union & women's movements	Urban	Working class	Mostly white
Citywide	CAUSE (Campaign Against Utility Service Exploitation)	Los Angeles, CA	1975	Energy crisis, anti-war movement	Urban	Middle & working class	Mostly white
Citywide	Nine-to-Five	Boston, MA	1973	Women's & labor movements	Urban	Middle & working class	Mostly white
Neighborhood	ROAR (Restore our Alienated Rights)	Boston, MA	1974	Neighborhood protection	Urban	Working class	White
Neighborhood	Co-op City*	Bronx, NY	1974	Tenants movement	Urban	Working class	¾ White ¼ Black
	II. *Electoral efforts*						
	Chrystal City (Cristal)	Zavala County, TX	1970	MAYO (Mexican American Youth Organization) La Raza Unida Party	Rural	Low	Chicano

ff	Membership	Size	Funding	Issues*	Media Profile
		280 just starting. 2 states, NC & SC	Dues	Occupational health & safety, compensation, factory condition improvement	High profile; good coverage
5		400 active members, thousands involved	Foundations	Jobs for local Black residents on the construction, land & water rights compensation	Low profile
		300 dues-paying, 1000 participants	Dues	Wage discrimination, working conditions, unionization, affirmative action in hiring & promotion	Medium profile
		23 member organizations	Fundraising	Lifeline rates for water, gas & electricity, fight against Alaska Pipeline costs passed on to consumers	High profile; use TV especially
groups, unions		450 dues-paying. 800 on mailing list.	Dues	Wage discrimination, working conditions, unionization, affirmative action in hiring & promotion, maternity benefits, job training	Medium profile
0 lunteers		1000. 400 active. 200 marshals	Contributions	Fight against forced busing, neighborhood preservation, electoral politics. ABC's (antiabortion, busing, communism)	Very high profile; national coverage
full-time		55,000 people. 15,372 units	Withheld rents	Rent strike	Very high; Nat.-local
ost all ected & pointed ficials		10,000. 500 active. "Ciudanos Unidos"	Taxes, federal funds, foundations	Housing, schools, health care, economic development (CDC), unionization of Delmonte	High profile

	Type of Group	Location	Age	Origin		Constituency	
	III. *Alternative institutions* A. CDCs	Headquarters	Date of Origin	Historic Antecedents	Rural or Urban	Class*	Race
Multicounty	MACE (Mississippi Action for Community Education)	Greenville, MS	1967	Civil rights, voter registration, SNCC, MS Freedom Democratic Party	Rural	Low	Black
	SEASHA (Southeast Alabama Self-Help)	Tuskegee, AL	1967	Civil Rights, OEO educational program	Rural	Low	Black
Citywide	SSUS (Spanish-speaking Unity Council)	Oakland, CA	1963	Social work & services	Urban	Low	Hispanic
	Chicanos Por La Causa, Inc.	Phoenix, AZ	1968	Civil rights, Martin Luther King/JFK inspiration	Urban	Low & moderate	Chicano
	HOPE (Hispanic Office of Planning & Evaluation)	Boston, MA	1970	Civil rights. Social service	Urban	Low & moderate	Hispanic
	MAUC (Mexican American Unity Council)	San Antonio, TX	1968	Civil rights	Urban	Low	Chicano
Neighborhood	Bedford-Stuyvesant Restoration & Development	Brooklyn, NY	1967	OEO, Senators Kennedy & Javits	Urban	Low	Black & some Puert Rican
	TWO (The Woodlawn Organization)	Chicago, IL	1959	Alinsky school	Urban	Low	Black

	Size	Funding	Issues*	Media Profile
ff	Membership			
ices ganizers	12,000. 14 counties	Ford Foundation	Equalization suit (Hawkins v. Shaw), electoral politics (former MS Freedom Democratic party), economic development, water and utilities	Very low profile; avoid media
–25	8,000. 2 counties	Ford Foundation, federal programs, OEO	Feeder-pig co-op, credit union, housing, voter registration, Black land retention	Low profile; little media
	13 organizations. 47 at peak	Ford Foundation, federal programs	Information & job referral, business consulting, humanpower training, housing & building management	Very low profile; almost no media
	366 (just began)	Ford Foundation, federal programs, OEO, CSA	Zoning, housing, education, airport location, services, community economic development	Low; prefer more/better coverage
	300, plan membership drive	Ford Foundation, federal programs, revenue sharing	Education (College-Bound program), anti-Southwest Corridor, prison, project	Low profile; little media
0 +	None	Ford Foundation, federal programs, revenue sharing	Housing, hospital care, mental health, police brutality, acoholism	Medium profile; runs own radio & TV spots
0 now, 0 peak	None. 26 "member" directors	Ford Foundation, federal programs, revenue sharing	Neighborhood physical & economic development, job creation, housing, rehabilitation, tax issue, social programs	High profile; lots of media
88 staff TWO & /CDC). 5 staff in rganizing services	115 groups, now beginning individual membership	Ford Foundation, federal programs, revenue sharing, social services money	Real estate/land use, economic development, housing, job training, employment, crime, shopping center employment	High profile; uses the media

	Type of Group	Location	Age	Origin		Constituency	
	III. *Alternative Institutions* A. CDCs	Headquarters	Date of Origin	Historic Antecedents	Rural or Urban	Class*	Race
Neighborhood	SECO (Southeast Community Organization)	Baltimore, MD	1970	Organizer training, civil rights, "New Pluralism"	Urban	Low & moderate	white ethnic
	WLCAC (Watts Labor Community Action Council)	Los Angeles, CA	1965	United Auto Workers	Urban	Low	Black
	TELACU (The East Los Angeles Community Union)	Los Angeles, CA	1965	United Auto Workers	Urban	Low	Chicano
	III. *Alternative Institutions* B. Cooperatives						
	SCDF (Southern Cooperative Development Fund)	Lafayette, LA	1969	Civil rights; rural co-op movement	Rural	Low	Black
	FSC (Federation of Southern Cooperatives)	Epes, AL	1967	Civil rights; rural co-ops	Rural	Low	Black

		Size	Funding	Issues*	Media Profile
aff	Membership				
		70 groups	Ford Foundation, federal programs, revenue sharing	Expressway fight, neighborhood housing services, economic development	Increasing; cultivate media
0 aff, 0 ployees		25 clubs	Ford Foundation, federal programs	Small business development, housing, Martin Luther King Hospital, humanpower training, seniors program	High profile; uses media
staff		15 clubs	Former Ford funding, federal programs	Economic development, research & planning, loan package, voter registration, incorporation	Low profile; little media coverage
		35–50 co-ops	Ford Foundation, federal programs	Preventing Black land loss, creating humanitarian Moshav-style alternative, helping member co-ops with credit union, getting Blacks elected	Low profile; favorable coverage
		30,000 families, 120 co-ops, 14 states	Rockefeller foundation, federal programs	Preventing Black land loss, providing "populist/socialist" technical assistance to co-ops, comprehensive rural economic development strategy, training center, demonstration farm (1,300 acres)	Low profile

Appendix B
*Access to Media**

James R. Bennett

MEDIA

Commercial Broadcasting

American Broadcasting Company
1331 Avenue of the Americas
New York, NY 10019

CBS Television Network
51 W. 52nd Street
New York, NY 10019

Mutual Broadcasting System, Inc.
135 W. 50th Street
New York, NY 10020

National Broadcasting Company,
Inc.
30 Rockefeller Plaza
New York, NY 10020

Westinghouse Broadcasting
Company
90 Park Avenue
New York, NY 10016

Public Broadcasting

Public Broadcasting Service
4475 L'Enfant Plaza West, SW
Washington, DC 20024

National Public Radio (NPR)
2025 M St., NW
Washington, DC 20036
  See article in *Saturday Review* by
  Karl Meyer (July 21, 1979)

The Advocates
P.O.B. 1978
Boston, MA 02134

Black Perspective on the News
4548 Market Street
Philadelphia, PA 19139

Consumer Survival Kit
Maryland Center for Public
  Broadcasting
P.O.B. 1978
Owings Mills, MD 21117

---

* This list first appeared in *The Humanist* 39 (Nov./Dec., 1979), pp. 52–
54, and is reprinted by permission.

Firing Line
P.O.B. 5966
Columbia, SC 29250

The MacNeil/Lehrer Report
Box 345
New York, NY 10019

Nova P.O.B. 1000
Cathedral Station
Boston, MA 02118

Magazines and Newspapers

*Ulrich's International Periodicals
Directory* (journals)

Ayer's Directory of Publications
(newspapers)

SELF-REGULATION

National Association of Broadcasters
1771 N Street, NW
Washington, DC 20036
The Code Authority of the National
Association of Broadcasters handles
complaints from the general public,
based upon standards embodied in
the Radio Code and the Television
Code of the NAB. When the complaint alleges a possible violation of
Code standards, the Code Authority
may investigate the matter with the
station. (Not all broadcast stations
subscribe to the Codes, however.)
The main office of the Code Authority is in New York City, 477
Madison Avenue, 10022.

National Advertising Division
(NAD)
Council of Better Business Bureaus,
Inc. (BBB)
845 Third Avenue
New York, NY 10022
Statement from the NAD: "The
goal of the National Advertising Di-
vision of the Council of Better Busi-
ness Bureaus, Inc. is to assure truth

and accuracy in national advertising."

National Advertising Review Board
(NARB)
850 Third Avenue
New York, NY 10022
"If an advertising problem cannot
be resolved by the NAD, it comes
before a five-member panel of
NARB for final disposition. The
NARB is composed of fifty men and
women representing national advertisers, advertising agencies, and the
public sector."

National News Council
One Lincoln Plaza
New York, NY 10023
For complaints regarding news items
distributed nationwide by AP, UPI,
the networks, or a national maga-
zine or newspaper, the National
News Council will possibly take up
the matter with the alleged offender.
Their reports are published in the
Columbia Journalism Review.

GOVERNMENT AGENCIES

See the *Directory: Federal, State,
County, and City Government Con-
sumer Offices,* published by the De-
partment of Health, Education, and
Welfare. For a copy write:
Superintendent of Documents
U.S. Government Printing Office
Washington, DC 20402

The most relevant federal governmental bodies are:

Consumer Product Safety Commission
1750 K Street, NW
Washington, DC 20207

Department of Commerce
Office of the Ombudsman for
Business
Fourteenth Street, NW
Washington, DC 20230

Department of Health, Education, and Welfare
Office of Consumer Affairs
330 Independence Avenue, SW
Washington, DC 20201

Federal Communications Commission (FCC)
1919 M Street, NW, Room 258
Washington, DC 20554

Federal Trade Commission (FTC)
6th and Pennsylvania Avenue, NW
Washington, DC 20580

Office of Telecommunications Policy
1800 G Street, NW
Washington, DC 20504

Senate Subcommittee on Communications
Russell Senate Office Building
Room 130
Washington, DC 20510

House Subcommittee on Communications
Rayburn House Office Building
Room B 333
Washington, DC 20515

Corporation for Public Broadcasting
1111 16th St., NW
Washington, DC 20036

And write your congressman:

U.S. House of Representatives
The Capitol
Washington, DC 20515

U.S. Senate
The Capitol
Washington, DC 20510

GOVERNMENT PUBLICATIONS

Consumer Information

Consumer Information Center
Pueblo, CO 81009
An index of selected federal publications of consumer interest. And

ask for Federal Information Center pamphlet No. 245D.

Guide to Federal Consumer Services
Department of Health, Education, and Welfare
Office of Consumer Affairs
(address above)

PRIVATE ORGANIZATIONS

Accuracy in Media, Inc.
777 14th Street, NW, Suite 427
Washington, DC 20005
Founded to combat inaccuracies and distorted reporting of the news by the major media. You can subscribe to their *AIM Report* for $15.

Action for Children's Television
46 Austin Street
Newtonville, MA 02160
Publishes a newsletter; has a film available, *But First This Message.*

Alternate Media Center
144 Bleecker Street
New York, NY 10012
Resource for video information, particularly in the use of cable access; publishes a series of workbooks on access and maintains an exchange and rental catalog-library of tapes.

Cambridge Documentary Films, Inc.
P.O. Box 385
Cambridge, MA 02139
A nonprofit filmmaking and distribution organization.

Council on Children, Media, and Merchandising
1346 Connecticut Avenue, NW
Washington, DC 20036

Great Atlantic Radio Conspiracy
2743 Maryland Avenue
Baltimore, MD 21218
Political radio group producing weekly programs and a monthly review of underground and alternative media.

H.A.R.T. (Help America Reduce Televiolence)
P.O. Box 1701
South Bend, IN 46624
"Instructions for Writing Network and Sponsors," a newsletter *Hart Beat,* and other resources. Membership $10.

Media Mix
221 W. Madison Street
Chicago, IL 60606
Claretian Publications publishes a newsletter called *Media Mix*. Reviews films, filmstrips, tapes, records, books, and games. Published eight times a year for $9.

National Association for Better Broadcasting
P.O.B. 43640
Los Angeles, CA 90043
"NABB's objectives are primarily educational. A major goal is the development of public awareness of the public's rights and responsibilities within the established American concept of broadcast service. The Association is strongly opposed to censorship. Since its inception NABB has been a national leader in efforts to reduce violence in television entertainment. The association publishes a quarterly newsletter which includes in its winter issue each year NABB's long-established annual evaluations of network and syndicated program series. It also produces and distributes other printed materials."

National Citizens Committee for Broadcasting
1028 Connecticut Avenue, NW, Suite 402
Washington, DC 20036
Publications: *Media Watch* (NCCB newsletter free with membership), *Access,* and *Citizen's Media Directory* ($7.50 book).

National Organization for Women
425 13th Street, NW
Washington, DC 20004

Network Project
101 Earl Hall
Columbia University
New York, NY 10027
Non-profit research and action group that published bi-monthly reports costing $2 (White House Role in Media, etc.; no new numbers of the reports are being issued); also has a series of radio documentaries on cassette dealing with television and communication.

Newsreel
630 Natoma Street
San Francisco, CA 94103
Provides films and media production services for political organizers and educators.

Plain Talk, Inc.
1333 Connecticut Avenue, NW
Washington, DC 20036
"A nonprofit public-interest group working for plain English in all writing."

Public Media Center
2751 Hyde Street
San Francisco, CA 94109
"A Handbook on Free Access to the Media for Public Service Advertising" ($3.00) and other anti-doublespeak public-service material.

The RAP Collective
P.O. Box 736, Stuyvesant Station
New York, NY 10009
Distributes free mimeographed information sheets to newspapers.

The Satellite Video Exchange Society
261 Powell Street
Vancouver, British Columbia
Canada V6A 1G3
Maintains a nonprofit library of noncommercial videotapes; encourages exchanges for sharing resources.

Slide Tape Collective
36 Lee Street
Cambridge, MA 02139
Helps people make, distribute, copy, and exchange slides and tapes.

TeleVISIONS Magazine
Washington Community Video
  Center
P.O. Box 21068
Washington, DC 20009
A quarterly magazine on all aspects of television and other media.

Truth in Advertising, Inc.
4600 Kawanne Avenue
Metarie, LA 60002
Privately funded by Hugh Exnicios. To become a volunteer monitor or report a deceptive ad, write or call toll free 1-800-535-7094.

Viewer's Disgust
P.O. Box 1039
Palo Alto, CA 94302
Against violence on television with a national volunteer approach of direct protest to sponsoring companies. Join for $4.50.

Zodiac News Service
950 Howard Street
San Francisco, CA 94103
An alternative news service, airmailed daily to over four hundred progressive FM, top-forty, and college radio stations and community papers.

PROFESSIONAL ORGANIZATIONS

National Council of Teachers of
  English
Public Doublespeak Committee
William Lutz, Chairman
1111 Kenyon Road
Urbana, IL 61801 or
Department of English
Rutgers University
Camden, New Jersey 08102

NCTE Doublespeak Award
Donald Lazere
English Department
California Polytechnic State University
San Luis Obispo, CA 93407
An award for misuse of public language. Send Lazere your choice examples.

Public Doublespeak Newsletter
Don L. F. Nilsen, Coeditor
Department of English
Arizona State University
Tempe, AZ 85281

NCTE George Orwell Award for
  Distinguished Contributions to
  Honesty and Clarity in Public
  Language
Del Kehl
English Department
Arizona State University
Tempe, AZ 85281
Send Kehl your nominations. The first award went to David Wise for *The Politics of Lying.*

Doublespeak Media Spots
  Subcommittee
Francine Hardaway
Scottsdale College
9000 E. Chaparral
Scottsdale, AZ 85252
For the preparation and dissemination of radio and television public-service spots to enable the general public to more critically analyze the language used by politicians, candidates for office, advertisers, etc. Contact Hardaway if you want to contribute.

PROFESSIONAL ORGANIZATIONS AGAINST CENSORSHIP

National Council of Teachers of
  English
1111 Kenyon Road
Urbana, IL 61801

NCTE has published several pamphlets, a guide to teachers and librarians faced with a censoring parent or administrator, and has issued strong position statements.

Speech Communication Association
Commission on Freedom of Speech
5205 Leesburg Pike
Falls Church, VA 22041
They publish *Free Speech.*

American Civil Liberties Union
22 East 40th Street
New York, NY 10016
The largest and most effective action organization in support of the First Amendment, they work primarily through the courts. And they need your financial support.

Office for Intellectual Freedom
American Library Association
50 East Huron Street
Chicago, IL 60611

National Ad Hoc Committee
    Against Censorship
50 East Huron Street
Chicago, IL 60611
Supported by the ACLU, AAUP, ALA, National Council of Churches, etc. They publish a newsletter and pamphlets, *Lobbying For Freedom* (72 pages).

Project Censored
Professor Carl Jensen
Sociology Department
California State College
Rohnert Park, CA 94928

RELIGIOUS ORGANIZATIONS

United Methodist Communications
475 Riverside Drive, Suite 1370
New York, NY 10027
See their policy statement: "The Church in a Mass Media Culture." Major activities: "1. Research into the effects of television on children and adults through the Media Action Research Center, Inc. 2. Television Awareness Training. 3. Dialogue with media leaders concerning program content with special emphasis on gratuitous violence and exploitative sex. 4. Production of alternative programming on television such as Six American Families and children's television public-service spots which teach alternatives to violent behavior."

United Presbyterian Church, U.S.A.
Office of Information
1935 Interchurch Center
475 Riverside Drive
New York, NY 10027

Presbyterian Church, U.S.
Office of Information
Presbyterian Center
Office of the General Assembly
314 Ponce de Leon Avenue, NE
Atlanta, GA 30308

Christian Church (Disciples)
Office of Communications
P.O.B. 1986
Indianapolis, IN 46206

United Church of Christ
Office of Communications
289 Park Avenue, South
New York, N.Y. 10010

Office of Film and Broadcasters
U.S. Catholic Conference
1011 1st Avenue
New York, NY 10022

National Catholic News Service
1312 Massachusetts Avenue, NW
Washington, DC 20005

ACTION MANUALS

Bennet, Robert W. *A Lawyer's Source Book: Representing the Audience in Broadcast Proceedings.* New York: Office of Communications, United Church of Christ, 1974. A how-to book for attorneys representing citizen groups written in generally accessible terms.

Cirino, Robert. *We're Being More Than Entertained.* Honolulu: Lighthouse Press, 1977. (Box 8507, Hawaii 96815)
Offers his proposal for access to media earlier sketched out in an article in *College English*: liberal, socialist, conservative, libertarian points of view given equal time and opportunity. "... the new United States Broadcasting Corporation (USBC) will operate on the assumption that the different representative viewpoints can only compete equally for public approval if each is allowed to produce and control its own news and entertainment" (p. 207).

Drury, Treesa, and William Roper. *Consumer Power.* Los Angeles: Nash, 1974. In addition to chapters on major frauds and dangers, one chapter tells "How to Fight Back," another "How to Organize for Consumer Action," and there are appendices on state consumer offices, state attorneys general, and consumer leagues.

Hirsch, Glenn, and Alan Lewis. *Strategies for Access.* San Francisco: Public Media Center, 1976. Write: 2751 Hyde Street, San Francisco, CA 94109. How to create your own PSAs, how to get them on the air, etc.

Johnson, Nicholas. *How to Talk Back to Your Television Set.* Boston: Little, Brown, and Company, 1970. Also Bantam paperback, 1970. Former FCC commissioner gives advice to citizens.

Kaye, Evelyn. *The Family Guide to Children's Television.* New York:

Pantheon Books, 1974. Much useful information for citizen groups, not limited in application to children's programs.

Michael, James, ed. *Working on the System: A Comprehensive Manual for Access to Federal Agencies.* New York: Basic Books, 1974.

Murray, Michael. *The Videotape Book.* New York: Bantam Books, Inc., 666 Fifth Avenue, New York, NY 10019. Video and information theory for novices; includes discussion of community video work.

Nader, Ralph, and Donald Ross. *Action for a Change: A Manual for Organizing Student Public Interest Research Groups.* New York: Grossman, 1972.

Public Citizen's Action Group
133 C Street, SE
Washington, DC 20036
Write for their manual.

Rivers, William L., and William T. Slater, eds. *Aspen Handbook on the Media.* 1975–1976 Edition. Palo Alto, California: Aspen Institute Program on Communications and Society, 1975. Highly useful source for a student concerned with public policy and broadcasting. Lengthy index of organizations.

Robinson, Richard. *The Video Primer.* Order from Quick Fox Inc., 33 West 60 Street, New York, NY 10023.

Ross, Donald. *A Public Citizen's Action Manual.* New York: Grossman, 1973.

Shapiro, A. O. *Media Access: Your Rights to Express Your Views on Radio and Television.* Little, 1976.

Schrank, Jeffrey, *T.V. Action Book.* Evanston, Ill.: McDougall, Littell & Co., 1974. A textbook which discusses the use of the television channels — programming, ownership of stations, the Fairness Doctrine, advertising. A substantial part of the book is a logbook to help students analyze local television.

White, Jack, et al. *The Angry Buyer's Complaint Dictionary*. New York: Wyden, 1974 (distributed by David McKay).

PROGRESSIVE PERIODICALS

The following is a list of some of the most important progressive periodicals in the nation. Most of them have been a constant source of material for this volume and can be found in any good college library. They are important, not only for keeping abreast of events not reported in "establishment" news sources, but for the discussion of the crucial issues of our times.

Periodical List

American Scholar
Atlantic Monthly
Dissent
Harper's
The Humanist
Monthly Review
Mother Jones
Nation
New Left Review
New Republic
New Yorker (especially "Letter from Washington" column)
New York Review of Books
Partisan Review
Progressive
Saturday Review
Skeptic
Social Policy
Socialist Review
Society
Village Voice
Washington Monthly
Yale Review

Name Index

Subject Index

Cover photo: Camerique

ISBN 0-205-07553-3
EDP 8175535